Securing Southeast Asia

This book analyses civil–military relations in Southeast Asia in the wake of the largely unexpected September 2006 coup in Thailand. It explores the impact and utility of the 'security sector reform' agenda on the region and assesses whether it is likely to help make Southeast Asia more stable and less prone to similar military interventions. Four of Southeast Asia's most important countries are examined: Malaysia, the Philippines, Indonesia and Thailand. This book provides an overview and update of developments in Southeast Asia's most important militaries, as well as a detailed analysis of their relationship with national governments. It also considers Southeast Asia's place in the 'war on terror' and the impact this may have on the region as a whole. A key feature of this study is the detailed exploration of the place of regional security sectors in their unique, historically determined national contexts. Consequently, this book offers a rare theoretically informed comparative study of the promise and pitfalls of security sector reform in the strategically important Southeast Asian region.

Mark Beeson is Professor of International Politics at the University of Birmingham. His research is centred on the politics, economics and security of East Asia. His latest book is *Regionalism, Globalization and East Asia: Politics, Security and Economic Development* (Palgrave, 2007).

Alex J. Bellamy is Professor of International Relations at the University of Queensland. His research is centred on the normative dimensions of military power. His latest book is *Just Wars: From Cicero to Iraq* (Polity, 2006).

Routledge Security in Asia Pacific series

Series Editors
Leszek Buszynski
International University of Japan,
and
William Tow
Australian National University

Security issues have become more prominent in the Asia Pacific region because of the presence of global players, rising great powers and confident middle powers, which intersect in complicated ways. This series puts forward important new work on key security issues in the region. It embraces the roles of the major actors, their defence policies and postures and their security interaction over the key issues of the region. It includes coverage of the United States, China, Japan, Russia, the Koreas, as well as the middle powers of ASEAN and South Asia. It also covers issues relating to environmental and economic security as well as transnational actors and regional groupings.

Securing Southeast Asia
The politics of security sector reform

Mark Beeson and
Alex J. Bellamy

Routledge
Taylor & Francis Group

LONDON AND NEW YORK

First published 2008
by Routledge
2 Park Square, Milton Park, Abingdon, Oxon OX14 4RN

Simultaneously published in the USA and Canada
by Routledge
270 Madison Ave, New York, NY 10016

Routledge is an imprint of the Taylor & Francis Group, an Informa business

Transferred to Digital Printing 2009

© 2008 Mark Beeson and Alex J. Bellamy

Typeset in Times New Roman by
Newgen Imaging Systems (P) Ltd, Chennai, India

British Library Cataloguing in Publication Data
A catalogue record for this book is available from the British Library

Library of Congress Cataloging in Publication Data
Beeson, Mark.
    Securing Southeast Asia : the politics of security sector reform /
Mark Beeson & Alex J. Bellamy.
        p. cm – (Routledge security in Asia Pacific series ; 6)
    Includes bibliographical references and index.
    1. Civil-military relations – Southeast Asia. 2. Southeast Asia – Politics
and government. I. Bellamy, Alex J., 1975– II. Title.
    DS525.7.B44 2007
    355'.033059–dc22   2007012127

ISBN10: 0–415–41619–1 (hbk)
ISBN10: 0–415–49174–6 (pbk)
ISBN10: 0–203–93488–1 (ebk)

ISBN13: 978–0–415–41619–1 (hbk)
ISBN13: 978–0–415–49174–7 (pbk)
ISBN13: 978–0–203–93488–3 (ebk)

Contents

Acknowledgements

A number of people have helped us in the preparation of this book, and we would like to acknowledge their contribution. We are, of course, solely responsible for any errors of fact or interpretation in what follows, but we would like to thank Michael Connors, Bob Elson, Jane Hutchison, Francis Loh, Marcus Mietzner and Kevin Smith, for reading and commenting on parts of the book.

In addition, we would like to thank and acknowledge the many people we interviewed in connection with this book, some of whom wish to remain confidential. Of those we can mention, we would like to thank, K.S Balakrishnan, Ken Brownrigg, Suchit Bunbongkarn, Chayachoke Chulasiriwong, Sunait Chutintaranond, Richard Ellis, Chris Forbes, David Garnock, J. Kristiadi, Chandrun Jeshurun, Andi Mallarangeng, Ana Marie Pamintuan, Arsa Sarasin, Stuart Jarvis, Mohamed Jawhar bin Hassan, Keiran Miller, Makmier Kelial, Steve McLean, K.S. Nathan, General Niyom, Sukhumbhand Paribatra, Edy Prasetyono, Ariston Delos Reyes, Johan Saravanamuttu, Philips J. Vermonte, Andi Widjajanto, Craig White and Zakaria Ahmad.

Supachai Watanangura and Chawannat Limtaskinkul offered generous assistance during the fieldwork in Thailand.

We would also like to acknowledge the invaluable research assistance of Bryn Hughes and David Hundt. Thanks to Peter Sowden at Routledge for his encouragement and assistance in bringing this project about. Finally, we wish to acknowledge the support provided by the Australian Research Council in funding this research, without which it would not have been possible.

Introduction

Southeast Asia is something of an anomaly. Superficially, since the end of the Second World War it has enjoyed many of the conditions often thought necessary for capitalist democracy and stable government. In practice, however, governance in the region has often been characterised by authoritarianism and a pronounced tendency for the security sector to play a dominant role in political and economic life. This was exemplified most clearly by the 2006 military coup in Thailand and by a series of apparent coup attempts in the Philippines. According to one scholar, the region's states have chosen 'cohesion over consensus' (Janowitz 1981: 16).

For much of their history, security sectors in Southeast Asia have tended to play an active role in the political and economic life of the country, defending and sometimes promoting authoritarianism, and concentrating on securing particular regimes rather than the state itself or its citizens. Traditionally, a common refrain for observers of security sector politics in Southeast Asia has been to note the lingering military-sponsored authoritarianism that has persisted long after the military's so-called return to barracks (e.g. Olsen and Jurika 1986). Indeed, it is not uncontroversial to argue that since 1945 Southeast Asians have been more threatened by their own security forces than both those of other states (see Burke and McDonald 2007). Recently, however, there has been evidence of an important shift in the way that the region's security sectors are governed, the values they subscribe to and the roles they fulfil. In what has become a landmark study, Alagappa (2001) concluded that profound changes were afoot. In Indonesia and Thailand he observed a discernible shift towards the 'old professionalism' model of civil–military relations.

The phrase 'old professionalism' was first coined in relation to Huntington's (1957) discipline-defining work and refers to the idea that the military ought to be a professional institution shaped by the values of expertise in the use of violence, social responsibility (understanding its role as being to act as guardians of the state and society), and corporateness (having a sense of self-identity based on the profession's values). Alagappa argued that in Thailand and Indonesia, the militaries had narrowed their role and withdrawn from politics – a conclusion we now know to have been premature, especially in Thailand's case. In Malaysia, a long-standing tradition of 'old professionalism' was identified, but in the Philippines, by sharp contrast, significant problems were thought to remain. An attempted military coup in 2003, and a threatened mutiny in 2006, appeared to confirm that the security sector remains both divided and deeply engaged in politics.

Given this complex backdrop, the aim of this book is twofold. First of all, we want to make sense of these apparent changes to security governance in Southeast Asia. How profound have reforms been? Are there limits to reform? Are we sure that change in the security sector always occurs in one-direction? Has change at the rhetorical level influenced the actual behaviour of the region's security forces? Second, after establishing that security sector reform (SSR) is an important and worthwhile endeavour, we want to understand the drivers and inhibitors of reform in Southeast Asia. Are the principal dynamics internal or external? To what extent has reform been internalised by prominent regional actors? What conditions make reform more or less likely? What types of reform are most appropriate and most useful in a Southeast Asian context?

The nature of the problem

The principal role of most of Southeast Asia's militaries has traditionally been the protection not of the state, nor of its citizens, but of a particular regime and/or the interests of the military itself. As we set out in more detail in Chapter 3, the glue that brought the state leaders together in 1967 to form the Association of Southeast Asian Nations (ASEAN) lay not in a common history or culture, but in their shared experiences of trying to govern fragile states. Although ASEAN's goals were primarily the promotion of economic, social and cultural cooperation, the prime preoccupation was regional peace and security. The leaders of the new ASEAN members recognised that regional peace and security depended on stability and security *within* states. Thus, at the first ASEAN summit at the heads of government level (held in Bali, 1976), the closing declaration maintained that, 'the stability of each member state and of the ASEAN region is an essential contribution to international peace and security. Each member state resolves to eliminate threats posed by subversion to its stability, thus strengthening national and ASEAN resilience' (in Leifer 1989: 66).

It is important to reiterate that it is not the impersonal state that regional elites have traditionally sought to secure but rather their own regimes. As Michael Leifer (1986) put it in relation to the formation of ASEAN, 'the prime object of the regional exercise was the promotion of a structure of relations which would serve to reinforce the domestic basis of conservative-minded governments by reducing external frictions between them'. ASEAN was formed against a background of ongoing dispute about borders and legitimacy within a context of recent decolonisation and the arrival of sovereign statehood. Throughout much of the cold war and even now for many of the region's states (particularly those discussed in detail in this book), the paramount concern has been with the consolidation, legitimisation and security of particular regimes and ruling elites. Seen this way, the common perception of threat that brought the leaders together to form ASEAN in 1967, and that continues to shape much regional cooperation, was not only fear of an expansionist China or Vietnam but the presence of opposition movements that threatened regimes from within (Ganesan 2000: 260). ASEAN's primary goal was therefore the promotion of regional peace and security through the collective legitimisation of states with limited cooperation to protect the security of the region's regimes from *internal* challenges. Quite often, under the banner of regime protection, Southeast Asian militaries have abused the citizens under their ostensible care.

This idea is clearly demonstrated by briefly considering two recent or ongoing cases that we will explore in more depth in the second part of the book. A 2004 incident in southern Thailand, which received considerable international attention, illustrates how the Thai government has used the need for national cohesion and internal order to justify human rights abuses committed by the military. In this particular instance of a decades' old conflict between the mainly Buddhist government and the mainly Muslim southern provinces, a crackdown by government security forces on protests by Muslim youths led to the deaths of six Muslim youths by shooting and the deaths of around 80 others by suffocation (during transport) (Agence-France Presse 2004a). After the event, former Thai prime minister, Thaksin Shinawatra – later removed from power by the military – praised the efforts of the government's security forces and claimed the actions were justified (Voice of America Press 2004). And despite general condemnation from many voices in international society – including Muslim leaders and other civil groups in Thailand (Agence-France Presse 2004a) and the US State Department and Philippines government which both expressed 'concern' – these egregious human rights abuses have been allowed to go unchallenged (Agence-France Presse 2004a, 2004b).

Similar events have marred Indonesia's recent past. Most remarkable perhaps was the violence of 1999 (both sanctioned and committed by the Indonesian military) unleashed upon East Timorese civilians prior to and especially following their vote for independence (e.g. Parry 2002). East Timor, however, is only one of several regions where the Indonesian armed forces have used violence against civilians as part of its campaigns against regional insurgencies. Although the two sides have recently concluded a political settlement, in the province of Aceh Indonesian government security forces have been accused of committing numerous atrocities on the Acehnese population, including the massacre in 1999 of a Muslim teacher, Teungku Bantaqiah, and 56 of his followers (Human Rights Watch 2000). In West Papua, moreover, reports about the murder of pro-independence supporters by government security forces are not uncommon and the violence has even increased in recent years (Human Rights Watch 2003).

Virtually every state in the region, with the exception of Singapore, has confronted a significant internal threat from ethnic secessionists, religious radicals or communists and responded with military force. Ethnically inspired conflicts have persisted to this day in Indonesia, Burma, the Philippines and Papua New Guinea and new ones have emerged in Thailand. Although the end of the cold war has seen the demise of externally backed communist insurgencies, many states in the region have been confronted with emergent threats from radical Islamic terrorism. Like the communist threat, radical Islam combines a physical threat to the regime and the state's citizens with an ideological threat. The first type of threat is obviously manifested through acts of terrorism such as the 2002 Bali bombing.

Insurgency groups such as the *Moro Islamic Liberation Front* in the Philippines, and *Jemaah Islamiyah* (JI) across the region, pose an important challenge to the legitimacy of the state itself. Radical Islamic groups throughout the region insist that the state should be organised along Islamist lines and should be founded on religious law. Moreover, they insist that the religious leadership should replace traditional political elites at the head of the state and that states should not foster relationships with the US and its allies. Radical Islamic politics have proven particularly divisive in secular-based states such as Indonesia, Thailand and the Philippines, though it is important to note that Islamic parties have been relatively unsuccessful in national elections (Rabasa 2003).

There have been many recent manifestations of this type of threat, producing an outpouring of scholarly literature (e.g. Pearson 2002; Jones 2004). In August 2004, three people were killed by Islamic separatist terrorists in Thailand's southern provinces (*Bangkok Post* 2004). In September 2004 a bomb was exploded in front of the Australian Embassy in Jakarta, killing at least seven and wounding over 180 people (*Jakarta Post* 2004). And in February 2005, bombs were set off in two cities in the Philippines (*Manila Standard* 2005). In many cases, this resistance to the state's legitimacy is further enabled by links between the various groups. For instance, a recent report by the International Crisis Group (2004) supported the idea that there were links between the Filipino Muslim separatists of the *Moro Islamic Liberation Front* (MILF) and *Jemaah Islamiyah* (JI), *Abu Sayyaf Group* (ASG), and even Al Qaeda. Evidence suggests that working relations exist among these Islamic groups to the extent that JI's Mindinao cell, for instance, reportedly planned many of the major terrorist acts that occurred in the Philippines between 2002 and 2003. Thus, while the presence of radical Islamic groups in the Philippines, Indonesia, and Thailand has been disrupted by recent counter-terrorism efforts, it continues to be a potential source of violence against the state.

Whilst each of these threats has some substance to them (some more than others), our concern here is not with the validity of the threats but with their *effects* on the role and structure of the military in Southeast Asia. First of all, then, it seems clear that the region's militaries are primarily focused on preserving the status quo against internal threats. This, in turn, has led to two other important trends in Southeast Asian civil–military relations: military intervention in civilian affairs and a form of corporatism that rests on, among other things, a system of patronage and corruption.

At the most abstract level, some writers have suggested that societies in Southeast Asia exhibit a tendency towards greater acceptance of political and military authority that is greater than those exhibited in the West. Philip Eldridge (2002), for instance, argued that Asian societies are more amenable towards deference to authority and paternalism, and that as a result Asian citizens are more willing to surrender their individual rights in return for community harmony and state security than their counterparts in the West. Although the so-called Asian values debate has undoubtedly overplayed Asian exceptionalism in this regard, it is clear that underlying societal and cultural factors may help to shape regional ideas about the nature of political power. Thus, although the concept of a 'nation-state' was imposed on Southeast Asia by European colonisers, it is argued that the region's predilection for paternalism has been translated into a powerful form of nationalism predicated on the state (Pye and Pye 1985: vii). This has had two primary consequences for regional patterns of civil–military relations: first, the inability of the civilian sector to assume authority over the military sector and, second, the establishment of particular types of civil services that cannot be simply caricatured as 'weak', as tends to happen when Western analysts discuss state capacity beyond the first and second worlds. The effect of these two factors has been to fashion patterns of civil–military relations that conform to neither the Western model (direct civil authority over the military) nor its opposite (military rule).

According to Alagappa (1988), civilian political institutions in many postcolonial states were relatively weak and confronted with innumerable challenges. Not least, the four Southeast Asian states we focus on were confronted with the task of simultaneously establishing effective governance, resolving ethnic and political disputes, nation-building, establishing a degree of security from external threats, to say nothing of the need to spur economic development. In all four cases, the military sector had important assets that were lacking in the civilian sector. First, the military had material capabilities including the means of coercion. Second, they had nationwide bureaucratic networks. Finally, and perhaps most importantly, the military was the first physical embodiment of new statehood and nationhood. Within this context, the region's militaries 'strayed' (though we would contend that the region's militaries were never 'classically professional' in the western sense) from what might be understood as 'classic professionalism' and adopted what Alagappa labels 'new professionalism' (Alagappa 1988: 17). Rather than adopt a politically neutral, instrumental and primarily external role, Southeast Asian militaries assumed a developmental role in the political, social and economic sectors. What this precisely meant for individual states in Southeast Asia depended, crucially, more on the *relationship* between military and civilian elites than on their relative power. These relationships were predominantly carved out during the process of decolonisation and were in many ways determined by the nature of those processes. The process of decolonisation itself helped to entrench the internal focus of most of the region's militaries, contributing to the obstacles to security sector reform.

There are, we suggest, four distinct models of civil–military relations in Southeast Asia based on this practice of developmental professionalism and determined by the nature of the relationship between civil and military elites. These models are

- Military rule: the government is run by military officers.
- Concordance: civilian and military elites are part of a common ruling epistemic community and cooperate closely. The civil and military sectors are only formally separate.
- Polyarchic: civilian and military elites establish separate power bases and represent different interests.

- Constitutional: a broadly Western model where the military is governed by laws. In practice, informal relations may resemble elements of the concordance model.

The meaning of the first type, military rule, is relatively self-evident but it is worth noting that with the exception of Burma, exclusive military rule has in the main been rare and brief in Southeast Asia. For example, although Thailand has endured sixteen successful coups in its recent history, governments have tended to be organised along concordant lines with military officers cooperating with civilian allies. Likewise, in the Philippines, government has tended towards polyarchy rather than settled military rule. We will now briefly outline the latter three models.

Directly challenging the liberal insistence that military and civilian institutions be clearly separated with the former subordinated to the latter, 'concordance theory' suggests that the state functions best when civilian and military elites establish a cooperative relationship (Schiff 1995: 7). The quintessential illustration of the possible interlinked evolution of military, civilian and – crucially – economic power occurred in Indonesia. As Robert Elson (2001: 191) points out, in Suharto's Indonesia, 'army officers were permitted, even encouraged, to establish or extend business to provide new sources of funds for their operations and, indeed, for the private gain of the officers concerned'. It entrenched a system that became an institutionalised part of civil–military affairs and a central part of economic activity. Consequently, it will prove resistant to easy reform or substitution.

Since independence, many Southeast Asian states have tended towards a con-cordance model whereby civilian and military elites form common interlinked epistemic communities marked, for example, by membership of common political parties. This is most often the case where post-colonial states were products of armed struggles against colonial powers. In such cases, nationalist movements comprised both military and political elements that worked together closely. This created a military–civilian elite that formed the government in the immediate post-colonial period. Again, perhaps the best example of this type of relationship is Indonesia. From the outset, the armed forces of Indonesia (*Angkatan Bersenjata Republik Indonesia* or ABRI)[1] considered that it was the 'progenitor of the state' (Vatikiotis 1998: 30), the 'people's army' and the source and protector of Indonesian independence.

In such circumstances, the emergence of the doctrine of *dwifungsi*, or 'dual function', in which the military claimed both a traditional military role and a non-military position as a political entity becomes more understandable. Although the doctrine of *dwifungsi* pre-dates the Suharto era it became deeply institutionalised during this period. The key point to make at the outset is that, despite generally showing no great flair for commercial activities (Robison and Hadiz 2004: 54), the military arguably had little choice other than to become involved in the economy: by some estimates 60–65 per cent of the military's operating expenses come from 'off-budget sources' (Cochrane 2002). In other words, the inability of the central government to adequately fund Indonesia's substantial military has encouraged military elites to establish a web of relationships with business and public officials, allowing the military to consolidate its influence across all levels of Indonesian society (Callahan 1999).

Despite recent moves to wind back the military's overt political role by eliminating its reserved seats in the National Assembly, it remains one of the most important, capable and influential institutions in Indonesia. The continuing centrality of the military in Indonesian political and economic life can be seen in the TNI Reform Bill (2004), which was intended to substantially reconfigure civil–military relations and which self-consciously reflected ideas associated with security sector reform.[2] Under the proposed reforms the intention is that the military will withdraw from active involvement in business within five years. But given the dependence on non-government sources of funding noted above, this goal looks wholly unrealistic. Indeed, the parlous state of the Indonesian economy makes this unachievable, in the absence of drastic, politically- and socially-unacceptable cuts in military manpower. Even more fundamentally, perhaps, the military's territorial command structure – which, as we shall see in more detail in Chapter 6, has been central to the consolidation of power by regional commanders, and the associated development of local networks of political patronage and economic cronyism – will remain in place, albeit under another name.[3] In short, while there are some important changes in the rhetoric surrounding the reform process, there is a real possibility that they will prove little more than cosmetic, with the military remaining firmly entrenched at the centre of Indonesian political, economic, and social life (Scarpello 2004).

This tendency towards the establishment of elite epistemic communities crossing the civilian and military sectors facilitated the creation of 'military entrepreneurship'. What is more, as civilian rule has been consolidated, patterns of civil–military concordance have enabled the military to expand its commercial activities in the civil sector, leading one analyst to conclude that revenue raising itself had become one of the core functions of the region's militaries (Capie 1998: 21). This has encouraged the widespread view that the military plays an important role in encouraging economic growth, a view that has been widely disputed by writers who insist that the militarisation of the economy is antithetical to economic development. We will explore this issue in more depth in the next section. The point to make at this stage, however, is that militaries across the region generally occupy important places in national political and economic affairs, albeit usually less overtly than in Indonesia's case.

In Thailand, for example, while elements of the military may exploit their position to engage in illegal activities like smuggling and arms dealing, the superior performance of the Thai economy has meant that the government has been able keep the military relatively happy by expanding its budget (Ockey 2001: 200). Likewise in the Philippines, while the military became highly politicised during the Marcos years, and despite numerous interventions into Philippine politics, the military's role in the economy has generally been limited and not of itself a direct threat to the overall regime. The potentially constraining influence of a wider set of social circumstances is seen even more clearly in the case of Malaysia, where the dominance of indigenous Malays within the military has helped to bind it to, and underpin, successive Malay-led governments – a set of relationships that was legitimised by successful economic development (Loh 2005).

In some cases the interlinkages between civil and military agencies are not strong, however. This leads to the development of rival military and civilian centres of power. Hence, a polyarchic model of civil–military relations is created in which military and civilian elites develop more independently. In such systems there are often few informal interlinkages between the two sectors. The military becomes largely impervious to civilian control and in situations where military officers take civilian roles their primary allegiance often lies more with the military's corporate interests than with a common governing elite. Often these two centres of power cooperate, blurring the distinction between concordant and polyarchic types. However, disagreements arise over issues such as the social composition of the officer corps, political decision-making, military recruitment and military ethos (Schiff 1995: 7). In such cases, or in cases where the military believes that civilian actors are governing inefficiently or corruptly, the military may take over the reins of civil power.

In Southeast Asia this type of civil–military relationship became particularly prominent where developing states had no strong history of a common struggle against colonialism, or where civilian authorities lacked the material capabilities to exert authority throughout the state's territory. In such circumstances, the roles of nation-building and state-building were taken up by the military. In Thailand, the historically powerful position of the military was established at the time of its transition from an absolute monarchy to constitutional rule in 1932 (Bunbongkarn 1988). Despite moves towards reform in the 1990s, the 2006 coup demonstrates only too well that the military continues to believe that it has the right, indeed obligation, to interfere in democratic politics.

But while there has been significant change in some of the underlying political, economic and social dynamics in Southeast Asia, there is still a noteworthy gap between Southeast Asian practice and the normative expectations that underpin security sector reform. In the Western tradition, it is assumed that the military is a neutral 'tool' of government that is separate from the political and economic domains especially in the domestic realm, where it is expected that the military will remain 'in barracks' unless specifically requested to provide assistance to the civil authorities (Alagappa 1988: 17; Kennedy and Louscher 1991). Both the concordance and polyarchic models of civil–military relations contrast with this Western model, suggesting that alternative approaches to understanding security sector reform may be necessary. Before we go down that path, however, it is important to acknowledge the existence of a nascent third model of civil–military relationship that reflects the Western model more closely: the constitutional model.

The best example of a constitutional system of civil–military relations in Southeast Asia can be found in Malaysia, though even here there are significant problems especially related to the role of the police and judiciary (see Chapter 4). Malaysia is often described as a semi-democratic system in which elements of authoritarianism and democracy combine in a mutually reinforcing way that makes systemic change unlikely (Crouch 1996: 12). Malaysia's armed forces – and its system of civil–military relations – was influenced by the British military tradition. The British influence on the Malaysian military was more pronounced than the influence of other colonial powers in the region because of the relatively peaceful nature of the transition to post-colonial statehood. Moreover, upon independence, the UK and Malaysia concluded a military cooperation pact (the Five Powers Defence Arrangements) and the UK was instrumental in assisting the new Malaysian ruling elite by suppressing a communist insurgency in the 1950s. The protracted communist insurgency in particular gave the security forces a key role in suppressing internal opponents of the regime. These factors have enabled Malaysia to develop a system of civil–military relations based on the formal separation of civilian and military authorities (Machmud 1994). It is important to recognise, however, that this relationship is always contingent on the continuation of the wider ethnically determined social accommodation that is predicated on the continuing Malay dominance of not just the military, but of the wider politico-economic structures of governance that have prevailed for decades (Gomez and Jomo 1997; Nathan and Govindasamy 2001). It is also important to recognise that the existence of a professional military is not necessarily a guarantee, or reflection of, a more activist civil society or extensive individual liberties. On the contrary, a succession of authoritarian governments in Malaysia have used a compliant judiciary, the police force and the notorious Internal Security Act to achieve the sort of coercive social controls that have been achieved through the military elsewhere (Hilley 2001).

It is clear from the preceding discussion that there are significant problems associated with the military sector in Southeast Asia. This raises the question, of why we might think the use of the military for internal security, regime protection, and in civilian and economic affairs is a bad thing. Is it simply that it does not conform to Western expectations about the proper role of the military, or are these problems symptomatic of deeper issues? Our reasons for thinking that reform is important will become much clearer in the subsequent chapters, but in short there are three key considerations. First, the fact that the region's militaries are often used to violate the human rights of their own citizens is a problem in itself and is ultimately counter-productive, casting doubt upon the legitimacy of the military and, indeed, the state itself. Second, there is evidence to suggest that the problems documented above reduce the efficiency and effectiveness of the armed forces themselves. Indeed, as intimated above, the region's security forces have proven almost uniformly unable to defeat armed opponents not only partly due to perceived illegitimacy but also partly due to a lack of capacity on the part of the military and the state. Finally, with the partial exception of Thailand, there are grounds for thinking that the role of the military in civilian affairs inhibits economic development. We are not suggesting a causal relationship in this regard, but it would be similarly foolhardy to deny the correlation.

The purpose of the remainder of the book is to interrogate these issues more carefully to get a better understanding of the promise and perils of security sector reform in Southeast Asia.

Structure of the book

The book is conceptually divided into two parts. The first addresses the key conceptual and historical issues raised by the questions posed earlier and sets out our approach. We begin by identifying security sector reform as a distinct area of activity and charting the claims its advocates make for it. We argue that, theoretically, security sector reform can make at least three important contributions to international peace and security. First, through programmes of professionalisation and military education, reform aims to make security forces better able to fulfil their tasks in an effective, efficient and legitimate manner. However defined, professional security forces are more capable than their unprofessional counterparts. Second, reform of the security sector makes an important contribution to wider processes of democratisation and whilst the idea that democracies do not fight one another is far from the cast-iron law some of its proponents suggest, it is certainly the case that democratically governed regions tend to be less violent places than regions with other forms of government. Security sector reform assists democratisation by constraining the anti-democratic tendencies of the security forces, protecting democratic institutions and by helping to spread and 'lock in' democratic values. Finally, security sector reform can make a direct contribution to economic development. It has become apparent that military involvement in politics and economics inhibits rather than encourages economic growth, especially once the development process is established and the task of economic management becomes more complex (see Chapter 2). The Thai military's capacity to manage the economy whilst maintaining the confidence of international investors will be an important test of this possibility.

There are also a number of problems, however, associated with importing an essentially Western framework into a non-Western environment. After identifying some of the problems in generic terms, in Chapter 2 we assess different ways of understanding how particular patterns of civil–military relations are formed and how they change. We argue that patterns of civil–military relations are established by a combination of material and ideational factors that operate at international, national and bureaucratic levels. The ideational factors create expectations about what the security sector ought to look like, what it should do, and how it should relate to other sectors of society. Because embedding a process of security sector reform involves changing established ideas, the final part of Chapter 2 identifies different types of change and sources. In short, we argue that change may be 'fundamental' or 'fine-tuning', either involving amending certain practices to accommodate a changed environment or achieving established goals more efficiently. Drivers of fundamental change include external shocks, external bribery or coercion, the accumulation of fine-tuning changes, and the resolution of legitimacy crises. 'Fine-tuning', on the other hand, is much less dramatic and may be driven by epistemic communities seeking new solutions to old problems within well-defined parameters.

Establishing the factors that influence security governance and change provides only part of the way around the problems associated with simply applying an essentially Western framework to a non-Western environment. In addition, we need a keen awareness of the historical forces that have shaped the Southeast Asian security sector and this is the purpose of Chapter 3. Here, we argue that the forces of colonialism, globalisation and American hegemony have had a profound impact on the way that security is conceived and pursued, with the result that local elites remain deeply sensitive to questions relating to boundaries, sovereignty and regime maintenance. This constitutes an important challenge to those wishing to propagate security sector reform (SSR), and an important potential limitation on the extent to which local elites are likely to hand over control of the sector to democratic institutions.

The second part of the book examines four case studies in Southeast Asia in order to identify key possible impediments to SSR, and to provide a comparative account of these obstacles. The research focuses on the experiences of four Southeast Asian states – Malaysia, the Philippines, Thailand and Indonesia – which are important for two principal reasons. First, they are the region's largest and most strategically important states. This was true before 11 September 2001, but Southeast Asia's prominent role in the subsequent 'war on terror' has given them renewed significance. Second, the four countries contain a number of similarities and differences that provide points for comparison. On the one hand they share some broadly similar recent historical legacies, on the other, they have distinctively different contingent factors that will allow us to compare and highlight critical variables.

The cases range from Malaysia where there is a tradition of military professionalism and subservience to civilian authority, to the Philippines, where security sector agencies continue to interfere in the political process and exert considerable autonomy. Of the other two cases, Thailand provides a paradoxical example wherein it has engaged in perhaps more overt security sector reform than any of the states but without reforming the fundamentals of the way the military sees its role in relation to the monarch, the government and the people – a paradox that became only too evident in the coup. Indonesia, meanwhile, exhibits many of the traits seen in the Philippines but has shown in recent times a proclivity to reform, though the actual substance remains weak.

While Malaysia's armed forces have tended to respect the authority of civilian institutions, there are particular issues that need investigating if impediments to SSR are to be identified and assessed. The most distinctive characteristic of the Malaysian security sector is that it is dominated by ethnic Malays. Significantly, therefore, although Malaysia has considerable formal state capacity, our earlier research leads us to expect that in the absence of a more wide-ranging process of political and economic transformation, narrowly conceived SSR is unlikely to impact positively on the dependent variable (Beeson 2000). It is also important to recognise that although security sector institutions exhibit the formal trappings of independence and accountability, they are heavily politicised – a fact indicated by informal recruitment policies that offer rewards to those either attached or sympathetic to the ruling elite.

In the middle of the spectrum are two states with long traditions of military involvement in civilian politics that have embarked on significant reform programmes: Thailand and the Philippines. In Thailand, the SSR process has been developing and growing for several years. The intervention of the Thai king during the last coup attempt in 1992 proved something of a watershed in civil–military relations leading to a prolonged and ongoing period of reform (Huxley 2001) but the subsequent 2006 coup raised important questions about the depth of the transformation and the continuity of older patterns of politics. The key empirical questions are centred on: organisational conservatism in military culture; the informal methods used by the army to influence political processes after its formal exclusion from civilian politics; competition between different elements of the security sector for resources and political influence; the security sector's continuing involvement in economic activities; the relationship between the state and civil society and the continuing monopoly of knowledge on the security sector held by the state and ruling regime; the impact of the financial crisis on the capacity of bureaucratic institutions to fulfil their roles.

Indonesia provides a striking illustration of our contention that there are significant impediments to SSR. Indonesia's armed forces (TNI) have a long-established 'dual function', in which the military's external security role is supplemented by participation in government and the economy (Vatikiotis 1998). Although there have been significant attempts to change this role following the ousting of the Suharto government, vested interests and patrimonial relations within the security sector remains an important obstacle to SSR. The military's continuing political influence, especially when combined with a need to fund many of its own activities – itself a reflection of the Indonesian state's chronic *in*capacity – means that SSR faces obstacles that are distinctive and not captured by the existing literatures on civil–military relations or SSR. By applying the framework of analysis to the Indonesian case, the key issues that emerge are: the formal and informal role of the military in civilian politics; problems with the lack of transparency and accountability at all levels of the security sector; the economic role of the military and its partial self-sufficiency; the Islamicisation of the military; the state's capacity to implement policy in the light of the above; and the absence of non-state expertise and freedom of expression on security matters.

In the Philippines, the question of institutional capacity and its influence on the security sector has generally proven more critical than in the other cases. Economic problems that confront the state limit the capacity of the state's institutions and the military to implement reforms whilst providing a backdrop for endemic corruption. In addition to general questions revolving around state capacity and institutional transformation, research based on the framework of analysis will focus on: the impact of the US and organisations like the World Bank on the international context of SSR; attitudinal changes within the security sector following the unsuccessful coups of the late 1980s and early 1990s; the ability of insurrectionary forces to undermine SSR by maintaining high levels of threat perception within the Manila government; and the enduring legacy of corruption. In short, the demise of the corruption-plagued Estrada government, and the Arroyo administration's difficulty in pushing more general reform processes provides a stark reminder that the potential for SSR cannot be considered in isolation from wider societal and economic factors.

In the final, concluding, chapter we ask what all this means for security reform in the region and offer tentative answers to some of the questions posed at the outset.

1 Security sector reform in a Southeast Asian context

The purpose and principal argument of this chapter develops in two stages. First, we suggest that the Security Sector Reform (SSR) agenda contains ways of overcoming problems associated with the security sector in Southeast Asia, but that as presently conceived the agenda is flawed in important respects. Second, to sustain the case for not rejecting SSR as a whole because of the problems we identify, we explore the ways in which SSR has already been adopted to some extent in the region and argue that rather than jettisoning SSR, what is required is a more regionally sensitive approach.

Security sector reform

The theory and practice of SSR is relatively new. Its origins lay in the growing recognition within the Western 'development' or 'aid' community that development and security are interdependent. Long-term development or democratisation programmes could not succeed, it was argued in the 1990s, without the provision of stable security by legitimate and democratically accountable security forces. According to this perspective, Western aid donors therefore have a responsibility to promote good governance in the security sector in order to assist broader development programmes sponsored by a range of non-governmental organisations (NGOs), individual states and international institutions such as the World Bank (Ball 1998). There has been a growing awareness in the development and aid communities that not only do 'repressive or corrupt security structures ... undermine the stability crucial to maximising the benefits of aid programmes' (Cooper and Pugh 2002: 5) but also that positive reform of the security sector can provide a catalyst for wider 'good governance' and democratisation programmes. Since the 'security first' initiative in Mali in 1992, a 'new aid paradigm' (Duffield 1999) has developed which recognises that self-sustaining security depends upon the creation of a legitimate, democratically accountable and effective indigenous security sector. Whereas during the cold war the security sector was shunned by the development and aid communities as the source of the underdevelopment problem, there is an increasing awareness that development and security are interdependent and that armed forces and police forces can make a positive contribution to wider processes of democratisation and development (see Duffield 2001).

This chapter aims to introduce the concept of SSR to a Southeast Asian context by showing how the issues it raises are pertinent for the way that security is pursued in the region, by identifying some of the specific problems that may arise from attempts to pursue a SSR agenda. We argue that thinking about SSR makes at least three important contributions to the way we ought to think about, and pursue, security in Southeast Asia:

- First, it prompts *a renewed focus on the importance of civil–military relations* and particularly on the role of the military in domestic societies;
- Second, it speaks to *a broader human security agenda* by making the point that there is not only no security without development and democratisation, but also no development and democratisation without security;
- Finally, it raises important questions about *the effectiveness of externally sponsored development programmes that take place within insecure environments* and the broader impact of defence measures such as arms sales and transfers, training assistance and defence diplomacy on development and democratisation.

The birth of SSR: the new aid paradigm

The 'new aid paradigm' centres upon the merging of security and development identified by Mark Duffield. According to Duffield (2001: 16), there has been a noticeable convergence between the two to the extent that they are now seen as interdependent. Such convergence 'embodies the increasing interaction between military and security actors on the one hand, and civilian and non-governmental organisations on the other' (16). Thus, 'proponents of the new aid paradigm accept that a prerequisite for social development and human rights protection is the security and stability that comes through an effective, impartial and humane introduction of law and order, alongside the extension of sound governance to the military sector itself' (Cooper and Pugh 2002: 14). Such convergence is evidenced by the growing interest in security issues on the part of predominantly Western organisations such as the World Bank (1997b), International Monetary Fund (IMF), the European Union, the UK's Department for International Development (DFID), Saferworld and others, and the simultaneous growth of concern amongst UN peacekeepers, military organisations such as NATO and individual states about democratisation and development (e.g. Thakur and Schnabel 2001; Asmus 2002). The basic point is that these very different types of organisations (though noticeably all dominated by Westerners) have begun to work together more closely because of a shared recognition that rather than being mutually exclusive, their concerns (development and security) are actually interdependent. Such linkages, however, are hardly new. The links between security and economic development were expressly made by the founders of ASEAN who saw its primary aim as being the creation of a secure environment conducive to economic development (Acharya 2001: 141). However, at its inception ASEAN understood a 'secure environment' to mean a degree of negative peace or simply the absence of war. At the time there was no indication of a belief that the *structure* and *function* of a state's security forces had an impact on democratisation and development.

Foreign assistance to another state's military is hardly new either and was common practice during the cold war. During this period, both superpowers offered military aid for the purposes of nation or state building and legitimisation. Throughout Latin America in particular, the US donated large sums of money to construct armed forces capable of defeating communist insurgents, thus helping to defend, indeed sometimes create, non-communist (though usually not democratic) states (Fischel and Cowan 1988: 38). Such aid consisted of arms transfers, covert training and joint operations. In the decade leading up to 1989, for example, the CIA channelled US$2billion worth of weapons to groups fighting Soviet forces in Afghanistan (Cooper and Pugh 2002: 13). Such aid was offered without much, if indeed any, consideration of the wider impact of assistance. This led to what Chalmers Johnson (2001) described as the 'blowback effect' in the 1990s: groups funded and supplied by the CIA during the cold war used those resources to work against US interests after the cold war. Al Qaeda is perhaps the best known consequence of the 'blowback' of US military assistance.

For their part, Western development and finance agencies were not much interested in security matters during the cold war. Their view, not wholly inaccurate, was that militaries, militias and their superpower supporters were some of the most significant barriers to economic development. Organisations such as Save the Children, Oxfam, CARE, Medecins sans Frontieres, UNICEF and others often operated close to war zones delivering emergency assistance or worked on long-term development programmes in states with oppressive military regimes. Neither of these contexts was conducive to close relations between international development agencies and the military; the guiding principles developed by such agencies (restraint, consent, neutrality) stood in stark contrast to the values espoused by the military (Slim 2001). Moreover, during the cold war, emergency assistance in response to natural and man-made disasters was delivered quite separately from long-term development aid, diminishing the likelihood of agencies or militaries establishing the relationship between development and security. To the extent that there was any appreciation of a link between the two, there was a wide assumption in the development community that protracted social conflict was produced by underdevelopment (Duffield 2001: 27). There was certainly very little appreciation that the reverse might also be true.

This began to change after the cold war partly as a result of changes within the development community and partly due to changes within the theory and practice of security. The proliferation of so-called new wars (Kaldor 1999) and, more importantly, the proliferation of international agencies working in environments of protracted social conflict, helped to increase awareness on the part of aid and development agencies of the fact that their projects could not succeed without the provision of basic levels of security. In places like Sierra Leone, Bosnia, Somalia, East Timor, Aceh, Papua New Guinea, and the Solomon Islands there was growing recognition within the development community that the delivery of aid and assistance in insecure or unstable environments was not only ineffective but could potentially lengthen violent conflict and reward warlordism (e.g. Shearer 2000; Bruderlein 2001). Moreover, in places where there is underdevelopment but no protracted social conflict, such development aid may prop up the systems of patronage and corruption that help sustain underdevelopment whilst creating wealthy local elites. Partly as a response to this, and partly as a response to wider global change, development agencies in the 1990s began to insist that development depended upon two other factors that had not enjoyed a prominent role in their activities or thinking during the cold war. The first was democratisation. Although democratisation has been a prominent element of Western rhetoric since 1945 it did not feature heavily in its military assistance programmes during the cold war. Nevertheless, the removal of the ideological opponent to liberal capitalism saw the West promote democratisation as a good in itself (Abrahamsen 2000: 44). The second key factor was security. On the one hand, many of the ideological and practical barriers between development agencies and international militaries were eroded by the ending of the controversial military assistance programmes and proxy wars. On the other hand, there was widespread recognition that across the world violent conflict and illegitimate security actors were often the cause of underdevelopment and therefore could not be ignored. This was true not only in humanitarian crises but also more generally.

For its part, the theory and practice of security also changed significantly in the 1990s to the extent that, not only were the maxims of cold war security politics (the 'balance of power', 'deterrence', 'mutually assured destruction') discredited and exposed as actually a significant part of the problem, but also new maxims appeared, and some long-forgotten ones reappeared, ('human security' and 'security communities' (e.g. UNDP 1994; Adler and Barnett 1998; Bellamy 2004)); all of which helped to change the perceived role of the military in global politics. The pursuit and study of security underwent two principal changes in the 1990s: deepening and broadening. First, approaches to security were deepened by an understanding of the constitutive role of security studies. Security, it was argued, was a far from neutral pastime. Instead, it was about awarding social value that permitted authoritative and exceptional behaviour in response to threats that were in fact constructed by security theorists and practitioners (Booth 1991; Campbell 1992; *inter alia* Dillon 1996; Krause and Williams 1997; Buzan and Wæver 1998; Smith 2000). The pursuit of security in response to particular threats was not an instrumental reaction to objective threats; it was rather a normative response to socially constructed danger. This epistemological point opened up the possibility of thinking about alternative threats to security and different ways of ameliorating them: the broadening of security. The pioneering work in this area was Barry Buzan's *People, States and Fear* (1991), which identified five broad dimensions of security (military, political, societal, economic and environmental). Since then there has been growing recognition that more people in the world are threatened by their own security forces than by other people's (Booth 1995), that military threats to security are only one – and in most places of the world not the most significant – of the causes of human insecurity (Thomas 1987, 2000), and that armed forces can play important positive roles in society. For instance, the human security concept now frames a great deal of activity on the part of the UN and states such as Canada and the UK (see Bellamy and McDonald 2004). Furthermore, the notion that the military can play a wider social role is enshrined in both the current NATO strategic concept and the primary objectives of the emerging European intervention force, both of which identify peacekeeping, humanitarian activities and military assistance to civilian authority as core military purposes.

The 'new aid paradigm' therefore emerged out of significant shifts in the way that very different types of actors, predominantly in the West, thought about development, crisis assistance, democracy, the use of military power and the meaning of security more broadly. On the one hand, development and humanitarian organisations began to realise that (1) short-term aid and long-term development were not always discrete activities, (2) the lack of security constituted a major barrier to successful development and democratisation and thus (3) engagement with the security sector was important. On the other hand, states concerned with providing military assistance began to see (1) the 'blowback' effects of unrestricted military aid, (2) the failure of traditional maxims of security to actually provide humans with security, (3) the fact that security can be constructed in different ways that incorporate threats other than the direct threat of military invasion by foreign powers and (4) that the armed forces could play important positive social roles.

SSR as policy framework

The study of the 'security sector' (as opposed to the traditional focus on civil–military relations), therefore, is a rapidly emerging field that had its roots in development studies, security studies, practical policy and in the 'new aid paradigm' specifically. The driving force behind the idea can be found in the adoption of SSR as a major policy goal by Britain's Department for International Development (DFID) in 1999. The basic rationale for this focus was that 'unprofessional or poorly regulated security forces often compound rather than mitigate security problems' (Hendrickson 1999: 9). The UK's former development minister, Clare Short identified five key areas of SSR that DFID intended to promote. They were

- Supporting the establishment of structures of proper civilian control over the military;
- Training members of the military in international humanitarian law and human rights;
- Strengthening national parliamentary overseeing of the security apparatus;
- Supporting civilian organisations that might act as watchdogs over the security sector;
- Supporting the demobilisation and reintegration of ex-combatants (Cooper and Pugh 2002: 16).

Within post-conflict programmes such as that in East Timor and potential programmes in Cambodia and Vietnam, SSR may also include building local capacity for reconstructive activities such as de-mining and encouraging armed forces to play a role in promoting regional stability through defence diplomacy and building peacekeeping capabilities (Bellamy 2003). These policy initiatives form the hub of the security sector reform agenda. The key normative objective underpinning them is the maximisation of the efficacy of the armed forces in the pursuit of their legitimately and democratically decided goals through programmes designed to improve the professionalism and democratic control of armed forces (see Cottey *et al.* 2002; Forster *et al.* 2002) and the minimisation of the potential threat to human security that they pose (Germann 2002: 10). As Malcolm Chalmers (2001, 2002) has explained, SSR is concerned with moving a state's armed forces – its practices, doctrines and management structures – towards *Western* norms of behaviour.

Viewed this way, the foundational logic behind SSR is reminiscent of the democratic peace thesis and shares many of its problems. The democratic peace thesis insists that democratic states do not wage war on each other (Levy 1988). That is not to say that democratic states do not wage war, or, make less use of their military or are less warlike in their relations with each other, only that democracies tend not to fight *each other* (see Russett 1993; Elman 1999). Advocates of this approach generally present one of two explanations as to why this might be though they are in no way incompatible. These two explanations are broadly referred to as structural/institutional accounts and normative accounts (Owen 1994). Structural or institutional accounts explain the democratic peace by pointing to the institutional constraints placed on decision-makers in democracies. Legislatures, the rule of law and electorates mitigate against rash decisions to go to war (Owen 1994: 90). We can add to this the plethora of international institutions and regimes that tie democratic states into international society and give political leaders international as well as domestic responsibilities (see Keohane and Nye 1977; Krasner 1983). In contrast, normative explanations of the democratic peace focus on the ideas and norms that underpin liberal democracy. Democracies practice compromise in their internal politics, believe that it is imprudent to fight each other, and confer legitimacy upon other states believed to be democratic. Moreover, states that trade extensively with each other are less likely to fight because such war is costly and irrational (Owen 1994: 90; Hegre 2000).

SSR therefore promises to assist the process of building democratic peace by fostering armed forces that reflect and promote liberal democratic values. It contrives to do so by enhancing human security, democratisation and broader development programmes in places where there has either been 'protracted social conflict' (Azar 1991), as in East Timor or Cambodia, or a track record of illegitimate and ineffective governance, as in many other parts of the Southeast Asian region.

As Figure 1.1 shows, SSR aims to promote democratic peace by contributing to three interrelated processes. First of all it aims to enhance the physical security of a state's inhabitants. As we noted earlier, one of the cornerstones of the 'new aid paradigm' is the idea that the lack of physical security can be an important impediment to broader processes of development and democratisation. This point holds in times of protracted social conflict also where there is open military confrontation.

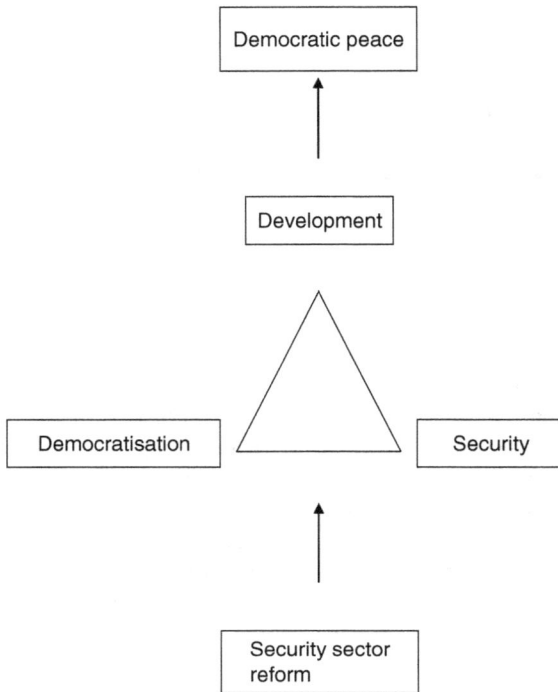

Figure 1.1 SSR and the democratic peace.

In such situations the safety of international and indigenous aid workers and the fiscal security of long-term development programmes are jeopardised by 'generalised lawlessness'. On the other hand, community security is associated with local commitment to development projects and deeper collaboration between local communities and international donors (Anderson 1999: 64–65). It is also true that a basic level of physical and legitimate security is an important ingredient for the success of development and democratisation programmes in places that are not suffering from protracted social conflict (World Bank 1994; Buzan and Herring 1998). As DFID (1999) put it, 'an essential condition for sustained development and poverty elimination is security'.

SSR aims to enhance security in two principal ways. First, through professionalisation programmes it attempts to create armed forces capable of carrying out their tasks in an effective, efficient and legitimate way. Traditionally, professionalisation has tended to be equated with the 'professional' attributes of individual soldiers. Professional soldiers are volunteers who form an epistemic community with shared values and rules (Janowitz 1960; Edmonds 1988). Others argue that professional soldiers accept that they have a duty to fulfil the demands placed upon them by civilian governments (Huntington 1957). Still others argue that military professionalism is all about developing the technical expertise and social awareness necessary to prosper in post modern times (Freedman 1998; Moskos *et al.* 2000). By themselves, each of these conceptions of professionalism is inadequate. For example, the first proposition implies that all conscripts are unprofessional (therefore we must conclude that the French and German militaries were unprofessional until very recently), whilst all volunteer soldiers are 'professional' (a conclusion that is unsatisfactory when we think about the human rights abuses and economic activities perpetrated by Tentara Nasional Indonesia 'volunteers'). A more useful way of thinking about professionalism and processes of professionalisation is offered by Forster *et al.* (2001). They argue that professional armed forces are defined by four core characteristics, which SSR programmes seek to instil. They are

*   *Role:* 'professional armed forces have clearly defined and widely accepted roles in relation to both external functions and domestic society' (5).
*   *Expertise:* 'professional armed forces have the expertise necessary to fulfil their external and domestic functions effectively and efficiently' (6).
*   *Responsibility:* 'professional armed forces are characterised by clear rules defining the responsibilities of the military as an institution and of individual soldiers' (6).
*   *Promotion:* 'professional armed forces are characterised by promotion based on achievement' (6).

This leads us to the second security function of SSR. According to Samuel Huntington (1957), professionalism entails the creation of a professional class or 'epistemic community' (Haas 1992) that operates according to the rules and social norms that constitute a 'profession'. This contributes towards the minimisation of corruption, the prevention and punishment of crimes by members of the armed forces, the prevention of human rights abuse and the politicisation of the military by a particular governing regime. SSR therefore attempts to limit the negative impact that a state's armed forces can have on its own people through direct oppression and human rights abuse and indirectly through corruption and the distribution of resources to itself – both of which have been core features of the domestic role of the military in states such as Indonesia and the Philippines (Kebschull 1994; Singh 2000).

The second way in which SSR contributes to the building of democratic peace is through its direct assistance to broader processes of democratisation. The provision of legitimate and legal internal security by professional armed forces is clearly an important precondition for democratisation more generally; the fate of Cambodia after UNTAC's withdrawal in 1993 and Thailand's return to military rule in 1991–1992 provide testimony to what happens when democracy is installed without requisite levels of security and military professionalism. Professionalisation, it is argued, provides an important normative barrier to military intervention in politics, permitting the creation of strong civilian institutions such as parliaments, judiciaries and bureaucracies that reinforce civilian supremacy over the military (Finer 1962; Perlmutter 1977; Huntington 1995). These institutions, in turn, 'lock in' the military's subservience to civilian and democratic control. The 'locking in' of a certain pattern of relations happens where 'an initial arrangement effectively maintains itself over time, even in circumstances where the reasons for the arrangement no longer apply, because the costs of change are prohibitively high' (Brown 2002: 39). This has two effects in relation to civil–military relations. On the one hand, it protects civilian institutions from the threat of military coups – 'coup-proofing' as the traditional civil–military relations literature refers to it (e.g. Quinliven 1999). On the other hand, such professional militaries may become powerful bulwarks of democracy and secularism – a particularly important and positive characteristic in states that have little experience of liberal democracy.

As such, SSR may contribute towards wider programmes aimed at fostering 'good governance'. Good governance refers to the efficient, effective and legitimate use of resources by governing elites in particular countries. As we noted earlier, the 'new aid paradigm' insists that the key problem confronted by those interested in fostering economic development was not merely poverty or the lack of scarce resources but endemic inequalities and social injustice. Whilst such inequalities are partly caused by global economic structures, they are exacerbated in many developing states such as some of those in Southeast Asia by the lack of good governance. SSR can contribute towards good governance by bringing the military under the ambit of parliament, curtailing so-called off-budget expenses, and creating transparent methods of governance and management that filter into other areas of government (Hendrickson and Ball 2002).

Finally, SSR can contribute to development. In places formerly stricken with protracted social conflict (such as Indonesia and the Philippines), SSR can contribute directly to demobilisation and post-conflict peacebuilding. There has been increased recognition that one of the main reasons why violent conflict recurs in places like Cambodia, Aceh and other Indonesian islands is that there has never been a sustained policy of demobilising belligerents and reintegrating them into society. Ongoing conflict delays and retards development programmes whilst at the same time indicating that the civilian economy is incapable of absorbing large numbers of adults and youths into the workforce. Because professionalisation usually implies a *reduction* in the actual size of the armed forces and the monopolisation of legitimate violence within a state, SSR depends on the successful rehabilitation of former soldiers into civilian life. Consequently, foreign donors involved in professionalisation programmes ought to be responsible for the welfare of demobilised persons not least because successful demobilisation is an important element of the professionalisation process. They need to ensure that the local economy *can* absorb former soldiers in meaningful ways that imply a sustained commitment to economic development (Colletta *et al.* 1996; Spear 1996). More generally, the provision of a basic level of internal and external security and the curtailing of the negative aspects of the security sector's role in developing states mark in themselves a significant contribution to development, as is recognised by the 'new aid paradigm'.

SSR therefore claims to contribute to the construction of democratic peace by assisting in the provision of legitimate physical security, contributing to embedding democratisation, and creating an environment conducive to long-term development programmes. The agenda insists that in each of these areas, an illegitimate, non-transparent, politicised or cadre controlled armed force acts as a powerful impediment to progressive change, a claim sustained by a cursory glance around Southeast Asia.

How, though, does thinking about SSR contribute to or challenge more traditional approaches to civil–military relations? Edmunds (2001: 1–2) argues that SSR introduces at least three new and important lines of thought. First, it takes us beyond the pattern of thinking about a civil–military dichotomy in which an interventionist military struggles with a civilian elite for power. Instead, the military may actively contribute towards the internalisation of good governance practices and democratisation by local elites. In many parts of the post-colonial world the indigenous military was a constitutive element of the state building process populated by members of the national liberation movement charged with constructing civilian bureaucracies. Often, therefore, the question is not necessarily the degree of civilian control or management over the military, for in many non-democratic regimes the civil–military distinction is blurred. Rather, the central question is how *democratic* that control is.

Second, it forces us to consider wider issues of state capacity – taking us back to van Doorn's (1975) understanding of the need for effectiveness within legitimate armed forces. Armed forces do more than merely defend the state's borders. They can contribute towards the overall capacity of the state, fulfil normative roles and facilitate regional and global cooperation in a number of ways.

Finally, taking up the DFID agenda discussed earlier, Edmunds argues that thinking about SSR widens our engagement with the internal functions of the security forces, and not just their ability to threaten civilian governments through coups. Indeed, this approach suggests that there is a need to look beyond ideas such as 'coup-proofing' towards an understanding of the wider contribution that the armed forces can make to democratisation and good governance programmes. Thinking about SSR therefore ought to prompt a discussion about what a particular military is for and the role it plays in wider society. This again takes us beyond the simplistic idea that militaries need to be 'constrained' by civilians towards a more thorough appreciation of the positive and negative impacts that the armed forces can have on human security, democratisation and development.

This brings us to two general questions. First, how do we define the security sector? The whole purpose of thinking about a security sector is to acknowledge that there is more in the equation than a military formation, but by moving beyond this traditional focus the potential list of entities that might fall within the security sector is immense, potentially invalidating the usefulness of the concept itself. For the purposes of this book, therefore, the 'security sector' is taken to consist of: *Organisations that are able to employ lethal violence in a way considered legitimate by the political community and the mechanisms used to control those organisations.*

There are several reasons for adopting this apparently narrow definition. First, practical policies that come under the rubric of SSR are primarily concerned with issues related to armed forces and militia groups and not issues of policing and wider aspects of human security, though it is important to acknowledge their interdependence and there are certainly areas where the relationship between the roles ascribed to the military and police overlap. Issues relating to the police are particularly pertinent in the Malaysian case, for example (see Chapter 4). Second, this definition opens up the study to include the numerous security/intelligence services and paramilitary (both non-state and state-based) organisations that operate in Southeast Asia.

This raises a second question of what, precisely, policies aimed at promoting SSR consist of. There have been a number of attempts to identify the remit of SSR practices and policies. Nicole Ball (2000: 18), perhaps the leading figure in this area, has identified five types of assistance that foreign donors can offer in order to facilitate and encourage SSR. They are: the strengthening of civil institutions; the professionalisation of civilian defence and security personnel; the professionalisation of security forces; the institutionalisation of mechanisms to develop security policy and identify security needs; and the provision of assistance to overcome the legacies of war. SSR certainly includes the areas of reform identified by DFID (earlier) and Nicole Ball, but we can broaden these out into three generic areas of concern: control, capacity and cooperation. It is worth elaborating a little more on what we mean by this.

Control – SSR is about establishing civilian *and democratic* control over instruments of lethal force. This involves making security forces accountable to democratically elected civilian authorities; general adherence to the rule of law – both domestic and international; making the security sector adhere to the same principles of financial management and transparency as the non-security sector; creating and embedding clear lines of authority which establish civilian *and* democratic control of the military; building capacity within civilian government and civil society to scrutinise defence policy (building an epistemic community for defence); creating an environment conducive to the participation of civil society in security matters; and ensuring that the training of professional soldiers is in line with the requirements of democratic societies (Ball 2002: 5).

Capacity – it is about building organisations, 'which accept that their role is to fulfil the demands of the (civilian and democratic) government of the state [or political community] and are able to undertake military activities in an effective and efficient way and whose organisation and structure reflect these twin assumptions' (Forster *et al.* 2001: 5). SSR aims to create professional armed forces that are able to fulfil their functions (which consist primarily of the provision of internal and external security) in an effective, efficient and legitimate manner. It also aims to create systems of security governance that have a sufficient level of expertise and capacity to implement the security policies of governments in efficient and effective ways.

Cooperation – it is about reducing regional and internal security dilemmas by reorienting organisations, promoting confidence, and establishing cross-border working partnerships. As Edmunds argued (2001), since Morris Janowitz (1960) identified the 'constabulary concept', it has been recognised that militaries can play a normative international role. They can, for instance, promote cooperation and integration through defence diplomacy, joint exercises, training and education, and combined actions against common threats such as people smuggling, piracy and international terrorism (see Hills 2000).

The pitfalls

There are, however, several problems with this new focus on SSR. These include theoretical problems and more specific problems with the way that SSR programmes might be implemented in non-Western regions like Southeast Asia. Broadly speaking, the normative claims at the heart of SSR are grafted onto the back of the normative claims made by the democratic peace thesis. As such, the idea that material resources and intellectual weight should be given to SSR as opposed to more traditional aspects of civil–military relations draws the same criticisms as the democratic peace thesis, particularly when we talk about the need for states to incorporate SSR concerns into their broader development and democratisation strategies. Three arguments in particular are of relevance here.

The first of these generic criticisms is that some writers argue that there is little evidence to support the existence of a democratic peace. Many critics doubt the empirical evidence for the claim that democracies do not fight each other. Some argue that the evidence is too scant to prove that peace could be attributed to chance (Spiro 1994; Cohen 1995). Others point out that the definitions of 'democracy' and 'war' are so vague that they can be manipulated to provide favourable evidence for any thesis (see Russett 1993: 16). A third group of critics point out that there are plenty of cases where democracies *have* fought each other, the most commonly cited case being the Spanish–American war in the nineteenth century (Layne 1994). This criticism poses a fundamental challenge to SSR because it challenges the basic assumption that underpins it: that only *democratic* armed forces create the degree of legitimate security needed to foster long-term development and democratisation. The claim here is that democracy does not account for peace and hence development and security (see Cohen 1994). Whilst in Asia there are plenty of cases where corrupt and non-democratic militaries act as a brake on social, economic and political development (Indonesia perhaps being the best example) there are also cases where non-democratic militaries that break Western norms about the relationship between the military and civilian power actually foster secularism, developmentalism, and at least a basic level of political and civil rights (Thailand to an extent). When thinking about supporting SSR programmes, there is therefore a need to bear in mind that the causal links demonstrated in Figure 1.1 are not unproblematic.

A second set of criticisms hold that SSR is an agenda imposed by the West and that democratic ideals do not take root if they are imposed (through aid conditionality for instance). Critics argue that it is not possible to understand democratisation and development processes without recognising that both are intimately linked with colonisation (Barkawi and Laffey 1999: 411). They point out that not only were liberal democratic values imposed on the rest of the world by Western imperial states, but also many one-party systems evolved from the demands of fighting anti-colonial wars (e.g. Ho Chi Minh in Vietnam). They argue that the appearance of democratic peace emerges from the fact that liberal democracies are embedded in a web of political, social and, most crucially, economic relations that support capitalist power (Barkawi and Laffey 1999: 419). Seen in this way, the aim of SSR is not the furtherance of international peace and global development but rather the expansion and strengthening of international capitalism and a Westphalian society of states in a Western European image. As such, regional opponents to SSR might plausibly argue that it is an illegitimate foreign imposition.

Third, and linked to the first two, far from breeding security, SSR and the promotion of liberal democracy may foster instability. The promotion of liberal democracy associated with SSR (which entails the privileging of demands for political and civil rights at the expense of those for socio-economic and cultural rights) may actually encourage instability and violence by dissolving the 'patrimonial glue' that binds many states together (see Abrahamsen 2002). Moreover, the forced reform of the armed forces may actually create instability and help establish atavistic relations between civilian and military power, particularly if the reform process is not indigenously owned and internalised.

These three generic problems with the SSR agenda translate into specific problems about the actual relationship between SSR and wider processes of democratisation and development and problems associated with (1) adding security sector conditionality to foreign aid programmes and (2) ensuring that SSR processes are effective in themselves.

Neil Cooper and Michael Pugh (2002: 19–24) have summed up several additional relevant criticisms of the SSR agenda. They are that the focus on the security sector risks overlooking other important factors crucial to the development and democratisation programmes; there is a danger that the SSR programme will be hijacked by actors pursuing the 'traditional' cold war agenda of military assistance and the patron–client relations it engendered; the SSR discourse may be used to legitimise policies such as arms sales that may not contribute to democratisation and development; SSR tends to overlook the relationships between local, regional and global actors and to focus on the donor and overcoming the 'weakness' of the 'recipient' state.

Two further problems can be added to this list. The first is the question of ownership. Reform programmes that are widely seen as external impositions may be ineffective. Within liberal political thought there is a long-standing belief that imposed democracy cannot be internalised by societies that it is imposed upon. John Stuart Mill (1874: 238–264), for instance, argued that democracy not won by the people would be fragile. This freedom would be self-contradictory because it is won by 'foreign' agents and therefore represents the replacing of one form of foreign rule (colonialism) with another. Whilst there have been cases of imposed democracy taking root (post war Germany and Japan being the best examples) the general argument holds a salutary lesson for SSR. For SSR programmes to be effective they need to be 'owned' and internalised by the groups most affected by them. Armed forces can only be professionalised and brought under democratic control effectively if the relevant armed forces and civilian authorities are themselves committed to doing so. There are a number of strategic benefits to both groups that may flow from a successful SSR programme. In theory at least, it delivers a more effective, capable and legitimate armed force. The danger, though, is that if the process is viewed as an external imposition rather than an externally supported domestic initiative, local actors are likely to pay mere lip service to reform. Throughout Southeast Asia and elsewhere, such lip service is evidenced by the fact that states have impressive constitutional arrangements for civilian scrutiny of the military but in many cases this does not translate into *actual* civilian or democratic control over the military (see part 2).

A further potential problem is that SSR may actually inhibit wider processes of development and democratisation by effecting the prioritisation of military over civilian aspects of governance. According to much of the SSR literature, one of the principle concerns of the reform process is to actually *reduce* defence spending. Both the IMF and World Bank have identified excessive defence spending in developing countries as a major barrier to development and democratisation. However, leaving aside the domestic social and political problems that may be prompted by reductions in defence spending, international agencies have been unable to accurately identify what *excessive* military spending actually is (see MacDonald 1996). Simple measures of the proportion of GDP spent on defence, used by Western states to evaluate defence spending levels, are often inappropriate in places with relatively low GDP's but relatively significant security concerns. Moreover, one of the cornerstones of the SSR agenda is the idea that it produces more efficient armed forces. That is, armed forces capable of accomplishing their tasks more effectively but with fewer resources. The argument follows that if a state abolishes national service it can create a smaller but more effective professional armed force at lower cost. However, the practical experience of states such as Afghanistan and East Timor who have embarked on such a path is that small professional armed forces are actually *more expensive* than larger conscript based forces. Wages and the standard of living for soldiers have to increase, expenditure on equipment increases exponentially, and participation in multinational operations provides extra costs for very little material gain (though significant normative gains) (Hood 2005; Sedra 2006).

What all this suggests, therefore, is that whilst the potential to influence broader processes of democratisation and development through SSR may be significant and appealing to regional political elites and foreign donors alike – not least because of the clear correlation between a basic level of security and the success of other policies and programmes – the contribution that SSR might make is neither as self-evident nor always wholly positive as its advocates suggest. That is not to say that SSR should be stillborn. Instead, we are suggesting the need for contextual sensitivity in the way in which SSR programmes are put together and the way that they are related to wider development and democratisation programmes. Not least, such programmes need to be based on an understanding of the wider role of the military in domestic society, the socio-economic context, the cultural and normative traditions within the military, and the relationship between the military, the civilian state and civil society.

SSR in Southeast Asia

To summarise the argument so far, we contend that there are significant problems relating to, and emerging from, the role of the military in Southeast Asia and its relationship to both the civilian authorities and the wider population. Such problems pose a threat to human rights and human security in addition to inhibiting economic development and processes of democratisation. Since the mid-1990s, the SSR agenda has emerged in the West as a way of dealing with such problems by promoting the wholesale reform of the security sector along three axes – improving democratic and civilian control over the armed forces, improving their capacity through professionalisation and improving regional relations through security cooperation. However, we noted that there were some generic problems with the SSR agenda relating to both its central causal claims and its likely effectiveness and impact, especially in non-Western settings. Whilst these problems cast doubt upon the ability of the extant SSR agenda to transform security politics in Southeast Asia, we think that they constitute a case for thinking more carefully about SSR in a Southeast Asian context, not a case for rejecting SSR itself. The key reason for this, as this section demonstrates and as the second part of the book will amplify, is that the language and some of the policies related to SSR have been taken up by Southeast Asian elites. Although at a very early stage, there is some evidence of it having positive effects in terms of addressing the problems highlighted in the introduction, in precisely the ways predicted by SSR advocates in the West. As indicated above, the purpose of this section is to briefly demonstrate that the SSR agenda is being adopted, at least in part or in rhetoric, and has had some discernible effects. Of course, we will elaborate on both themes in much more detail in the second part of the book.

While the East Timor case stands out as the lone case of explicit externally driven SSR in the region, it is certainly not alone if one thinks about the whole panoply of the reform agenda (see Huxley 2001). In the Philippines, Thailand and Indonesia there have been moves since the 1990s to develop at least civilian (though not necessarily democratic) control of the military. In Thailand, for example, Prime Minister Chavalit (1996–97) intervened in military decision-making to assert civilian primacy and promote his own supporters. Such moves entrenched greater civilian control over the military but failed to uphold the ideal of 'depoliticising' the military (Huxley 2001: 9–12) or tackle deep structural issues relating to the role of the military, providing catalysts for the 2006 coup. The fall of Marcos (Philippines, 1986) and Suharto (Indonesia, 1998), moreover, opened up the possibility for military reform in both countries, even though this possibility failed to fully materialise at the time largely because the military remained an independent political, economic and social actor and because there was little incentive to reform. In Malaysia, Singapore and Brunei, where civilian control of the military is entrenched, there have been positive steps towards greater transparency and accountability. However, in the Philippines, Burma, Cambodia (to a lesser extent Vietnam), Papua New Guinea and the Solomon Islands the security sector continues to act as a powerful barrier to development and democratisation through their endemic corruption, human rights abuses, inefficiency, lack of professionalism and the absence of transparency or accountability.

There are at least two reasons why the region's states would want to engage with the SSR agenda. First, American and European military assistance is to some degree tied to fulfilment of SSR related goals. While it should be noted that some significant setbacks in SSR have occurred since 11 September 2001 – for instance Foot (2004) observes that the US has expediently turned a blind eye to human rights issues in Southeast Asian countries generally in order to advance its 'war on terror' agenda – efforts related to the 'war on terror' have nevertheless presented important opportunities to advance SSR. In the Philippines, reform of the military has been externally driven by the US interest in curtailing 'internal security threats' (i.e. Islamic terrorism) there. The 2003 Joint Defence Agreement between the US and Filipino governments tied military assistance aimed at enabling the Filipino military to better respond to Islamic and separatist terrorism to progress in wider reforms in the military sector. Furthermore, the US has made the delivery of aid to Indonesia conditional on measures to improve the transparency of Indonesia's military budget as well as progress on human rights (Antara 2004). Second, as well as improving the military sector's transparency, SSR is also interested in improving its effectiveness. Political leaders therefore have a vested interest in pursuing SSR even though this might also constitute an important limit on its emancipatory potential.

Before we continue, it is important to add the caveat that although several of the region's states are talking the language of SSR, substantive reform has been limited. In some places civilian control may have been bought at the expense of democratic control whilst in others (Thailand), civilian control itself proved much more fragile than most commentators believed. Moreover, in most Southeast Asian states outside the scope of this study, such as Burma, Vietnam, Laos and Cambodia especially, the SSR agenda has had virtually no impact. What follows therefore are four areas of emerging reform in Southeast Asia that have potential to stimulate wider SSR processes and address some of the problems described at the beginning of this chapter.

Military Professionalism. Indonesia's move towards a professional army was driven primarily by a significant increase in the proportion of officers given professional military education at Indonesian and foreign military academies in the 1960s and 1970s, new practices of promotion by merit and the depoliticisation of the officer corps (Honna 1999: 254; Kammen and Chandra 1999: 81–82). This new, though still relatively small, group of military professionals have fostered a strategy of *'regenerasi'* (regeneration) aimed at professionalising the Indonesian military. According to observers, this has had several direct and indirect positive effects. First, it has reduced the ability of senior officers to use military power to run corrupt regional fiefdoms, lessening the military's role in regional politics, its direct implication in human rights abuse and its exploitation of resources and personnel for the private benefit of military officers. Second, the creation of a professional ethos within the officer cadres has made it easier for advocates of reform within the military to make their case both in public and within military and government circles. Finally, the formalisation of a merit-based promotion system has created incentives for officers and members of lower ranks to follow orders and abide by the law (Kammen and Chandra 1999: 83–84). Coupled with these shifts in behaviour is an equally crucial infusion of the 'discourse of professionalism' which is helping to legitimise and internalise these practices (Honna 2003). Together these developments point toward the potential for an Indonesian military less antagonistic to the human security of Indonesian citizens.

Socio-Economic Role of the Military. Although traditional approaches to civil–military relations insist that the military sector ought to play no domestic role beyond emergency assistance to the civilian power, it is important to recognise that some of the wider roles and functions fulfilled by militaries in Southeast Asia can help to improve socio-economic conditions in some areas. For instance, through the adoption of mandates with development, relief, and economic foci, an increased willingness by the military to protect and rehabilitate affected populations can be fostered. Evidence indicates that this has already occurred, albeit sporadically, throughout Southeast Asia. The Philippine military, for example, has a long history of 'civic action' missions whereby the military has been employed for public works projects (Berry 1986: 226–229). Armed forces have been used to provide the necessary manpower and expertise to build much-needed infrastructure and move other common public goods to the benefit of the broader population. In Thailand, the military has also been involved in the promotion of the people's welfare (Bungbongkarn 1988: 134–137). In the late 1950s for instance, the military provided rural economic development assistance as part of its effort to win 'hearts and minds' during a counter-insurgency campaign (1988: 140–142). Again in the 1970s the military offered rural assistance as part of its fight against communist insurgency movements. Bunbongkarn (1988: 160) concludes that through programmes which tie the building of infrastructure and regional development assistance with the maintenance of order, the Thai military has acted as an important bridge between urban rich and rural poor populations, an outcome which is clearly consistent with emancipatory goals. Finally, the extensive involvement of militaries from across the ASEAN region in the provision of humanitarian assistance for the victims of the December 2004 tsunami illustrates well the fact that, appropriately engaged, the militaries of Southeast Asia can provide essential emergency assistance to the region's most needy. Armed forces from around the region were employed widely to alleviate the human suffering and insecurity caused by natural disaster (Agence-France Presse 2005).

Democratisation and Transparency. Security sector reform in the region also enables emancipatory reform in a number of areas of public life, making a direct contribution to human security. Three areas in particular stand out. First, military advocates of reform may also be powerful advocates of wider political reform. Somewhat ironically, between Thailand's two most recent coups, senior military officers played a vital role in arguing the case for anti-corruption and government transparency (Soontornpipet 2004). Second, the withdrawal of the military from politics enables civil society to play a much more important role in politics. On the one hand, the withdrawal of the military has itself opened avenues for civil society engagement. On the other, in some cases the military has actually encouraged this engagement as a means of making the civilian political authorities accountable. Finally, a point that should not be undervalued, the depoliticisation of the military can facilitate wider moves towards the establishment of an independent bureaucracy, helping to transfer power from the bureaucratic elite to the political elite (Ganesen 2001: 3). Wider moves toward democracy have taken many forms. Together, these developments indicate ways in which military reform itself can indirectly support broader patterns of democratisation.

International Cooperation. International security cooperation provides avenues through which military forces can actively help to 'mitigate' or occasionally 'transcend' regional security dilemmas (see Booth and Wheeler 2007). On one hand, SSR benefits can come from 'carrot' style approaches designed to encourage state militaries to reform. The US Justice Department, for example, has committed $40 million for a project to bring Indonesia's police more into line with Western democratic norms (McBeth 2003: 18). This type of cooperation can be seen in other examples. For instance, the US has financed and guided the creation of a 400-person counter-terrorism unit in Indonesia (McBeth 2003: 18) and the US and Filipino militaries have engaged in joint war exercises (Manilla Bulletin 2004). And while the purpose of these interactions is largely to combat terrorism in the region as part of the US 'war on terror', a likely side effect is that an improvement of their sometimes strained relations can open up further possibilities for SSR, increasing the potential for the military to play a positive role vis-à-vis human security. Recently, for example, the US based its resumption of military ties with Indonesia upon progress on SSR, particularly budget transparency and issues pertaining to human rights, demonstrating that whilst strategic interests may be the main driver of foreign engagement in the region, such engagement may help to stimulate measures that may enhance human security, however marginally.

Finally, military cooperation can be driven by assistance for humanitarian causes. The reaction and involvement by a number of state militaries to the tragic 2004 tsunami, as mentioned above, illustrate this. Cooperation came in the form of direct assistance to the victims and it not only brought together the Indonesian military with the militaries of established democracies like Australia, Japan and the United States, but it also led to extended interaction between the militaries of Indonesia and its regional state partners comprising ASEAN (Agence-France Presse 2005).

From this brief discussion, which will be amplified in part 2 of the book, it is clear both that the language of SSR has been partially adopted by political and military elites in Southeast Asia and that this has been manifested in policy, albeit to a relatively small degree. This is to be expected if we accept the claim that as it is perceived to be a predominantly Western doctrine, SSR is likely to have little impact on policy outcomes in Southeast Asia. For that reason, we need a better understanding of the historical, institutional and strategic context in Southeast Asia in order to both understand the nature of the reform process in more detail and to identify 'entry points' by which actors both in the West and regionally might promote reform more effectively. This is the primary purpose of the following chapter.

2 Civil–military relations and institutional change

What factors shape the relationship between the security sector, other state institutions, the wider society and the region? Are civil–military relations determined by objective characteristics or ideational factors? How do institutional relationships change? Our argument, presaged in the previous chapter and further developed in the following chapter, is that history, culture, identity and institutional pathologies matter. These ideational factors shape the way actors see their role in the world and their relationship to others, as well as defining the range of policies and practices that may be deemed effective and/or appropriate in particular circumstances. Although instrumental and material factors play an important role in framing the range of options available to decision-makers, they are not determinative. They are filtered and mediated by a range of ideational factors. This is evidenced by the different ways in which Southeast Asian governments, militaries and societies have responded to broadly similar contextual circumstances (see Chapters 4–7).

As we demonstrate in the following chapter and the case study chapters that follow, institutions develop their own identities, ways of operating and views of the world that shape the way they think they ought to act and set limits to what is seen as politically feasible and desirable. The purpose of this chapter is to conceptualise the relationship between the security sector and other institutions and to identify, in broad conceptual terms, some of the drivers of change. All too often, treatments of the security sector in the non-Western world have focused on supposedly 'objective' factors and have overlooked the significant historical, cultural and ideational forces that shape civil–military relations. Taking a lesson from constructivist studies of non-military matters, we argue that it is important to understand these ideational forces not only because explanations that omit or downplay such factors are always incomplete, but also because proposals for reform need to be couched in terms that make sense and appeal to pre-existing beliefs, attitudes and practices (Finnemore and Sikkink 1998).

This chapter develops in three parts. The first considers traditional ways of thinking about civil–military relations in the non-Western world, some of which focus on purportedly 'objective' material conditions. We argue that such approaches are flawed for at least two reasons. First, they conflate correlation with explanation and symptoms with causes. For example, Finer insisted that 'where public attachment to civilian institutions is strong, military intervention in politics will be weak' (Finer 1962: 21). This seemingly simple law raises more questions than it answers: how do we measure public attachment? What counts as military intervention in politics? Is the relation between public attachment and military intervention causal? If so, in what direction does causation run? Weak public attachment to civilian institutions may just as easily be a symptom of military intervention in politics as a cause. Second, such accounts are predicated on the assumption that civilian and military elites are discrete, pre-formed, entities. As we noted in the previous chapter, however, one of the dominant models of civil–military organisation in Southeast Asia has traditionally been the concordant model whereby elites form alliances across civil–military boundaries. Thus, although the question of civilian control of the military is a pertinent one, it amounts to only a small part of the problem of security governance and, as Suharto's rule in Indonesia attests, there is no necessary correlation between a semblance of civilian control and democratic, transparent and legitimate control (see Chapter 5).

The second part of the chapter seeks to supplement traditional ways of understanding civil–military relations in the non-Western world by introducing a range of ideational factors. We suggest that although material factors are important, they are given social meaning by a variety of ideas that operate at and between different levels. For heuristic reasons, we divide these into three levels of analysis. At the international level, we suggest that ideas about the nature of the region, the types of security threats and the nature of relations with neighbours play an important part in the security sector's self-identification and the role ascribed to it by others. The next level down involves the 'strategic culture' of a state and society. For our purposes, a strategic culture is understood as a distinctive body of beliefs, attitudes and practices about the role and composition of the security sector and the appropriate use of force (see Johnston 1995; Katzenstein 1996; Booth and Trood 1999; Gray 1999). Such beliefs frame dominant opinions about the appropriate role and composition of the military and its relationship to other institutions and society at large. In short, they create expectations about what the military ought to look like, do, and how it should relate to other sectors of society. The final level of analysis comes down to the institutional level. Here, we explore how the 'pathologies' (Barnett and Finnemore 1999), rules and cultures of bureaucracies shape the way they view themselves and others and the way they think and act (Herzfeld 1993; Scott 1998), an issue we develop further in the following chapter.

The final part of the chapter turns to the question of reform – how are these beliefs, attitudes and practices at the national level changed along the lines intimated in the previous chapter? We suggest that there are two types of change, labelled *fine-tuning* and *fundamental* by Longhurst (2004: 18). 'Fine-tuning' involves the reinterpretation of already existing beliefs, attitudes and practices to address perceived new requirements. 'Fine-tuning' may involve, for example, the recalibration of the military's primary domestic role from one associated with the suppression of ethnic minorities to one associated with economic development. Although an important change, the new policy might remain consistent with the belief that the military has an important role to play in nation-building. We suggest that there are at least three key drivers of 'fine-tuning' changes: 'institutional learning' where bureaucracies learn or develop more effective ways of pursuing established goals (Haas 1992) in situations where the measure of effectiveness remains relatively constant; 'convergence' where beliefs, attitudes and practices are adapted, but not fundamentally changed, to better reflect shared international/regional understandings of 'desirable and acceptable' forms of behaviour (Higgott 1996: 21); and 'recalibration' where pre-existing beliefs and attitudes are applied to new external issues, producing new types of practices. The principal groups of actors involved in this type of change, we argue, are national and transnational epistemic communities of military officers and experts and domestic political elites. Such changes are relatively frequent and form the normal stuff of bureaucratic politics.

'Fundamental' changes are much less frequent and may involve the alteration or removal of a core belief, attitude or practice, sometimes in dramatic fashion. For instance, in the case outlined above, a fundamental change would involve the emergence of a belief that the military had a subordinate role, if any role at all, in nation-building. Sometimes, fundamental changes may involve the collapse of the strategic culture as a whole. Fundamental changes tend to be brought about by one or more of four factors: a rapid proliferation of fine-tuning that ultimately undermines a once dominant belief, attitude or practice; an external shock or environmental change[1] that renders an aspect of strategic culture anachronistic; foreign imposition by force or bribery; or a legitimacy crisis wherein a belief, attitude or practice can no longer be sustained consensually and must instead call upon either bribery or coercion to secure support and compliance, both of which are unsustainable in the long-term.[2] Such crises can only be resolved by the recalibration of the social bases of legitimacy (Reus-Smit 2007), in this case a reconfiguring of the belief, attitude or practice in crisis. In relation to the security sector, these types of changes are generally forced upon the sector either by fundamental changes in a society's political culture, significant processes of political agitation, external shocks over which the security elite had little if any agency or determined external pressure which either creates a legitimacy crisis or radically alters the balance of costs and benefits associated with a belief, attitude or practice.

Conceptualising civil–military relations and the process of change in this way is important for identifying the drivers of and obstacles to security sector reform in Southeast Asia and we will return to these themes in the conclusion.

Thinking about civil–military relations

Traditionally, theories of civil–military relations have been dominated by thinking about military professionalism and the civilian control of the military in liberal democratic states (Feaver 2003: 7). Much less attention has been given to non-Western experiences other than to hypothesise about why non-Western states have not developed patterns of civil–military relations identical to the West and about how they might do so. Consequently, predominant approaches to civil–military relations have tended to advise exporting the Western model, and see this as a template for the efficient and effective control of the military by civilians based on the concept of professionalism (Cohen 2002: 226). In this, they have much in common with the security sector reform agenda described in the previous chapter. The purpose of this section is to elaborate on some of the themes raised in the previous chapter in order to demonstrate that we cannot get a good understanding of security sector reform in Southeast Asia by simply grafting a successful Western theory onto a new set of empirical cases, because the assumptions, language and expectations that underpin these theories, though helpful, are by themselves ill-suited to the Southeast Asian context.

Questions about the civilian control of armed forces first came to prominence in the 1960s as scholars sought to make sense of the many military coups that seemed to plague Africa, Asia and Latin America (Edmunds 2007). According to Samuel Finer, the prevalence of coups was hardly surprising given that

> [t]he armed forces have three massive political advantages over civilian organizations: a marked superiority in organization, a highly emotional symbolic status, and a monopoly of arms. They form a prestigious corporation or Order, enjoying overwhelming superiority in the means of applying force. The wonder, therefore, is not why this rebels against its civilian masters, but why it ever obeys them.
>
> (Finer 1962: 5)

Morris Janowitz expressed a similar view when he identified a sense of powerlessness on the part of legislators in the face of the military (Janowitz 1960: 357). For many of these early scholars of civil–military relations, the participation of the military in politics was seen as advantageous because the qualities described above could play a useful role in fostering national unity in post-colonial states and furthering 'modernisation' and economic development. Moreover, it was no coincidence that many military dictatorships – including some of those in Southeast Asia – were bulwarks against the spread of communism.

As we noted in Chapter 1, some of the earliest forms of Western encouragement of security sector reform came in the form of military aid aimed at propping-up anti-communist governments. Giving expression to these attitudes, in 1963 Levy argued that 'the most efficient vehicle for the maximisation of modernisation with the minimisation of the uncontrolled spread of side-effects' was the armed forces (Levy 1963: 27). Problems with this paradigm were soon to emerge, however. Not least, military governments failed to deliver rates of economic growth commensurate with those achieved by civilian led governments. Far from fostering national unity, post-colonial states with military regimes tended to be less stable and more violent than other types of regime. Moreover, as Martin Edmonds argued, rather than promoting the 'national interest' or 'common good' military regimes tended to aggressively promote the institutional interests of the armed force and/or the personal interests of a few prominent individuals (Edmonds 1988: 201–203). Indeed, Edmonds suggests that such failings were 'a consequence of the internal characteristics of the military institution itself: a prioritisation of its own institutional interests; an antagonism towards the "political"; and an inclination towards order and control over political development' (Edmunds 2007: 17). As we described in the previous chapter, therefore, the armed forces in non-Western societies came to be seen as powerful inhibitors of economic and political development, though there remained a tension between the West's interest in promoting such development and its strategic interest in supporting anti-communist regimes. Being only too aware of this tension, many military regimes – with those of Southeast Asia at the forefront – emphasised their anti-communist credentials.

The retreat from modernisation theory, which we discuss in more detail in the next chapter, prompted a sea change in the way that many in the West thought about civil–military relations in the rest of the world. The critical questions became (and to an extent still are): (1) what factors explain weak civilian control of the military and (2) what factors contribute to the strengthening of civilian control? In answering the first question, the field has produced a number of models that claim to explain the phenomenon by identifying correlations between weak civilian control and other (mainly social and political) factors. The answer to the second question has been found almost singularly in the concept of professionalisation discussed briefly in the previous chapter. The remainder of this section addresses these two discourses and identifies a series of problems which the proceeding discussion aims to address whilst forwarding the normative agenda embedded in security sector reform.

Civilian control of the military ... and vice versa

There are a number of theories that set out to explain and predict the level of civilian control over the military and we will focus on only two of the most prominent, those put forward by Samuel Finer and, more recently, Michael Desch.[3] These provide a useful snapshot because, according to Desch himself, they reflect two very different ways of approaching this question with Finer offering what Desch labels a 'cultural' explanation and Desch offering an instrumental account. From our view, however, the two perspectives have more in common than they have differences and share several key problems.

Finer's (1962: 67) case starts with the proposition that there are three enabling conditions that permit the military to intervene in politics: motive, mood and opportunity. *Motives*, for Finer, include an impulse to prevent the state from descending into crisis or to protect national unity after a crisis has erupted; an entrenched belief that military intervention is necessary for the national interest – a judgement which, incidentally, can only be made by the military elite; a desire to protect the corporate interests of the armed forces or to protect their prestige or political and/or economic privileges; and the self-interest of prominent individuals who may use the armed forces as a vehicle for advancing themselves politically or economically, or both. Such motives, however, are evident in almost every military and to some extent every security sector is involved in the promotion of its corporate interests (cf. Huntington 1957). Indeed, the promotion and protection of corporate interests is often understood to be a normal part of democratic politics. For Finer, the second necessary requirement for military intervention in politics is *mood*, by which he means that militaries need to have either an abnormally high level of collective sense of self-worth and believe that they are 'superior to civilians' (Finer 1962: 67), an exaggerated sense of their own place in the national scheme of things or, more often, a combination of both. Motive and mood are not enough however. Militaries also need an *opportunity* to intervene in politics. Opportunities are created either when there is 'an increased civilian dependence on the military' or when the military enjoys popular legitimacy (Finer 1962: 72).

When they operate together, these enabling conditions produce very weak civilian control of the military but they do not necessarily explain military intervention in politics. According to Finer, an additional factor can inhibit military intervention – the prevalence of a norm of military subordination to civilian rule. That is, where there are strong societal expectations that the armed forces will be subordinate to civilian rule, military intervention in politics is unlikely. For Finer, therefore, the military's role in politics boiled down to societal expectations about the proper ordering of politics rather than down to military professionalisation. Finer was a bit sketchy, however, on where this norm would come from, how it would be sustained, and how it would come to be embedded. He argued that the norm was dependent on three subsidiary considerations relating to the civilian authorities: the government must be authoritative, legitimate and lawful (Finer 1962: 21). These three conditions equated to public support for civilian government and inhibited military intervention by imposing political costs on the military. Thus, Finer insisted that

> Where public attachment to civilian institutions is strong, military intervention in politics will be weak…Where civilian associations and parties are strong and numerous, where the procedures for the transfer of power are orderly, and where the location of supreme authority is not seriously challenged, the political ambit of the military will be circumscribed.
>
> (1962: 21)

Studying Malaysia among other countries, Claude Welch came to a similar conclusion, finding that the ineffectiveness of civilian governments will not prompt military intervention in cases where there is a strong public attachment to specific civilian leaders (Welch 1976: 313–315). From this perspective, therefore, civilian control of the military can be maintained by developing a strong norm of military subordination to civilians and tackling problems related to motive, mood and opportunity.

By contrast, Michael Desch argued that 'cultural' explanations such as Finer's lacked explanatory power and in its place offered an explicitly 'universal' theory that could be applied to any state and which, he claimed, had 'broad explanatory and predictive power' (Desch 1999: 11). Desch's model boils down to an observation – that the extent of civilian control of the military is determined by six variables:

1   How 'experienced' the civilian political leaders are.
2   The level of unity among civilians.

3   The nature of civilian control: is it objective (i.e. the military is distanced from politics), subjective (i.e. the military is politicised) or neither?

4   The level of unity among the armed forces.

5   The orientation of the military: internal, external or unclear?

6   The extent to which the 'ideas' of the military and civilians are divergent or convergent (Desch 1999: 16).

The nature of each of these variables are themselves manipulated by the structural environment of the international system and the nature of the external and internal threats that confront the state in question. Desch argues that states that share similar threat environments will have similar responses to the above six variables and that even among dissimilar states (such as an Islamic state and a liberal democratic state) this will produce similar patterns of civilian control over the military.

There are a number of problems with Desch's claims, not the least of which is that it is empirically problematic. Moreover, despite its rejection of 'cultural' explanations it includes a cultural aspect, the variables are not measurable with any degree of accuracy, and some of the variables may actually be symptoms of weak civilian control. However, our purpose here is not to critique individual theories, but first, to show why we cannot simply import these theories into Southeast Asia to help us explain and understand the politics of security sector reform and second, to make a case for the importance of history and context. There are at least three problems with the way that both accounts set about their problem, which we will need to overcome in the proceeding discussion.

First, and arguably most importantly, both accounts assume a rigid separation between soldiers and civilians and between military institutions and civilian institutions. As such, the emphasis is placed on measuring the strength of 'civilian' control of the 'military' and factors that prevent civilians from controlling soldiers. There are a number of problems with this view, particularly when applied to a non-Western context. It assumes the existence of two types of entity and identity – civilian and military – prior to their engagement with one another. In practice, however, a state's civilian and military institutions tend to be mutually constituted. Historical sociologists have pointed to war-making as providing a significant contribution to state formation. In order to mobilise people, organise and move them, generate funds, and develop the technology of war, states created bureaucracies and those that created effective bureaucracies enjoyed a decisive advantage over their competitors (Giddens 1985; Mann 1988; Tilly 1990). This was part of a broader process which involved the centralisation of the bureaucratic state and produced, among other things, a national education system, economic system and social rituals, naturalising vernacular languages and producing forms of high culture that legitimised the state and allowed it to function efficiently (Giddens 1985: 112) War-making was not the *only* driver of this process, however, and in many cases not even the primary driver. Other drivers included bureaucratisation caused by capitalism and class conflict and bureaucratisation as a direct response to new technology (Dandeker 1990: 3–6; Barnett 2002: 109). The key point here, though, is that a permanent armed force both constitutes and is constituted by the civilian bureaucratic state. Given this, it makes little sense to start from the assumption that the civil and military sectors are two mutually opposed black boxes. The place of the military within a state is negotiated across and within civilian and military institutions. There are other, more practical, problems with this 'black box' image of civilian and military institutions. For instance, in most cases where the military is involved in politics, it establishes and legitimises itself by forging alliances with civilian politicians, bureaucracies and/or economic elites. Sometimes, militaries intervene in politics to install particular civilian regimes, sometimes at the request of those politicians. Finally, as we mentioned in the previous chapter, in many post-colonial states with a history of armed resistance to colonial rule there was often no distinction between military and political leadership.

Second, these approaches confuse causes and consequences. For example, to borrow from Finer, is a military's self-identification as the leading institution with a special role to play in national development a *cause* of weak civilian control of the military or is it a *consequence* of the military fulfilling such a role historically? What if that self-identification is ascribed to it by civilian actors? Or, alternatively, is the relationship between the two set factors correlational rather than causal? The same is true of Desch's variables. Are radically different ideas about the proper running of the state amongst the military and civilian leaderships a cause or product of weak civilian control? If we assess the sets of variables in detail we find that they help us neither explain nor understand particular patterns of behaviour. Instead, they are descriptions of the types of political and social phenomenon that surround cases of weak civilian control of the military.

Finally, a problem we identified in the previous chapter was that these approaches ask the wrong question. One can have civilian control of the military and have all the problems identified in the previous chapter and introduction: abuse, corruption, the military defending particularistic interests rather than national interests, the security sector inhibiting economic development and undermining the rule of law and so on. The most obvious example of this is the former Soviet Union. Few militaries were under tighter civilian control than the Soviet military, yet almost all the problems associated with unreformed militaries were evident there. In Southeast Asia, Suharto's Indonesia provides an equally good example (see Chapter 5). According to at least two prominent commentators in the region, civilianisation is not necessarily conducive to professionalisation especially when civilian elites are fundamentally corrupt (Djiwandono and Cheong 1988: 11). Simply establishing the factors that encourage or inhibit civilian control of the military is therefore not telling us very much about the impact of the security sector on the human security of a state's citizens or its political and economic development.

In short, therefore, common Western theories that purport to explain and understand civilian control of the military obscure as much as they illuminate. Whilst they identify some useful factors, they obscure the mutual constitution of military and civilian institutions, the historical evolution of those institutions, the networks that cross-over between those institutions and the way in which soldiers and civilians collaborate in generating and reinforcing particular modes of behaviour.

Professionalisation

The second chief preoccupation for scholars of civil–military relations was to understand how militaries could be brought under civilian control and how that control could be maintained, a preoccupation that paved the way for the emergence of the security sector reform agenda in the 1990s (see Chapter 1). For theorists like Huntington the best route to embedding civilian control of the military was through the professionalisation of the armed forces. Like security sector reform, Huntington's agenda was underpinned by an implicit normative and strategic agenda. Normatively, Huntington saw professionalisation as directly connected to the 'third wave' of democratisation, much of which involved the transition from military to democratic governance in southern Europe and Latin America especially (Huntington 1993). Strategically, the agenda was underwritten by the Clausewitzian insistence that the use of armed force was a continuation of policy 'by other means' (Clausewitz 1993: 87). As such, the military instrument should be directly and clearly subordinate to civilian and diplomatic control. Thus, whereas theorists like Finer and Desch were primarily interested in explaining weak civilian control of the military, Huntington was mainly concerned with understanding the conditions in which the transition to civilian and democratic control could be made. Moreover, whilst the former theorists insisted that the critical factor lay in the legitimacy and capacity of the civilian institutions, Huntington found the pivotal consideration within the military itself and, more specifically, its officer cadre.

Huntington's classic work on civil–military relations insists that the best way to ensure civilian and democratic control of the armed forces is by fostering the sector's professionalisation (Huntington 1957: 7–10). Conversely, therefore, weak civilian control is caused by unprofessionalism and a tendency towards 'subjective' methods of control, the foremost of these being the politicisation of the officer class (Huntington 1957: 96). According to Huntington, a professional military has three defining characteristics, which he derives from broader ideas about the nature of 'professions' more generally. First, they have a specialised expertise in 'the management of violence' (Huntington 1957: 11). In other words, they constitute an epistemic community (see below). Second, they are motivated more by a sense of responsibility and duty than material gain. Finally, a professional military takes on the persona of a corporate body with a shared identity grounded in the idea of military professionalism itself.

By fostering these three ideals, civilian institutions can professionalise the armed forces, bringing them under civilian and democratic control and – just as importantly – embedding that control by making it a pivotal part of the armed forces' identity. Moreover, by creating a 'profession' in the armed forces, professionalisation also contributes to the creation of 'objective' methods of control whereby the military and political spheres are kept separate and distinct – the former sustained not by its role in politics, economics or national development but by its own professional ethos, identity and history (Huntington 1957: 80–83). As Feld argues, individual soldiers have a symbiotic relationship with the military structure. On the one hand, to function appropriately, a professional military requires individual soldiers to obey orders, fulfil roles, and act according to established rules and customs. On the other hand, however, the status, legitimacy and role of the individual soldier are themselves constituted by the military structure (Feld 1968: 56). Indeed, one of the original impetuses for the creation of a distinctive warrior class in ancient Greece was to validate and legitimise certain types of killing, separate those types from ordinary murder, and therein protect warriors themselves from retribution by the wider society (French 2005).

This requires a bargain struck between civilians and soldiers. In return for the military voluntarily choosing not to intervene in politics, civilians must desist from politicising the military (i.e. allowing narrow political interests to determine military promotions and appointments, procurement and force structure decisions, strategic policy and so on) and must recognise the authoritativeness of the military's expertise on matters related to the organised use and threat of violence. So significant was this side of the bargain for Huntington that he went as far as to suggest that political interference in military matters might constitute justifiable grounds for military disobedience (Huntington 1957: 77).

It should be clear from this brief discussion that Huntington's theory of professionalisation suffers from many of the difficulties we found with Finer and Desch. In particular, although it recognises a symbiotic relationship between soldiers and civilians that could certainly be read as implying that this relationship is mutually constitutive, it tends to assume that military and civilian bodies are distinct institutions and it doesn't enquire into their origins. There are other problems as well if we were to try to apply the theory to Southeast Asia. First, there are empirical problems. It would be fair to suggest that the armed forces in each of the cases studied in Part 2 of this book exhibited many, if not all, of the characteristics of a professional military. A very strong case could be in relation to Malaysia that would not be problematic for Huntington's theory because of the tradition of civilian control there, but an equally strong professionalism case could be made on behalf of the Thai military – yet it has a long tradition of involvement in politics exemplified by the 2006 coup. Second, Huntington's definition of professionalism is problematic in a number of ways. Viewed from a Southeast Asian perspective, where militaries have a long tradition of promoting their own corporate interests, Huntington's injunction could be read as endorsing many of the practices commonly understood as inhibiting professionalisation, in particular economic activities aimed at generating income for military procurement. Furthermore, Huntington's insistence that professionalism is related to the military forming a closed and privileged epistemic community on the management of violence runs directly counter to the argument amongst advocates of security sector reform that transparency and accountability requires that expertise on military matters extend beyond the military. All too often, in Southeast Asia as elsewhere, armed forces use their claim to authoritative knowledge to deny scrutiny of defence spending, to justify 'off-budget' expenses and to determine national and domestic security policies outside normal democratic procedures. Not only does the idea of the professional military as a wholly autonomous actor not reflect the way that civil–military relations works in mature democracies, it also seems inimical to the reform of the security sector in

Southeast Asia. Finally, Huntington's definition of professionalism is very narrow and doesn't tell us much about what types of expertise are required, how soldiers ought to be recruited and trained, or how these core values are instantiated and nourished.

From this brief discussion of some of the core theories of civil–military relations it is evident that we cannot simply import ideas into Southeast Asia in order to understand the processes of, and obstacles to, security sector reform. As an alternative, the following section therefore aims to set out in general some of the ideational factors that play a role in shaping the relationship between civilian and military institutions in Southeast Asia.

Ideational factors

Although we are concentrating in this section on the ideational factors that shape civil–military relations in Southeast Asia and establish the context for debates about security sector reform, that should not be read as an argument that material factors are unimportant. Clearly, material factors play an important role. A country's size, geographical location, material wealth and the nature of its neighbours all play an important part in limiting the range of plausible options that its decision-makers have. However, most 'material' factors are given meaning by ideas. For instance, the fact that a state's neighbour has preponderant military power does not necessarily mean that it poses a threat that must be balanced or challenged.

Decisions about threat involve value judgements about the nature and intent of the hegemony and the extent to which its values and identity correlates with the weaker state. A prime example in this regard would be Canada's relationship with the US. Canada shares the world's longest land border with the world's most powerful state yet since the late nineteenth century has chosen not to defend that border primarily because it does not see its neighbour as a threat (Shore 1998). Similarly, there are a number of ways in which a government can portray and respond to internal discord, even violent discord.

The resolution of many of the world's most protracted conflicts has depended on a re-articulation of the nature of the problem from military-oriented to politics-oriented. In relation to terrorism, for example, governments can choose whether to use the language of 'war' or whether to respond through the criminal justice system (see Heymann 2003). Prior to 9/11, democratic states generally chose the latter. Our point here is not that material considerations ('how much money do we have?' 'are terrorists blowing up buildings?') are unimportant but that they are given meaning by ideas and that governments and militaries can only form policies once they give meaning to these material realities. These processes often involve the weighing of different sets of interests and values from a number of different perspectives and – importantly – processes of political contestation within and between bureaucracies. In order to make sense of these phenomena, we have limited our discussion on the range of influences to three levels of analysis – the international and regional, national and bureaucratic.

International and regional

In recent years there has been a significant proliferation of work on how international and regional ideas and norms shape a state's security policy and hence influence its civil–military relations. Ideas that inhabit the international and regional spheres tend not to *determine* the way a state sets up its civil–military structure except in cases where foreign actors impose particular solutions, as the US did on Japan after the Second World War and the UN did on East Timor in its defence restructuring between 1999 and 2005 (Caplan 2005). Instead, such ideas amount to, in the words of Jeffrey Legro, 'collective understandings of the proper behaviour of actors' (Legro 1997: 87). These collective understandings inform the way that states react to one another. Where a particular action or policy corresponds to these collective understandings, other states are likely to endorse it and maybe offer material support, making it easier for the state in question to pursue its policy. In cases where an action or policy appears to defy those collective understandings, however, a state can expect opprobrium, non-cooperation and even material sanctions, significantly raising the costs of that chosen course of action. Thus, although international and regional influences do not determine a state's structure of civil–military relations they can *influence* it by affecting the balance of costs and benefits associated with particular courses of action. It is therefore important to understand the international context in which patterns of civil–military relations develop. These norms and ideas fulfil at least three specific functions (see Reus-Smit 2003).

First, they are *constitutive*. Armed forces are legally recognised entities that have certain international rights and responsibilities. Members of legitimate armed forces are entitled to protection under the laws of war and enjoy certain other benefits. These benefits are conferred by the society of states upon those entities that fulfil certain criteria. Notably they must be formally related to the legitimate sovereign, they must be uniformed and recognised in a particular way, they must be hierarchically organised and they must conduct themselves with due reverence to the legal and moral norms associated with the rightful conduct of armed force (for a discussion see Bellamy 2006). Militaries that fail to satisfy these three criteria may be denied recognition. This will severely limit the types of arms they can procure, will restrict the 'war rights' that their soldiers can claim (they may, for example, be deemed 'unlawful combatants') and will diminish their authoritativeness on international security issues. In short, to be recognised as such by other like-actors, a military must behave in a particular fashion.

The second function of norms, and the one most often referred to, is their role in *constraining* the activities of social actors. Given that armed forces are partly constituted by international norms they are also conditioned to act in particular ways and are constrained from acting in other ways by more than simple calculations of power. As Michael Barnett (1995: 50) put it, states are 'embedded in an increasingly dense normative web that constrain [their] foreign policy' and the same can be said for their armed forces. As with all societies, international society is 'rule-governed' and legitimacy within that society is obtained by acting in accordance with the rules. Thus, even powerful states do not act with complete disregard for international norms. Nor are norms simply swept under the table when political interests are at stake. Not only, therefore, must the military organise itself in a particular way to achieve external validation, but it must also behave in particular ways or risk de-legitimisation and a significant increase in the costs associated with its preferred policies.

Finally, norms provide a *framework for meaningful communication* between actors within the region and more widely. Norms create a meaningful language for world politics based upon established patterns of social interaction. In their discussion about diplomatic relations, for instance, states invoke a body of shared meanings encapsulated in the Vienna Convention. Norms frame the way that states justify their behaviour and provide a means for international society to evaluate those claims. That is not to say, however, that they are always consistent or straightforward. Norms often collide, forcing political leaders to make difficult choices between competing sets of values.

Nicholas Wheeler has suggested that thinking about the role of norms in terms of a game provides a useful analogy.[4] A football match, like international society, is constituted by rules. A referee is given the job of adjudicating and the players, by and large, play according to those rules and recognise the role of the referee. Importantly, as only one person among 22, the referee cannot physically enforce his or her decisions, so compliance is largely voluntary. The object of football is to win the game by scoring goals. Different teams adopt different tactics for doing so. Some will make extensive use of the 'offside' rule. Doing so involves difficult calculations about the rules and the most effective way of securing victory. The *practical* rules of the game give the players a common language that allows them to calculate strategies based upon expectations about what it means to be successful and what the other players will do. Moreover, both teams have a vested interest in abiding by these rules and acknowledging the status of the referee because their very existence as participants in a game depends upon them doing so. Football is not football without two goals, a ball, and a set of rules.

International norms therefore fulfil three important roles in shaping a state's civil–military relations. They contribute to the *constitution* of the armed forces, they *constrain* those actors' actions, and they provide a *framework for meaningful communication*. Because we are interested in how civil–military relations change, it is worth briefly commenting on different types of norms and their susceptibility to change. Ward Thomas (2001: 34) helpfully identified two kinds of norms: 'convention-dependent' and 'embedded'. Convention-dependent norms 'rely heavily on precedent and patterns of reciprocal adherence'. They are predicated on agreed moral principles but do not accord fully with the identities and interests of actors. To take an example that Thomas himself uses, norms about targeting civilians in wartime were weaker when they impaired the military effectiveness of great powers than they are today, because such norms sit easily with Western ideas about the efficiency of precision warfare. Alternatively, norms about the civilian and democratic control of armed forces were less important in Southeast Asian international relations when military regimes were seen as important bulwarks against communist expansion (see Chapter 3).

Convention-dependent norms are therefore based on reciprocity. Members of a society agree that such patterns of behaviour are a normative good but they are not constitutive because failing to uphold them will not result in either the rescinding of an actor's identification as a legitimate actor or the de-legitimisation of its preferred policies and the associated costs. To return to the football analogy, there is a norm that if the ball is deliberately put out of play in order to allow a player to receive medical treatment, the opposing team should return the ball to the team that kicked it out from the throw-in. Both teams, and the football community at large, recognise this norm as a moral good. However, failure to uphold it – for instance if a team believes it will be detrimental to winning the game – does not constitute a fundamental challenge to the rules of football. A powerful team may suffer less for its breach of the norm than a weaker team, which may for instance lose sponsorship because of its perceived unethical play, but it will nevertheless be open to scrutiny by other teams, pundits and the wider society. If a strong team were to ignore this norm it is likely that other teams would begin to ignore it as well until the norm itself fell into obsolescence. Such norms may therefore act as a framework for meaningful discussion and, when practised, constrain the behaviour of actors. However, they tend not to be constitutive and can become redundant through repeated non-compliance. As we demonstrate in the following chapter and throughout the second part of the book, this description closely reflects the status of the 'norm' of civilian and democratic control of the armed forces during the cold war especially, and afterwards too, as the regional response to the 2006 Thai coup demonstrates. Whilst generally accepted as a moral good, many actors also acknowledge that the norm is aspirational and secondary to concerns such as state-building, economic development and defeating communism or, more recently, terrorism.

By contrast, 'embedded norms' are built upon agreed moral principles, patterns of repeated adherence, and fulfil each of the constitutive, constraining and communicative functions outlined above. Embedded norms constitute the identities of actors and therefore help to frame their interests. A football team that picked up the ball on a regular basis and refused to be constrained by the referee's decisions is no longer playing football. By refusing to obey the game's constitutive or practical rules, the team has effectively brought the game to an end. In international society, states follow embedded norms as a matter of habit. Such norms frame the identities and interests of actors and provide a framework of meaning that is often unseen.

How do these international expectations about the identity of appropriate actors and rightful conduct translate into meaningful positions in relation to civil–military relations? According to an increasing number of writers, states inhabit regional security cultures or complexes and, occasionally, security communities. There is a particularly long tradition of thinking about regional security cultures in Southeast Asia (e.g. Ball 1993; Kerr 1998). The basic proposition is that regions establish common ideas and expectations about the nature of security issues within that region and the types of responses that are considered appropriate. According to Johnston, regional security cultures are best thought of as norms, ideas, identities and values that create durable and pervasive security preferences in a given region by forming judgements about the role, effectiveness and legitimacy of particular approaches to security (Johnston 1995: 36). Developing this idea, Haacke and Williams suggest that regional security cultures are founded on shared assumptions around two sets of foundational tenets and several operational issues. The foundational tenets refer to the relative importance of various referents of security (e.g. state, regime, community, particular value) and the nature of the political-security environment (i.e. is it difficult or benign? Multipolar or bipolar? Structured according to alliances? Framed by deterrence or pre-emption?) (Haacke and Williams 2006: 14). Operational issues involve agreements about what sorts of issues or problems can be classified as a security threat and 'which policy instruments are the most effective, feasible and legitimate in view of the security situation at hand, and what is the most appropriate relationship between individual members [states] and collective arrangements for dealing with security challenges' (Haacke and Williams 2006: 15). The key point here is that regional security cultures do not determine a state's defence and security policy but they do shape their normative and strategic context and thereby change the relative costs and benefits associated with particular courses of action.

To take an example relevant for Southeast Asia, during the cold war the region's security culture was dominated by the idea that states faced two key threats: first, there were threats to regimes from various internal opponents; second, there was a transnational communist threat inspired by China and Vietnam. Within this context, values such as democracy, human rights and civilian control of the military played almost no role in the regional security culture. Instead, the region's militaries played the role of regime protector – guarding the ruling regime against internal dissent – a role legitimated not only by other states in the region but also by powerful external actors such as Japan and the United States. Once the cold war ended, the balance of expectations began to change. Without imminent regime threats from communists and other groups, the regional security culture changed to embrace the idea that militaries ought to be democratically controlled by civilians, though this remains a 'convention dependent' or aspirational norm. That is not to say that the region's states embraced security sector reform overnight, just that the international costs associated with an overt military role in politics increased to the extent that the region's only long-term military government today (Burma) is an international pariah subject to economic and political sanctions and its other military government (Thailand) is under international pressure to hand over to civilians and the democratic process.

The precise nature of Southeast Asia's security culture is a matter for the following chapter, but it remains for us to reflect on the membership of this culture. Following Buzan and Wæver's work on the associated idea of 'security complexes', it is possible to identify three layers of membership. First, and most obviously, are those states that are actually in the region. As Buzan and Wæver argue, security challenges are like ripples in water, most intense near to the epicentre. In other words, the things that most concern the region's states are security matters that relate to their immediate neighbourhood. Second, there are powerful states in the neighbourhood that impact upon the security culture. Most obviously, the so-called China threat has had a profound influence on the types of issues identified as security threats and the types of strategies deemed appropriate for dealing with them (Shambaugh 1996; Ross 2005). Despite the fact that China's defence spending remains comparatively low and that it has taken great pains to reassure its Southeast Asian neighbours about the implications of its 'peaceful rise', it continues to generate a good deal of nervousness. Japan, on the other hand, has managed to reposition itself as a force for stability in the post-war period, despite recent moves to become a 'more assertive or "normal" military power' (Hughes 2005: 18). Finally, the global superpower, the United States, counts the whole world as its region. Given the immense material capabilities at its disposal, the US has the capacity to unilaterally alter the costs and benefits associated with particular courses of action and as we show in the second half of this book, US policy has played an important part in the calculations of Southeast Asian leaders.

In summary, world politics is comprised not only of brute material facts but also of ideas which give political meaning to those facts. Regional security cultures are sets of commonly shared ideas about what counts as a security threat and the most effective and appropriate means of meeting those threats. They are comprised of states in a given region and key external actors. They do not determine a state's defence and security policy but they affect the balance of costs and benefits associated with a given policy choice. Thus, for example, whilst the regional security culture was unable to prevent the 2006 military coup in Thailand, it did affect the economic and political costs associated with military rule, creating an impetus for return to civilian rule.

National level – strategic culture

At the next level down are strategic cultures. These are shared beliefs, attitudes and practices within a state about what counts as a security threat and what means may be used to address those threats. The idea of strategic culture was first mooted in the 1970s and found its origins amongst strategists who believed that American ethnocentrism 'skewed' its strategic thinking. In a now famous Research and Development (RAND) study, Jack Snyder warned that nuclear strategy was premised on flawed assumptions about Soviet rationality which held that the Soviets would play the nuclear game identically to the Americans. This type of thinking created expectations about Soviet behaviour that were not grounded in a deep understanding of how the Soviets actually thought about nuclear politics. Instead of 'rational man', Snyder argued that the Soviets had a particular way of thinking about nuclear issues that was shaped by a combination of history, ideology and institutional learning. For Snyder, this 'strategic culture' was a collection of 'ideas, conditioned emotional responses, and patterns of habitual behaviour that members of a national strategic community have acquired through instruction or imitation and share with each other with regard to nuclear strategy' (Snyder 1977: 8).

In the 1980s and 1990s, these ideas were taken up and developed by both hard-nosed realists and more constructivist-minded scholars. Colin Gray argued that all states have a 'national style' when it comes to security policy, defining strategic culture as 'modes of thought and action with respect to force, which derive from perceptions of the national historical experience, from aspirations for responsible behaviour in national terms. . .the civic culture and way of life' (Gray 1986: 36–37). Similarly, Ken Booth identified the role that the 'fog of culture' played in strategic policy in his call for the rational actor model to be replaced by an account of strategy that took culture, perception and identity into account (Booth 1979). There was therefore broad agreement that ideas play an important part in shaping security and defence policy and a number of recent works have attempted to afford the idea of strategic culture greater precision by, for instance, delineating it from strategic behaviour to develop a theory of causation (Johnston 1995) and linking it to wider theories about the social elements of world politics (Katzenstein 1996).

There is no need for us to go into too much detail about the theories of strategic culture other than to note that defence and security policy – including the domestic organisation and orientation of the armed forces – are shaped by historically embedded ideas. According to Colin Gray, strategic cultures exercise a 'semi-permanent influence upon policy behaviour' that provides an enduring explanation of strategic behaviour in the absence of 'new historical experience' (Gray 1986: 37). Thus, as Kerry Longhurst argues, strategic cultures are persistent over time though they are subject to change. Helpfully, Longhurst goes on to distinguish three elements of a strategic culture. First, 'foundational elements' are deep qualities that have historical origins and comprise core basic beliefs about the use of force and the proper role and structure of security agencies. These elements tend to give a strategic culture its distinctiveness and are highly resistant to change. Second, 'regulatory practices' are observable manifestations of the strategic culture. They are 'longstanding policies and practices' that apply the substance of a state's strategic culture to the external and internal environment. These are less resilient to change than the foundational elements. Third and finally are what Longhurst labels 'policy standpoints', which are 'the contemporary, widely accepted, interpretations as to how best core values are to be promoted through policy channels' (Longhurst 2004: 17). To offer a relevant example, a foundational element of Thailand's strategic culture during the cold war held that the proper role of the armed forces was to protect the Thai state as a capitalist, monarchical entity from internal and external enemies. This fed into a series of regulatory practices which held that the military should intervene in the political and economic life of the state to fulfil the foundational elements. At various points in history this prompted policy standpoints that suggested that the best way to secure core values was for the military leadership to develop economic development programmes, appoint the government and so forth.

Strategic cultures shape the way that policy elites perceive the security environment. They also shape the types of strategy that will be seen as either appropriate or effective in a particular set of circumstances. As with regional cultures, strategic cultures do not determine policy outcomes. There may be political disputes about how to interpret a given situation and strategic cultures are constantly open to change, a question we will address in greater detail in the following section. In relation to security sector reform, though, two points are important to make at this stage. First, genuine security sector reform is likely to involve changes to a state's strategic culture because it involves rethinking the role of the security sector and its relationship to other institutions and society at large. Second, in the absence of external shocks or coercion (see below), reform agendas that run counter to a strategic culture's foundational elements or regulatory practices are unlikely to change behaviour and very likely to be resisted. Alternatively, states might engage in surface level reform that does not alter behaviour in fundamental ways. In short, therefore, proponents of security sector reform have to pay careful attention to strategic culture.

Bureaucratic pathologies

The third set of ideational influences on a state's civil–military relations relate to the relevant bureaucracies themselves. It has long been recognised that bureaucracies, whether civilian or military, are not simply neutral instruments giving effect to government policy. Instead they contribute to the policy process by, among other things, delineating the realm of the possible, and they determine outcomes by the way in which they implement policy. In relation to security sector reform, for instance, it has often been noted that whilst governments may embrace reform at the declaratory level this does not always translate into actual changes in the way that the security sector is structured or behaves – a significant problem identified in the previous chapter.

According to Beetham (1996: 9–12), bureaucracies have four features in common. First, they are hierarchic in that each official has a specific role to play and is answerable to a superior. Second, they have continuity inasmuch as they provide on-going full-time employment and the possibility of career progress. The third feature is impersonality in that the work is conducted according to prescribed rules and procedures designed to eliminate arbitrariness. Finally, expertise, in that officials are organised according to technical functions and control access to knowledge on the basis of similar criteria. According to Max Weber, bureaucracies are the most efficient system of administration precisely because they are impersonal and rules-oriented (Weber 1978). From this view, their efficiency derives from the very fact that bureaucracies are not neutral bodies but are actors that have a shared culture, rules, working procedures and worldview, where individual success is measured in relation to these values.

What effect does this bureaucratic culture have on behaviour? Barnett and Finnemore (2004) have identified four specific effects that are directly relevant to understanding how the implementation of security and defence policy is shaped by particular sets of bureaucratic ideas. First, bureaucratic rules prescribe action for actors both inside and outside the organisation. They are the 'standard operating procedures' that allow the organisation to fulfil its role efficiently and they set out appropriate and inappropriate ways of responding to certain problems.

Thus, for example, an organisation whose culture is strongly predisposed towards nepotism as a means of career advancement is unlikely to embrace a merit-based approach without a concomitant shift in its culture. Second, this culture shapes the way that officials see the world and understand the problems that they confront and in this way it is closely allied to strategic culture. The culture provides labels that are used to describe and make sense of certain kinds of behaviour and also suggests types of responses. Third, bureaucracies tend to construct a view of the world that legitimates the widening role of the bureaucracy itself. For example, defence bureaucracies articulate a worldview that contains and expands the role of the military. After the end of the cold war, few defence bureaucrats argued that there was no longer a need for armed forces, even in countries whose defence sector was entirely predicated on the so-called communist threat. Instead new military roles were identified that re-legitimised the sector. Seldom, if ever, do bureaucracies achieve their designated goal and declare themselves moribund. Finally, the bureaucratic culture is constitutive of the institution itself. It is the culture itself that marks out one institution from another. One of the key themes running through the second part of this book is that security agencies tend to defend their special prerogatives and immunity from democratic control on the grounds that they are different to other types of government agency.

Bureaucracies themselves, therefore, have particular ways of seeing the world and standard procedures that help them to make sense of their own role, the nature of the problems they face and the most efficient and appropriate ways of achieving their goals.

Ideas and the constitution of civil–military relations

We have outlined some of the myriad ways in which ideas help to shape the way a state organises its security sector and the way that actors and bureaucracies in the security sector itself understand their purpose, role and the types of behaviour that are likely to deliver desired ends. We argued that whilst these different layers of ideas do not determine behaviour, they play a significant role in shaping behaviour by affecting the balance of costs and benefits associated with certain courses of action. Behaviours that accord with well established bureaucratic, strategic cultural and regional security culture norms are likely to be welcomed and receive support and, if properly calibrated, are therefore more likely to achieve the desired goal at a minimum cost. However, behaviour that runs directly counter to them is likely to incur opprobrium and even attracts sanctions of one form or another. The more power is attached to a particular actor, the more able it is to bear these costs. Thus, for example, a military that assumed power against a prevailing strategic culture of civilian control backed by regional norms to that effect may be able to preserve itself in power only through a mixture of bribery and coercion. The cost of maintaining this rule, both financial and political, would be much greater than the cost of maintaining civilian rule. As a result, such rule would be unstable and, in the long-run, potentially unsustainable.

We suggested in answer to the question asked at the beginning of this chapter, that a state's civil–military relations is shaped by certain material factors mediated and given meaning by different sets of ideas that operate at the international, national and bureaucratic levels. Between them, these ideas create expectations about the role of the security sector in general – its purpose, the threats it aims to counter, the means it might use, the way it ought to be organised and so on – the role of *particular* security sectors and the role of individual bureaucracies within those sectors. Because security sector reform is all about changing the security sector and because this necessarily involves change in one or more of the sets of ideas described in this section, we need to briefly elaborate on how these ideas change, the different types of change and the key drivers of change.

The politics of change

In this final section we briefly outline in conceptual terms the different types and drivers of change. As we set out at the beginning of the chapter there are broadly two types of change. The first are fundamental changes. Fundamental changes are quite rare and refer to the profound transformation of one or more of the security sector's key elements. Such changes may involve a fundamental rethinking of the military's role in politics, or a recalibration in the way that the military is structured and managed, or a pronounced change in its primary role. For instance, a military that in 1988 was entirely geared towards defending the state from an imminent Soviet attack would have undergone a fundamental role change if, by 1991, it saw its principal role as contributing to multinational humanitarian operations. The second type and much more frequent form of change is fine-tuning. Fine-tuning may involve amending certain practices to accommodate a changed external environment, changing institutional behaviour in order to accomplish established goals more effectively, or developing new practices within the same mindset as a result of learning.

What causes these different types of change? Fundamental change usually has four primary causes, the first two of which are related to material forces and the latter two the realm of ideas. First, *external shocks*. A dramatic and profound change outside the security sector might force fundamental change upon the sector. Thus, the end of the cold war would be an external shock producing fundamental change to a security sector exclusively geared towards cold war strategy. In the Southeast Asian context, such external shocks have included European colonisation, Japanese expansionism and, most recently, the 1997 Asian financial crisis. Such shocks render particular beliefs, policies or bureaucratic structures anachronistic in that the sector no longer reflects the world it lives in. Typically, because of the bureaucratic culture described in the previous section, the immediate response to an external shock is a period of policy inertia whereby bureaucracies either refuse to admit the change, attempt to apply old ideas to new circumstances or actively resist change and adjustment (Longhurst 2004: 18). Ultimately, however, institutions that fail to reform or adjust to the external shocks become less able to fulfil their purpose efficiently and effectively.

The second driver of fundamental change is *external bribery or coercion.* Powerful external actors might either simply impose fundamental change – perhaps by physically overturning a structure of governance – or they might alter the balance of costs and benefits associated with particular beliefs, policies or institutional structures so much as to leave policy-makers with very little room for manoeuvre. Most clearly, fundamental change may be imposed after a great power has defeated the regime, occupied the country and decided to reform and restructure the security sector. Undoubtedly the most striking example of this type of fundamental change would be the process of security sector reform currently underway in Iraq and, to a lesser extent, Afghanistan. A little more subtle are the range of multinational operations deployed under the rubric of 'transitional administrations', 'peacebuilding missions' or 'peacekeeping' that have security sector reform as part of their mandate. In Southeast Asia, the clearest example of this type of activity would be the role of the UN, UK and Australia in shaping the identity, function and structure of the East Timorese security sector. The UN played a similar role briefly in Cambodia (Doyle 2001). Alternatively, external actors might use bribery to enact fundamental change by radically altering the balance of costs and benefits associated with particular courses of action without necessarily imposing the change. In post-cold war Europe, for example, a combination of financial, political and technical measures provided by the EU and NATO persuaded virtually all the region's post-communist states to adopt Western methods and structures of security governance.

The third driver of fundamental change is less dramatic and obvious than the other two. Fundamental changes may be wrought over time by the accumulation of fine-tuning changes (see below). This can operate in at least two ways, one more obvious than the other. The more obvious way is best explained as a Kuhnian 'paradigm shift'. Discussing how scientific paradigms change, Thomas Kuhn argued that when a prevailing paradigm becomes buried under a pile of anomalous cases, the scientific community recognises that the paradigm is no longer suitable and a scientific revolution occurs (Kuhn 1996). The production of fundamental change through fine-tuning can occur in a similar way. When a dominant belief, policy attitude or institutional structure becomes buried by small adjustments and revisions to such an extent that the dominant idea or practice no longer makes sense, policy-makers effect a 'paradigm shift' – a fundamental change. The second, and less obvious, method of change is organic. That is, unlike the Kuhnian model there is no self-conscious paradigm shift but the 'old' ways of doing things change nevertheless. Thus, for instance, bureaucracies might not change their name, might not alter the wording of the way they see their role in the world and might not self-consciously change their operating procedures but fundamental change might occur incrementally nevertheless as new practices become normalised and old labels are afforded new value and meaning.

The fourth and final driver of fundamental change is the resolution of legitimacy crises. As we noted earlier, legitimacy crises occur when established practices of civil–military relations can no longer be sustained consensually. In other words, when domestic and international opinion about the way a security sector functions is so negative that the sector is forced to revert to bribery or coercion to sustain itself (Reus-Smit 2007). As we noted earlier, reliance on bribery and coercion is inherently unstable and in the majority of cases is unsustainable in the long-run. According to Reus-Smit, legitimacy crises are only resolved by the recalibration of the social bases of legitimacy. That is, only when the causes of grievance are removed in some consensually mediated process. Thus, for example, if a crisis of legitimacy is caused by military intervention in politics in the face of determined civil society opposition the crisis can only be resolved by either civil society voluntarily dropping its demand for the withdrawal of the military from politics (highly unlikely) or by the military acquiescing and reconstituting its relationship with the civil government. This is why we locate the driver of fundamental change in the resolution of such crises, not in the crisis itself because in the hypothetical case given above the military could choose to rely on alternative sources of power to legitimacy, such as brute force or bribery, thus limiting the potential for fundamental change.

All four types of fundamental change are likely to provoke both political and bureaucratic resistance. Externally driven change crashes against established patterns of behaviour embedded in regional security cultures, strategic cultures and bureaucratic cultures. Environmental changes may be more obvious in one area than another, provoking contestation both within and between the different levels. Actors will doubt the extent to which the world has changed, will argue about the meaning of change and dispute proposals for responding to change. Such arguments will contest both explicitly cultural ideas such as ideas about the proper role of the military, the nature of the state and apparently material issues such as the most effective way of securing common goals. Quite often, bureaucracies might adopt the new language and enact superficial reforms without actually altering the way they go about their daily business. For instance, it is not uncommon for a security sector to commit itself to professionalisation and promotion by merit whilst simultaneously continuing to appoint and promote on the basis of nepotism and patrimonialism (see Forster *et al.* 2002).

The second type of change is *fine-tuning*. Fine-tuning occurs 'when issues have arisen, from either domestic or international sources, that have challenged or at best sat uneasily with the established foundational elements' of a state's security sector (Longhurst 2004: 18). Such challenges will be understood through the lenses of the different levels of culture identified in the previous section. Beliefs, attitudes and practices will be amended to respond to the challenge but without a change to the fundamentals themselves. For example, a security sector whose primary role is 'regime protection' might alter its focus from transnational communism to international Jihadism in the light of the changing international environment. This role shift may involve other changes in the way that the security sector organises itself because of the different nature of the perceived threat. This would involve a number of fine-tuning reforms, maybe even a restructuring of the armed forces to deliver violence more effectively against the new threat. This would not, however, involve a fundamental change because the security sector's role would remain that of 'regime protector' and its primary means of fulfilling its role would remain the application of force. Alternatively, a military may respond to external and internal pressure to stay out of politics and 'return to the barracks' by doing just that, but may resist structural reforms aimed at fundamentally altering the way the military is organised and managed in order to prevent it returning to politics. In those circumstances, the return to barracks is best understood as 'fine-tuning' rather than fundamental change.

As we mentioned in the introduction, fine-tuning may involve 'institutional learning', 'convergence' or 'recalibration'. They can be generated by either of the two logics of action identified by March and Olsen which, as Krasner (1999: 5) argues, are all too often wrongly seen as incompatible. The first is a 'logic of expected consequences' which sees political action and outcomes as the product of 'rational calculating behaviour' designed to maximise performance given a set of preferences (March and Olsen 1989: 24–26). In other words, if we assume that particular institutions know what they want to achieve (and we argued earlier that identity and role changed fundamentally only infrequently), they will change how they go about achieving that goal over time as they discover more efficient and effective means. In other words, some – indeed most – fine-tuning changes involve recalibrations aimed at delivering the same, or more of the same, good at a lower cost. For instance, at the end of the cold war many defence ministries believed that it was now possible to deliver the same amount of security from external threats with much less expenditure on items such as heavy armour and such changes had important ramifications for the way the armed forces were organised.

The second logic is the 'logic of appropriateness'. The logic of appropriateness holds that the social and normative environment that action takes place in is important. Because, as we argued earlier, social norms constitute, constrain and provide frameworks of communication for actors, actions cannot be meaningfully divorced from their context. The logic of appropriateness therefore holds that, 'human actors are imagined to follow rules that associate particular identities to particular situations, approaching individual opportunities for action by assessing similarities between current identities and choice dilemmas and more general conceptions of self and situations' (March and Olsen 1998: 951). The logic of appropriateness might affect fine-tuning by altering the balance of costs and benefits associated with certain courses of action, by encouraging a recalibration of an institution's identity in line with international norms (recall the constitutive role of norms discussed earlier) and by opening up paths to re-legitimisation – as, for example, the reform process in Thailand did for the Royal Thai Army after the 'shock' of the 1992 killings (see Chapter 5).

Arguably the key drivers of 'fine-tuning' changes of both types are domestic and international epistemic communities. An epistemic community is understood as 'a network of professionals with recognised expertise and competence in a particular domain and an authoritative claim to policy-relevant knowledge within that domain or issue-area' (see Knoke 1990; Haas 1992: 3). According to Peter Haas, epistemic communities are formed when professionals are brought together by four common concerns: shared normative beliefs, shared beliefs about causation, shared criteria for evaluating valid knowledge and a common policy enterprise. Because an epistemic community can lay claim to the production of valid knowledge within a particular area they can influence the construction of perceived interests and appropriate actions by establishing generally agreed notions of causation (e.g. activity x would not be in our interests because it would produce negative effect y) (Haas 1992: 15). Indeed, such communities may themselves articulate logics of expected consequences and appropriateness by constructing generally accepted 'commonsense' about particular topics. For instance, during the cold war, nuclear deterrence achieved the status of commonsense amongst many Western (and Eastern) policy networks largely because these ideas were enunciated, by and large without challenge, by a transnational epistemic community of strategists. Within their areas of expertise, epistemic communities also have the power to define plausible policy alternatives, shaping the scope of political debate and limiting the construction of national interests (Schattenschneider 1975: 66–70).

Thought of another way, the epistemic community can be understood as a group of people who contribute significantly to the construction of *epistemes* or 'regimes of truth' (Foucault 1970). According to Foucault, each community has its own regime of truth. Such regimes provide 'the mechanisms and instances which enable one to distinguish true and false statements, the means by which each is sanctioned; the techniques and procedures accorded value in the acquisition of truth; the status of those who are charged with saying what is true' (Foucault 1980: 131). Similarly, *epistemes* refer to sets of shared symbols and references, expectations based on knowledge about causation and predictability of action and intention (see Ruggie 1998: 55). Within its own subject area, the epistemic community holds a privileged position. It is recognised as the arbiter of truth and falsity on a particular subject, it articulates ways of evaluating knowledge claims and frameworks for understanding causation, and contributes to the construction of national interests and appreciation of logics of appropriate behaviour.

Because they are based on subject matter rather than citizenship or national identity there is no reason to assume that epistemic communities cannot be multinational and indeed most epistemic communities *are* multinational. For instance, there is a global community of military professionals schooled in the basic art of Clausewitzian warfare, the rules and logic of the Geneva Conventions and the fundamental principles of civil–military relations enunciated by Huntington, Finer and others. As a community, they build their own identity and interests that may be quite different to the perceived self-interests of the state they are housed in. Thus, the identities and interests of individual members of an epistemic military community may differ greatly from the perceived national interests of the state, and this may persuade state leaders to act in ways that seem inimical to the narrower interests and identities of the state. Such interests may be constructed through the 'supranational entrepreneurship' of senior officials in international organisations and other members of the epistemic community (Moravcsik 1999).

It is important to note that the limits of epistemic communities do not necessarily correspond with the boundaries of regional security complexes. Of course, on matters divorced from narrow security concerns (trade policy, for instance) there may be no congruence whatsoever between the security complex and epistemic communities. However, regarding even 'security' matters (however defined) there is no direct congruence between the security complex and the epistemic communities that operate within it. For instance, the epistemic community of military professionals, politicians and defence experts at the heart of ASEAN's security community comprises people from outside the region (especially the US, and also Europe, Japan, Australia). These networks therefore play an important role in introducing new ideas about both how to maximise performance ('expected consequences') and about the types of beliefs, attitudes and practices that are considered appropriate.

Conclusion

We posed a number of general theoretical questions at the outset of this chapter and have addressed them in a fairly abstract way as a precursor to the more detailed historical and empirical analyses of the following chapters. We argued that a state's civil–military relations are conditioned by a range of material and ideational factors and that the latter give meaning to the former. In other words, the different models of civil–military relationship described in the previous chapter are produced by a diffuse range of social factors that are embedded in history and various cultures. As such, at the beginning of the chapter we outlined a number of reasons for eschewing the temptation to simply apply one or more of the myriad Western theories of civil–military relations to the Southeast Asian case on the grounds that in their pursuit of objectivity these theories give scant regard to history and culture and the particularities of the Southeast Asian experience. If we take these particularities seriously we cannot even use some of the basic building blocks of the predominant theories because they are prefaced on untenable assumptions about the relationship between military and civilian institutions.

Rather than providing an alternative conceptual model, we proceeded by articulating in very general terms the forces and ideas that contribute to the shaping of a state's security sector. We suggested that these factors operated at a number of levels and informed basic judgments about the identity, purpose and role of the security sector which informed assessments about the nature of the security environment and most appropriate type of military organisation. Although some of these factors are more resilient to change than others we ended the chapter by setting out different types of change and reflecting on the likely drivers of change.

From this we can take a further insight on top of the idea that history matters, that civil–military relations are constituted at a number of levels and that we cannot simply apply a Western view of the issue into a Southeast Asian context: all proposed change causes friction (i.e. opposition) and reform is only likely when its tenets correspond in some way to pre-existing ideas. As Ward Thomas explains, 'norms are not continually re-created from scratch; rather, at any stage in history states operate within a pre-existing normative context that is both the product of past processes and the starting point for future ones' (Thomas 2001: 33). In other words, proposals for reform have to appeal to pre-existing ideas somewhere within the three levels described earlier in this chapter (international,

national, bureaucratic). If they do not, only an external shock or foreign imposition is likely to bring effect to reform proposals. We noted that one common practice in relation to externally sponsored security sector reform agendas has been to adopt the language of reform at the declaratory level without actually changing much in the way of behaviour or structure. In the chapters that follow we aim to shed more light on this by identifying precisely how civil–military relations are constituted in Southeast Asia, where the drivers for reform are coming from, what types of reform are underway, and where, precisely, does opposition to reform lie? These questions are taken up in the following chapter that sets out the region's historical context.

3 The historical origins of Southeast Asian security

Security sector reform is, as we have seen, something that was largely developed in 'the West'. Although 'the West' is an unsatisfactory shorthand for a complex array of historical processes and relationships,[1] it does serve one useful purpose here: like so much else that was originally developed in Europe or more latterly North America, SSR reflects a particular set of beliefs and/or practices that is being actively exported from one part of the world to another. In the case of SSR, it is accompanied by the hope, if not the expectation, that its adoption will improve the lives of those on the receiving end. The same sorts of hopes accompanied Europe's 'civilising' mission in Asia and elsewhere in the eighteenth and nineteenth centuries. While there are plainly significant differences in the relationships between what world systems theorists like to refer to as the 'core' and 'periphery' these days (see Chase-Dunn 1998), it is worth noting at the outset that there is likely to be a degree of sensitivity about replicating an historical pattern that not only has unfortunate precedents, but which inevitably carries with it a similar sense of superiority and inferiority. In other words, whatever the merits of SSR, its reception is bound to be overlaid with a good deal of historical baggage and possible antipathy.

One of the principal intentions of this chapter is to unpack some of this historical legacy so that we are better able to understand both potential sensitivities about what might be perceived in some quarters as 'neo-colonial' relations and – more importantly – the way Southeast Asia's distinctive political, economic and, above all, security histories evolved *before* they emerged as independent nation-states. Indeed, the fact that the region is populated by independent states at all is an artefact of European contact and colonisation, and indicative of just how profound an impact Southeast Asia's historical relationship with the West has had. It also explains why the region's militaries look more or less like their European counterparts in terms of their internal organisation and nominal responsibilities. However, this is where the easy correspondences end, and why we need to look more closely at the particular way apparently universal institutions like 'the military' have evolved in distinct, contingent national circumstances. To do this we need to think about the way institutions like the army have become socially embedded in a wider array of intersecting institutions, something that helps to account for their different national roles and capacities. Consequently, the first part of this chapter builds on the discussion of the previous chapter by presenting a brief outline of institutional theory and its utility in explaining national differences in superficially universal contexts.

One of our key contentions in this context will be that 'history matters'. We shall suggest that it is not possible to understand why, for example, Malaysia's military has come to play a very different role in that country's national life than militaries in other parts of the region unless we have some sense of the particular historical circumstances in which an independent Malaysia emerged and the specific role that various institutions have played. Consequently, this chapter provides a broad historical overview of the region's development that helps to account for the specific historical dynamics and patterns of social organisation that came to distinguish each of our case studies. As we shall see, the quite distinct circumstances that prevailed before and immediately after independence go a long way to explaining why the militaries of each country have behaved as they have. Indeed, we shall argue that not only do such historically specific circumstances help to explain the quite distinct roles played by each of Southeast Asia's militaries, but they have also imparted a degree of 'path dependency' to their subsequent development. The notion of path dependency not only helps us to understand the different trajectories of military and security development in Southeast Asia, but it also helps to explain why reform might prove difficult and be resisted – perhaps even violently resisted.

Consequently, we first outline why institutions are significant and how they shape and reflect the social life of a nation in ways that may be resistant to change. After this, we provide a sketch of the distinctive historical forces that have shaped the region's political, social and economic development, and explain how such processes have come to influence ideas about security and the appropriate role of the military. We detail how two pivotal historical forces – the expansion of capitalism and the deeply inter-connected export of the international state system – have profoundly influenced the course of development in Southeast Asia. We also detail how 'geopolitical' factors, especially the 'hot' and 'cold' wars that have been such a prominent part of the region's history, have influenced thinking about and the development of militaries in Southeast Asia. As part of this latter discussion, we consider the rise of American hegemony and its impact on the region, an influence that has recently become even more important and which operates in a number of ways that need delineating if we are to understand the constraints that face individual Southeast Asian nations.

Institutions and institutional theory

The military remains one of the most important institutions in the world. However, unless we have a vocabulary that allows us to differentiate between different types of militaries and – more importantly, perhaps – the various ways broadly similar military institutions are embedded in different societies, then we shall not be in a position to understand why they play different roles, and why some may be more enthusiastic about embracing externally generated reform than others.

In this section we outline some of the key ideas and approaches that have emerged from institutional theory[2] – especially its sociological and political variants – and suggest they can help us to develop our understanding of the role of the military in contemporary societies, especially in the so-called developing world.

Let us begin with some definitions and points of clarification that may aid subsequent discussion. First, it is useful to distinguish between organisations and institutions, although the terms are often used interchangeably. Oran Young (1994: 26) makes such a distinction and suggests that organisations are best thought of as 'material entities possessing budgets, personnel, offices, equipment, and legal personality'. A useful broad-brush definition of institutions, by contrast, suggests they are 'cognitive, normative, and regulative structures and activities that provide stability and meaning to social behaviour' (Scott 1995: 33). Institutions are, therefore, generic, socially constructed phenomena that enable people to know how to behave in specific contexts by routinising patterns of behaviour. However, it is important to recognise that such practices and structures are not simply restrictive or didactic. On the contrary, as John Searle (2005: 10) points out, 'the essential role of institutions and the purpose of having institutions is not to constrain people as such, but, rather to create new sorts of power relationships'. In other words, institutions are enabling and allow complex social interactions to occur which, to borrow from the jargon of economic intuitionalism, reduce 'transaction costs' and allow greater 'efficiency' (see Williamson 1993).

Plainly there is a debate to be had about how terms such as 'efficiency' are defined, but two points emerge from the institutional literature that are less controversial: first, institutions provide an effective way of coordinating and regularising certain social activities. This does not necessarily mean that such activities are 'functionally' necessary or vital to the survival of society, although they may be. Most societies could continue to exist without sporting activities of various sorts, for example, but without the existence of a tradable currency, a good deal of modern economic activity and organisation would be impossible (Cerny 1995). In this context it is worth noting that the necessity of national military institutions is not as self-evident as it may seem, and reflects a particular, historically entrenched way of thinking about security and international relations.[3] This highlights the important ideational aspect of institutions, described in the previous chapter, that is central to their second critical quality: they embody the 'rules' that govern social activities that people carry around in their heads, even when such rules are tacit and informal, and the participants are unaware of their existence.

Military organisations are particularly conducive to this sort of institutional analysis, which highlights the interaction between forms of social organisation and the ideas that inform their regulation, be they formal or informal, explicit or tacit. There are two aspects of this rule-governed behaviour that are especially pertinent to militaries and their organisational structures. As we noted in the previous chapter, what March and Olsen (1989) famously described as the logics of appropriateness and consequentiality capture the different modes of regulation that influence institutional behaviour and can be applied to the activities of militaries and their personnel. On the one hand, the logic of appropriateness refers to the obligations that flow from a particular social structure, which defines behaviour according to role, status and an understanding of 'appropriate' behaviour that has developed through socialisation processes. While the highly formalised social structures and relationships of the military are rather extreme versions of this, which frequently leave little room for personal autonomy or discretion, nevertheless it captures the sense of *obligation* that flows from specific social circumstances. The logic of consequentiality, on the other hand, refers to the normatively derived *choices* that are made as a consequence of expected outcomes.

As we shall see, this distinction helps to clarify both the underlying logic of SSR and its attempts to consolidate the logic of appropriateness, and the actual behaviour of Southeast Asian militaries – or more accurately, the elites that control military institutions in the region – which have frequently been driven more by the logic of consequentiality. Put differently, while the militaries of Southeast Asia may be replete with the formal aspects of military organisation that distinguish such institutions everywhere, and which are the subject of most analytical attention (see Chapter 2), to understand why they have behaved and developed in the way they have, we need to recognise the importance of informal influences and consequential thinking. Institutional analysis also offers a way of thinking about both the historical basis of consequential logic and the specific patterns of civil–military relations within which they are embedded.

In this context, one of the key insights to emerge from institutional theory is about the importance of history generally and about the possible importance of 'path dependency' in particular. Although it is possible to distinguish between those historical institutionalists who emphasise a 'calculus' approach that highlights the importance of institutional pay-offs to individuals, and a 'cultural' approach that stresses the importance of socially embedded, taken-for-granted routines (Hall and Taylor 1996: 939–940), there is general agreement that pre-existing institutions structure the behaviour of individuals and organisations. In this reading, institutions have an inherent 'logic' and 'relational quality' that embodies specific norms and practices which shape individual behaviour (Hall 1986). Much historical institutional analysis thus far has focused on politics and economics, and the key contentions have consequently been about specific national institutional structures and the 'policy logic' they generate. These are generally seen as 'a function of a country's distinct political and industrial development' (Zysman 1994: 245), and used to account for the very different patterns of political and economic organisation that distinguish areas like Western Europe and East Asia (Hollingsworth and Boyer 1997). However, it is our contention that such insights can be adapted to account for the equally distinctive patterns of military development and strategic thinking that distinguish Southeast Asia.

This is why the notion of path dependency is potentially so useful. At its simplest, path dependency refers to 'those historical sequences in which contingent events set into motion institutional patterns or event chains that have deterministic properties' (Mahoney 2000: 507). Put differently, specific, historically contingent circumstances not only vary from place to place, but they effectively delimit what is possible. At one level this might simply mean the capacity of one military to perform a particular function well or badly, or to project power more or less effectively. At another, equally important level, however, path dependency may help to account for the institutionalised norms, practices, world views and relationships that not only determine the ethos or role of a particular military, but may also shape the nature of its relationships with other social actors. Indeed, we would argue that it is useful to think of national militaries everywhere as being embedded in a complex array of inter-locking institutions that help to determine, and are reflective of, social norms and expectations about the role of specific institutions. This is not to suggest that such relationships and interactions are completely determinative, but that – in the absence of major systemic shocks – such structured patterns of relationships are likely to impart an overall 'direction' to both specific institutions and to the societies of which they are a part. As DiMaggio and Powell (1991: 11) put it, 'institutions do not just constrain options: they establish the very criteria by which people discover their preferences. In other words, some of the most important sunk costs are cognitive'.

Such institutional inertia helps to explain the persistence of some influential ideas or modes of behaviour when it might seem their time and appropriateness has gone (Goldstein and Keohane 1993). It also directs our attention to the way in which some institutions may be 'captured' by particularistic interests and exploited for their intrinsic properties, or utilised as part of a wider structure of exploitation and/or domination. The military is a pivotally important institution in this regard and, as we shall see, the history of Southeast Asia is replete with illustrations of its being put to tasks other than the defence of the state from external enemies. Our contention is that unless we can capture the specific, historically determined circumstances in which particular national militaries emerged, we will be unable to account for either their seemingly aberrant behaviour, or the resistance to new ideas and reformist impulses that may accompany it.

Institutional analysis is also helpful in explaining both the increasing influence of externally generated ideas like SSR, and the possible internal obstacles and limits to their adoption. Once again, institutionalists working on the transmission of economic ideas provide a useful template for thinking about the influence of ideas and norms in the security arena. At one level it is clear that international institutions are exercising an increasingly influential, relatively autonomous role in developing new policies, norms and practices that become international benchmarks, in a continuing process of 'disseminating new models of social organisation around the world' (Barnett and Finnemore 2004: 3). They are able to do so because of their perceived expertise, authority and – in some cases – enforcement capacity. The key point to make in this context is that externally generated policy ideas and norms will be mediated by domestic political structures and their adoption or rejection will depend in large part on the way they can be appropriated by indigenous political actors (Cortell and Davis 1996). For new initiatives and practices to be taken up and acted upon in a national context they need to 'become embedded in state institutions that have the organisational capacity to carry out the policies' (Sikkink 1991: 2). Part of this capacity is simply the sort of technocratic or Weberian competencies that distinguish effective from non-effective policy implementation and adoption (see Poliadano 2000). Part of this capacity, however, is about the internal structure and personnel of specific institutions, and the way they are embedded in wider social formations. In short, is there sufficient political support from powerful actors to allow ideas and polices to become institutionalised parts of particular social orders (Hall 1993)?

As we observed in the previous chapter, there have already been some sophisticated attempts to link ideas, norms and culture to different security practices (see Katzenstein 1996; Adler and Barnett 1998). Less attention has been given to the way such influences crystallise in generic institutions rather than formal organisations, especially in a Southeast Asian context. By applying some of the insights of institutional theory to Southeast Asia, we hope to show both how the region's militaries have developed, and why they may be resistant to certain reformist ideas as a consequence. To begin this process, we need to look more closely at the specifics of Southeast Asian history and the very distinctive circumstances in which individual national militaries emerged.

Southeast Asia in historical context

The importance of the social construction of institutions, and social facts more generally, is highlighted by Southeast's Asia's distinctive historical trajectory. Indeed, even to speak of 'Southeast Asia' as a discrete region is a relatively new development and one that is a function of the interaction between what we now think of as the states of Southeast Asia and the rest of the world. Only during the Second World War, when the British fought the Japanese in Burma and elsewhere, did it become common to use the term 'Southeast Asia' to describe the countries of what we now think of as the ASEAN grouping (see Emmerson 1984). At one level, then, the recognition of Southeast Asia as a distinct area represented an important ideational shift, but one that had little material impact. Other aspects of the interaction between Southeast Asia and the rest of the world had more immediate, tangible impacts, however, which initiated major processes of social transformation and institutional change. The most important and enduring of these – at least from the perspective of the development of the region's militaries – was Southeast Asia's incorporation into the international society of states.

Before we consider this in any detail it is worth emphasising a number of comparative points which emerge particularly clearly in the institutional literature. First, the modern state was the result of an extensive process of institutional selection and competition. Hendrik Spruyt (1994) has demonstrated how the state displaced other forms of social organisation because territorially based sovereign states were better able to mobilise social resources and rationalise economic activity. They also had the benefit of conferring legitimacy and regularising relations with other states. Spruyt suggests that once established, systemic change is only likely in the face of major exogenous 'shocks' (Spruyt 1994: 22). As far as Southeast Asia was concerned, European expansion and eventual colonialism, especially when combined with the spread of capitalist social relations, provided precisely the sort of shock necessary to overturn the existing order and institute major, long-term institutional change. This 'shock' was delivered in a highly truncated time frame giving the proto-states of Southeast Asia much less chance to adjust to the new international order of which they found themselves a part.

The other factor that made imperial expansion so irresistible, of course, was the effectiveness of the highly developed, established European states as an institution with which to mobilise military resources and encourage the development of military technology. Charles Tilly (1990) has explained how the interaction between economic and social development underpinned the rise of European states as major military powers. Simply put, the state form provided an unparalleled mechanism for mobilising social and economic resources for the conduct of war, in what became a self-reinforcing process. This not only made European states more effective mechanisms for controlling 'national' territory than anything that had preceded them, but it also made them highly effective vehicles for outward expansion and conquest. Indeed, when combined with the underlying dynamism of a rapidly developing capitalist system, the expansive dynamic that began in Europe in the fifteenth and sixteenth centuries, but which was consolidated and increasingly formalised in the high imperialism of the nineteenth century, proved well-nigh irresistible (Abernathy 2000).

Although the expansion of the European states system was not a coordinated, collective enterprise (Watson 1992: 256), but one that occurred under the auspices of individual imperial powers, its cumulative impact was ultimately to establish the state as the key organisational unit in the contemporary international system. Whatever the merits of such a system, before the peoples of Southeast Asia could be incorporated into it, they had to free themselves of the yoke of colonialism. But before we consider how they did this and the imprint this has left on the region's militaries in particular and societies more generally, it is worth emphasising how potentially attractive the state form was for the region's indigenous elites: it held out the prospect of international recognition, legitimacy and the prospect of imposing an over-arching, territorially demarcated order and identity where – in most cases – none had existed before. In such circumstances, it becomes easier to understand why the region's political elites generally took to the idea of sovereign, nation-statehood with such alacrity, and why they have invested so much effort in propping it up ever since (Beeson 2003).

Southeast Asia's imperial legacy

There is one important exception to the picture of relatively recent independence and state development following colonial occupation. Thailand is famously the only country in Southeast Asia that managed to avoid being colonised by a European power and it is as well to begin our discussion of the impact of European colonisation there as it represents something of a counterfactual case. Before considering the colonial period, it is important to highlight one important comparative point that separates Thailand from our other case studies. The Philippines, Malaysia and especially Indonesia can all be thought of as maritime states, in that they are archipelagos and have been profoundly affected by the inescapable nature of their geographies. The Philippines and Indonesia are composed of numerous islands – literally thousands in Indonesia's case – which make governance more complex. Even Malaysia must contend with a major divide between its major population centres on the main peninsula and on Sarawak. The sheer difficulty of melding a unitary and effective state administration out of such geographically dispersed elements is a formidable challenge, but when it is overlaid with a myriad of ethnic and religious cleavages, the task becomes even more challenging.

We shall consider the specifics of these internal dynamics in more detail in subsequent chapters, but the point to make at this stage is that Thailand's very different physical geography helps to account for its unique history and its avoidance of colonisation. Thailand is a mainland Southeast Asian state and the concentration of population and power this facilitated has given much greater continuity and sense of identity to the Thais. Siam, or modern Thailand, has been a recognisable, coherent entity since the twelfth and thirteenth centuries when it emerged as a significant force in mainland Southeast Asia. More recently, Thailand was able to avoid being colonied through astute diplomacy and an ability to exploit inter-colonial rivalries (Tarling 2001). Significantly, the Thai monarchy played an important role in this process and, as we shall see, it has remained an influential force in Thai society and an important source of historical continuity and identity ever since (see Chapter 5). And yet, it is important not to overstate Thailand's unique, independent status: certainly, it was not colonied, but it was forced to surrender some its territory to the colonial powers, and its continuing independence was in large part testimony to its capacity to adapt to the new, Euro-centric order. In other words, institutional adaptation and reform to more powerful external forces was the key to maintaining sovereignty. Thailand's experience in the nineteenth century has some striking parallels with the contemporary period, but before we consider them, we need to consider the impact of colonialism on our other three case studies where the consequences were far greater.

Indonesia, the Philippines and Malaysia were all colonised, but by different imperial powers, and provide an interesting comparative window on the dynamics of the colonial relationship generally, as well as the specific historical legacy that has shaped post-imperial development in each country. Of the three, Malaysia has had the most successful post-independence track record, both as far as general development is concerned, and in the specific area of civil–military relations. Nevertheless, Malaysia's comparatively successful development outcomes have been achieved despite rather than because of its colonial heritage – recent revisionist studies of the benefits of British colonialism notwithstanding (see Ferguson 2003). Indeed, no country has been more profoundly marked by the colonial experience as far as the basic social make-up of the country is concerned.

Before British colonisation, which happened in a fairly haphazard and incremental manner, Malaya was a thinly populated collection of estuarine communities without any central political structure. Britain was initially motivated by a desire to secure important trading ports like Penang and Singapore, and to exclude rival imperial powers as well as Thailand. The rapidly growing economic importance of what were then the Straits Settlements meant that the British were drawn into a deeper and more expansive administrative relationship that mirrored and facilitated its growing economic interests. The most important long-term consequences of this period as far as contemporary Malaysia was concerned was to distort the course of its economic development in line with the demands of its centre, and to profoundly reshape its population. Migrant labour poured into Malaya from India and especially China to work the plantations and run the expanding bureaucracy. Managing the consequences of this social transformation has remained one of the defining security and public policy issues to this day. The arbitrary boundaries that marked the outer limits of British interests in Malaya would eventually constitute the borders of independent Malaysia, but they would contain disparate ethnic groups that had little in common and little sense of shared identity.[4]

Indonesia's post-independence rulers were faced with even more daunting challenges of nation-building, but these would be compounded by a history of 'indirect' colonial rule (Trocki 1999). Pre-colonial rule among the peoples of the modern Indonesian archipelago was based primarily on personal relations, and the ideas of states and territories were not simply alien but essentially unknown (Tarling 1998). The sort of arms-length imperial rule favoured by the Dutch in Java and elsewhere did little to displace extant patterns of authority and allegiance (Elson 1999). While this may have made Dutch rule less disruptive and traumatic than elsewhere in the region, the traditions of personal loyalties and patronage that underpinned patron–client relations[5] were not displaced, nor was the basis for a competent, technocratic Weberian-style state established. In other words, from its independent inception, the Indonesian polity has been overlaid by earlier patterns of political and personal relationships which became an institutionalised part of the emergent order.

The persistence of patron–client relationships and the importance of personal connections is even more evident in the Philippines. Again, as in Indonesia, earlier patterns of social organisation were not completely erased as Spanish colonisation was a slow and incremental affair that remained incomplete. The Sultan of Sulu, for example, never submitted to Spanish rule, and the seeds of Philippine insurrection and rebellion, which have provided the backdrop to its distinctive and continuing security concerns, were planted long ago (Osborne 2000: 78). The Philippines also has the dubious distinction of having had two imperial rulers, with the Americans replacing the Spanish after the latter's defeat in the Spanish–American War. The most important consequence of America's relatively brief phase of direct colonial control was to establish a pattern of cooperation and cooption which effectively institutionalised the power and position of a small local elite (Thomson *et al.* 1981). In addition to entrenching a local oligarchy, the other major legacy of American imperialism was – in line with its ideological preferences – to bequeath the Philippines a small and highly ineffective state apparatus that was subject to capture and manipulation by the local elites (Hutchcroft 1998). The inadequacy of inter-connected processes of political and economic development lies at the heart of the Philippines' post-independence problems and, as we shall see, helps to account for the prominent role played by the military in national political life.

The points to emphasise from this very brief snapshot of the impact of the colonial powers in Southeast Asia is that the entire region, including Thailand, was profoundly affected by the experience, and that the subsequent course of post-independence development has been shaped and constrained by this earlier period. At one level, this can be seen in the dramatic transformations that occurred in the region's social structures. And yet while the impact of European economic and political practices was undoubtedly profound, it was incomplete and overlaid on existing patterns of social organisation, which have imparted a significant degree of path dependency to subsequent development. Not only do political practices and economic structures in Southeast Asia often have distinctive qualities that distinguish them from the European exemplar, but they are also different from each other. Because of this fundamental, historically contingent differentiation, the institutions that emerged from Southeast Asian societies have varied as a consequence, too. We shall explore the implications of these variations in detail in subsequent chapters. Before doing that, however, it is important to say something about the impact of the overall international security environment out of which the region's militaries have emerged.

Nation-building and the cold war

While we now think of Southeast Asia as composed of independent nation-states, it is important to re-emphasise that this is not only a relatively recent development, but it was also one that was often achieved in the face of significant opposition on the part of the former colonial powers. The majority of our case studies were relatively fortunate in this regard: only in Indonesia was the process of de-colonisation especially difficult and violently opposed by the imperial power. The Philippines, by contrast, was granted independence as early as 1946, following the return of the victorious Americans. Even in Malaysia, where there was a sustained communist insurgency, eventual independence for Malaysia was always an integral part of British foreign policy; the only questions were about when and under what circumstances (Stockwell 1999: 49). Indeed, the long-term impact of the insurgency in Malaysia was to entrench an anti-communist leadership with strong ties to Britain when independence was eventually achieved. In Thailand, of course, there had been little disruption to indigenous patterns of rule; but even here it would be quite misleading to suggest that the region was the same place it had been before the Second World War. Even before the fighting was concluded across the region, it was clear that Southeast Asia in the post-war period would bear little resemblance to its pre-war position.

At one level, this transformation had ideational roots. The Japanese occupation of Southeast Asia and the decisive defeat of the European powers that preceded it, unambiguously ended the idea of European superiority and fatally undermined the legitimacy of European rule. The fact that the Europeans had been ejected from the region by another Asian power meant that there was no going back to the old order and that the entire region would be redefined as a consequence (Beeson 2007). But it took the Dutch in particular some time to realise that their position in Indonesia had become unsustainable and deeply resented by much of the local population. As we shall see in more detail in Chapter 6, this period proved crucial in cementing the military's place at the centre of Indonesia's post-independence national order. And yet, the evolution of an indigenous military capacity might not have proved decisive – at least in the relatively short-term – had it not been for another feature of the emerging post-war order: the emergence of the United States as a proto-hegemonic power.

The rise of the US to 'superpower' status in general and the development of the cold war in particular were important globally, of course, but they had an especially pronounced impact on Southeast Asia. In this context, Southeast Asia's independence movements might have expected to benefit from America's rise to prominence. After all, American history *ought* to have made its policy-makers temperamentally opposed to anachronistic colonial empires and supportive of independence movements everywhere (McDougall 1997). In reality, however, it was as much the inability of the Dutch to achieve a decisive military outcome against local opposition that encouraged a change in America's foreign policy toward the region (McMahon 1999: 53). This shift in regional priorities was reinforced by the logic of the rapidly developing cold war, which added another, more tangible dimension to the reconfigured ideational and normative environment as part of its evolving global strategy, the US wanted to establish independent, pro-Western, successful capitalist economies as a way of containing communist expansion (Gaddis 1982). Although American priorities were primarily centred on Europe, it was clear that Southeast Asia had – like East Asia more generally – become an increasingly important theatre of superpower confrontation and contestation (Hess 1987).

The impact of this overarching geopolitical context on individual countries will be detailed in subsequent chapters. At this stage it is important to highlight the more general consequences of this period on the national and transnational development strategies of the Southeast Asian states. Of most significance in this context is that the cold war period produced a unique set of threats and opportunities as far as the newly (or soon to be) independent states of Southeast Asia were concerned. Unsurprisingly, perhaps, given the fragile nature of Southeast Asian state-hood and the preoccupation with security concerns that distinguished the cold war period, 'threat perceptions' received the most attention. What was distinctive about the position of Indonesia and the Philippines, and also of the comparatively more stable regimes of Malaysia and Thailand, however, was how much such threats had *internal* origins. Indeed, the most striking feature of the security situation generally in our four case studies is that, the alarmist predictions of the Pentagon's 'domino theorists' notwithstanding, they have not confronted major external security challenges that threatened the integrity of the state since the end of the Second World War. Even the 'confrontation' between Indonesia and Malaysia was a relatively bloodless affair that ultimately led to the institutionalisation and regularisation of intra-regional relations under the banner of the Association of Southeast Asian Nations (ASEAN) (Haacke 2003).

What distinguishes all our case studies, therefore, has been a preoccupation with internal security issues that were much more immediate threats to regime survival and national security than any likely external danger. Indeed, the supposed instability of the external international order was actually exploited with skill to reinforce and legitimate internal control and order. As such, Southeast Asia is something of a mirror image of the conventional understanding of the state's place in the international system: in Southeast Asia, it has generally been the internal political space that has been potentially unstable and even anarchical, while the interstate system of which Southeast Asian states are a part has generally been a source of stability, order and legitimacy. This not only helps to explain why Southeast Asians have been keen to develop regional institutions like ASEAN that are consciously designed to consolidate the inviolability of the domestic sphere (Acharya 2001), but it also explains why regional militaries have come to occupy such a pivotal place in consolidating such an order.

Political and economic consolidation

While the role of the Southeast Asia's militaries is the principal concern of the chapters that follow, at this point it is important to place their role and position in the wider context of the region's post-war development. Such an analysis not only helps us to better understand the particular constraints and capacities that shaped security outcomes in different countries, but it also provides a more generalised insight into the region's relationship with major external actors like the US.

Although it is now common to depict the US as enjoying an historically unparalleled position of dominance (Brooks and Wohlforth 2002), its recent pre-eminence was not as complete or assured for much of the post-war period. While the cold war was in full swing, countries that were either closely aligned to the US, or at least not actively opposed to it, had some prospect of benefiting from American largesse as it competed with the Soviet Union for influence across the world. This possibility was especially clear in East Asia where Japan became the principal focus of US assistance and efforts to consolidate capitalism in the region (Schaller 1982). Although Japan was clearly the main beneficiary of this process, and came to occupy a dominant economic position in the region as a consequence, it is equally apparent that most of the non-communist parts of East Asia also benefited directly or indirectly from the massive stimulus provided by American aid and the economic demand that the Korean and Vietnam Wars generated. But as Richard Stubbs (2005) points out, as far as regional elites were concerned, at least, the benefits of this period extended beyond the narrowly economic: because the US was preoccupied with potential Soviet expansion and the 'loss' of client states to the communist orbit, the Americans were prepared to tolerate – even support – 'benign' forms of authoritarianism.[6] The emergence of the 'strong' states that are such a feature of East Asia's post-war development becomes easier to understand in this context.

In all our case studies, authoritarianism and non-democratic forms of rule have been the norm for much of the post-war period. Even now, the stability of democracy is uncertain or incompletely realised (Case 2002) as the 2006 coup in Thailand demonstrates only too well. We shall discuss the specific forms of political rule in greater detail in subsequent chapters but there is a general point to make that flows directly from the post-war developmental experience and which helps to explain the persistence of non-democratic political structures. As Muthiah Alagappa points out (2001: 435), at the heart of many of Asia's authoritarian regimes – in which the military has frequently been an explicit part, or implicit guarantor – there has been an 'interplay of coercion, political legitimacy, and economic development'. While the region's regimes have been able to maintain the remarkable rates of economic growth and development that have been so characteristic of the post-war period, they have enjoyed a degree of legitimacy that has reduced pressure for political reform (Acharya and Stubbs 1999). Indeed, some observers have argued in place of the sort of political emancipation and reformist pressure that we might have 'normally' expected to occur alongside economic development (Rueschemeyer *et al.* 1992; Przeworski *et al.* 2000), in Southeast Asia 'the middle class produced by the developmental state is effectively in its thrall' (Jones 1998: 156).

While this picture may be changing as the consolidation of democracy in Indonesia and the Philippines appears to suggest and the Thai coup notwithstanding, the lack of pressure from Southeast Asia's emerging middle class does go someway to explaining the persistence of authoritarianism in the cold war period. The other factor that helps to explain the durability of authoritarianism at this time was regional rather than national, and had more to do with geopolitics than any strictly domestic factors: regional cooperation in response to the specific security dynamics of the cold war period provided a degree of legitimacy and solidarity for the region's authoritarian regimes (Yuen 1997). The establishment of ASEAN noted above may have been ostensibly about encouraging regional political, economic and cultural development and cooperation, but its principal motivation was to enhance security – both external *and* internal. In this context, it is revealing that the ASEAN Secretariat was intentionally designed to be small, relatively powerless and a direct repudiation of the model developed by the European Union.

While the internal benefits of ASEAN membership were potentially crucial, most analytical attention has focused on the conventional 'external' manifestations of interstate cooperation. But even in this context, there were complex motivations at work which reflected the intersection of domestic and international issues and highlighted the inherent artificiality of this division (Walker 1993). At one level, intra-regional cooperation was aimed at improving relations within Southeast Asia itself in the aftermath of the confrontation between Indonesia and Malaysia. At another level, however, the formation of ASEAN represented an attempt to establish a greater international presence and independence for Southeast Asia as an increasingly coherent collective actor. It is striking that despite the fact that both Thailand and the Philippines were allied to the US and thus involved in the Vietnam War, ASEAN reflected the ideas of the more independently minded Indonesian government, which had been such a conspicuous champion of the non-aligned movement (Yahuda 2003: 68).

In the longer-term, then, the significance of ASEAN, as far as the region's security environment generally and the role of its various militaries in particular are concerned, is twofold. On the one hand, ASEAN has clearly given Southeast Asian states a prominence and influence that they would not have enjoyed otherwise. This is not to suggest that they have been able to encourage the major powers of the region or the US to behave in ways that they might not have done otherwise, but they have clearly had an influence at the margins: both the ASEAN Regional Forum and the Asia Pacific Economic Cooperation (APEC) forum are predicated on the so-called ASEAN Way of consensus, informality and non-binding agreements. On the other hand, and more importantly for our purposes, ASEAN was instrumental in enshrining the doctrine of non-interference in the domestic security concerns of member states (see Acharya 2001: 57–60). Not only did this mean that some of the region's more repressive and unrepresentative regimes remained relatively insulated from unfavourable external criticism, but so did their respective military establishments.

Southeast Asia and the evolution of American hegemony

Southeast Asia's social, political and economic development since independence has occurred in a specific set of geopolitical circumstances. The defining feature of this period has been the existence of American hegemony, initially as part of a bipolar contest with the Soviet Union, and latterly as the central component of a 'unipolar' order in which it has been able to exert an increasing influence over the world's interconnected security, political and economic architectures (Ikenberry 2004; Beeson 2006b). Consequently, one of the central claims of this chapter in particular and of this book more generally is that to understand the development of Asian militaries, we must understand the evolution of the wider international order of which they are a part.

The ideological significance of nation-building

The intersection of political and strategic goals is most apparent during the cold war period when overt ideological contestation was far more prominent and geopolitical imperatives trumped all other considerations. The parallels with the current period and the 'war on terror' make the cold war period and its distinctive dynamics especially relevant and illuminating as a consequence. It is important to remember that the ultimate triumph of liberal-capitalism was far from assured in the immediate aftermath of the Second World War, and even in the 1960s it was far from clear – especially to American strategists – that much of Southeast Asia would not be 'lost' to communism. Given that there are similar concerns about the possible rise of radical Islam in all of the countries with which we are concerned, the cold war period provides a particularly fruitful point of comparison for contemporary developments.

In the late 1950s and early 1960s when Southeast Asia's newly independent but fragile states were struggling to come to terms with the twin challenges of nation-building and economic development, there was concern amongst American policy-making elites not just about their immediate potential vulnerability to communist infiltration and take-over – as there is now with radical Islam – but also about the underlying values of the population as a whole (Berger 2003). In the earlier period it was not Islam specifically that was considered to be the primary problem, but an adherence to 'traditional' values that were seen as being anachronistic, inappropriate and incongruent with 'modernity' (Latham 2000). Certainly, some religious traditions were seen as hangovers from a pre-modern era and part of outdated belief systems that were impediments to 'development', but Islam was not seen as a force for social mobilisation in the way that communism potentially was at that time. Indeed, it is instructive that one of the leading analysts of the 'problem' of political modernisation recognised just how brilliantly effective communist organisational strategies could be as vehicles for mass mobilisation. This was why Huntington suggested in his highly influential *Political Order in Changing Societies*, that

> In modernising society, 'building the state' means in part the creation of an effective bureaucracy, but, more importantly, the establishment of an effective party system capable of structuring the participation of new groups in politics.
> (Huntington 1968: 401)

For Huntington, then, the inculcation of 'modern' values and political structures was not just a simple-minded belief in the superiority of 'Western' ideas generally or the American-style economic structures and political liberalism more generally, but a recognition of the possible attraction of competing ideational and organisational systems. Consequently, what mattered was the creation of effective institutions, even if these were at odds with some of the declaratory rhetoric of America's cold war propaganda. For this reason Huntington was quite comfortable with the idea of non-democratic, one-party rule, as this could provide the required stability in the expected transition to modernity, a theme we noted in both Chapters 1 and 2. Significantly for our purposes, Huntington (1968: 203) believed that 'in the early stages of modernisation, military officers [could] play a highly modernising and progressive role'.

The possibility that regional militaries could play this sort of 'progressive' social role, whilst simultaneously shoring up domestic stability and warding-off external threats, explains America's practical support to the region's militaries and the prominence given to it as a key social institution by strategic thinkers and academic analysis. One of the most prominent theorists of 'modernisation' in an Asian context – Lucian Pye – also stressed the potentially positive role the military could play as an agent of necessary change, if the countries of Southeast Asia were to overcome their backwardness and acquire the trappings of modernity and the benefits of development. For Pye, the military was a definitively modern organisation and as such could act as a force of social transformation and acculturation, overcoming particularistic ties, personal loyalties and ethnic divisions, and replacing them with a 'rational outlook' and a range of skills that could be applied in administration or business. In short, 'the good soldier is also to some degree a modernised man' (Pye 1962: 80).

In part, therefore, military modernisation was seen as a potentially vital instrument in the long-term development of the region. A transformation in pre-modern belief systems would not only make the peoples of the region more Western and thus more sympathetic to the US, but they would also help to bring about the economic transformation of the region. For it must be remembered that in the aftermath of the Second World War it was far from clear – especially in Southeast Asia – that capitalism was going to deliver the developmental goods. Indeed, in some parts of the region, it remains far from clear to this day, a reality that contin-ues to undermine the legitimacy of both national governments and the overarching, US-dominated order of which they are a part (Beeson 2004). The important com-parative point that emerges from the cold war period is that – then, as now – the military was seen as a potentially indispensable part of broader regime stability in the face of perceived threats and thus worthy of active support (Janowitz 1964).

As we shall see, American foreign policy has undergone some important changes in the post-cold war era, in a process Mark Berger (2006) describes as a shift from a US-led modernisation project, to a US-led globalisation project. What is clear is that at different moments, geopolitical imperatives have shaped both the practice of American foreign policy and the thinking that inspired it. At their most dramatic such impulses culminated in the misguided, traumatic and the abortive attempts at nation-building and consolidation in Vietnam (Kolko 1985). But even in Indonesia and the Philippines, the regimes of Suharto and Marcos prospered partly as a consequence of American tolerance, if not active support of the US. Likewise, American support provided a vital prop for various military regimes in Thailand. Indeed, during the cold war period, superpower contestation offered some degree of potential leverage to the smallest of states: even if they did not directly benefit from American aid and support – and many did – they were comparatively free of direct intervention in their domestic affairs, as long as they were allied with, or broadly sympathetic to, the US.

This overarching geopolitical context, in which the US was prepared to tolerate, if not actively encourage, the development of authoritarian regimes as long as they were anti-communist, was dramatically reconfigured by the abrupt, and largely unexpected ending of the cold war. But given that the so-called war on terror appears to be recreating some of the dynamics, relationships and structures of the cold war period (Glassman 2006), it is worth briefly spelling out some of the features of the interregnum during the 1990s. If nothing else, this decade provides a useful comparative basis for thinking about the new ideological and strategic environment that has evolved in the aftermath of 9/11.

The 1990s interregnum

In the 1990s, when in the immediate aftermath of the cold war geo-economics appeared to have eclipsed geopolitics as the primary concern of policy-makers in the US and elsewhere (Luttwak 1990), a new array of external pressures were brought to bear on the Southeast Asian states, which suddenly found themselves stripped of their strategic significance. Two features of this period are especially significant when thinking about the prospects for importing and adapting an essentially externally developed reformist agenda like SSR: first, the circumstances in which particular ideas can be most successfully proselytised and second, the more general influence of the international system in which American hegemony plays a pivotal role in helping to 'constitutionalise' a particular regulatory and normative order (Gill 1998).

Optimism about the prospects for – even the inevitability of – institutional development in line with American 'best practice' reached fever pitch in the aftermath of the cold war. Francis Fukuyama's (1992) thesis about the 'end of history' is perhaps the best known exemplar of this tendency, but it is important to recognise that it was part of a more generalised shift in the ideational atmosphere which confidently predicted the irresistible spread of democracy and economic reform (Ohmae 1990; Huntington 1991). We now know, of course, that many of these predictions were wildly overblown and that the institutional differentiation, especially in East Asia, has proved far more durable than some observers expected (Beeson 2002). Indeed, at the height of the 'East Asian miracle', many influential Asian leaders and commentators were celebrating the distinctive and supposedly superior qualities of 'Asian values', which they contrasted unfavourably with those of a decadent and declining Western world.[7]

We now also know that these claims were similarly overstated. And yet despite the fact that claims about the efficacy of Asian values were clearly undermined by the impact of the economic crisis which broke out in 1997, it is noteworthy that many of the East Asian institutions that came in for such sustained criticism in the aftermath of the crisis were not eliminated or entirely discredited. Although a discussion of the East Asian financial crisis lies well beyond the scope of this book,[8] it had such a profound impact on the region – not the least of which was on its reputation and international standing – that a few points are worth briefly making as it contains some wider lessons about the prospects for reform more generally in a region where externally imposed ideas have often been fiercely resisted (Beeson and Islam 2005).

The first point to make is that the crisis provided precisely the sort of 'external shock' that might have been expected to have induced fundamental change of the type identified in the previous chapter. And while the crisis did bring down governments in Thailand and Indonesia, as well as triggering important changes at the formal level, many of the underlying patterns of power, patronage and interest – particularly those related to the security sector – either remained in place or rapidly adapted to the new environment. This was particularly the case in Indonesia which was the most badly affected by the crisis, and which might have been expected to have experienced the most change as a consequence. However, as we shall see in Chapter 5, despite the fall of Suharto, many of the economic, political and military structures he helped to create remain in place and continue to determine policy direction and implementation in Indonesia (Robison and Hadiz 2004).

So if some of the region's domestic institutions proved surprisingly resistant to change, what of external influences? At an ideational level, it is difficult to exaggerate the effort influential external actors and agencies made in attempting to discredit the 'East Asian model' and the close business-government relations with which it was associated (Hall 2003). Cleary this had some impact, especially when it came from powerful international organisations like the International Monetary Fund (IMF), which had the power to grant or withhold vital bail-out funds. Indeed, it was this latter form of direct economic leverage that was the most effective instrument in encouraging domestic reform in the region, something that was plainly recognised by the US. Significantly, the US chose not to rely on moral suasion or the alleged superiority of Western models of economic and political organisation. On the contrary, the US operated through the IMF to impose reform on a region that had proved reluctant to abandon practices that had proved highly successful both in terms of encouraging economic development, and in entrenching the position of regional political and economic elites (Wade 2001).

The East Asian financial crisis and its aftermath suggests that, even when there is an apparently powerful stimulus that might be expected to encourage institutional change, we should not expect this to occur easily or automatically. Where powerful vested interests are able to resist or adapt to such pressures, it is entirely likely that they will do so – even where substantial direct leverage is applied to encourage compliance with a new regulatory or normative order. The crisis period highlights the potential difficulties and obstacles confronting any reform process or agenda that has to overcome entrenched centres of power. This merits particular emphasis in the light of the expectations noted above about the inevitability of change in the contemporary post-cold war era. While it is true that all states are being influenced by, and forced to respond to the array of external and internal pressures generated by 'globalisation'[9] – including the very way security is conceived and achieved (Clark 1999) – it is not clear that this will lead to similar outcomes in different parts of the world. On the contrary, as we have seen in the context of ASEAN, different security regimes are likely to develop and be sustained because of the very different circumstances and state capacities that obtain in various parts of the world.

Again, this latter point merits emphasis as it is central to explaining the different security regimes, architectures and practices that are found in Southeast Asia at both the domestic and regional levels. For all the discussion of new modes of transnational governance, the rise of non-state actors and policy networks, and the transmission of new norms and regulatory standards,[10] it is important to remember that the non-state sector in East Asia is generally significantly less developed than it is in Western Europe, which provides the model for much of the theorising about new modes of transnational governance (Beeson and Jayasuriya 1998). The point to stress here is that not only is the institutional infrastructure in East Asia generally much 'thinner' than in Europe, but there are consequently fewer points of entry for reformist ideas and policies, and fewer non-state actors to champion them in the absence of governmental support. In general, there is little to suggest that the limited regional institutionalisation that has occurred in East Asia has the capacity to either overcome nationalist sentiment or to supplant the historically entrenched importance and position of the region's 'strong' states (Katzenstein 2005).

This possibility becomes especially pertinent when we think about the post 9/11 political and security environment. As we have seen, when the US was freed from the geopolitical imperatives of the cold war during the 1990s, it had little hesitation in attempting to utilise its immense political and economic leverage to impose its policy preferences on other parts of the world. Even in these highly favourable circumstances, however, there were plainly limits to this process, and domestic institutions proved to be important and surprisingly durable intervening variables that helped to determine how such reformist pressures would be realised. In the post 9/11 world when security concerns have re-appeared at the top America's policy agenda, the cultivation of allies around the world has become important once again – America's recent proclivity for unilateralism notwithstanding.[11]

In this context, Southeast Asia has rapidly come to assume a particular prominence because of its supposed status as 'terrorism's second front' (Gersham 2002). While claims made about the extent of terrorist groups in Southeast Asia are often unsubstantiated and reminiscent of the rhetoric of the cold war (Hamilton-Hart 2005), there is less doubt about the war on terror's impact on American foreign policy. In the aftermath of 9/11, the US moved rapidly to shore up relations with Southeast Asian states with large Muslim populations, or which were seen to be potential sources of terrorist activity. Even Malaysia, which had hitherto been marginalised as a consequence of Mahathir's anti-Western rhetoric, enjoyed a significant rapprochement with the US, and a reduction in criticism of Malaysia's domestic politics (Nesadurai 2006). Even more significantly in the context of long-term inter-regional relations and the prospects for SSR, the US has also re-established ties with Indonesia's Tentara Nasional Indonesia (TNI). Despite concerns about the TNI's responsibility for human rights abuses in Timor, Aceh, Papua and elsewhere, and despite the fact that it has been suggested that the Indonesian army has actually been responsible for allowing, if not directly encouraging, the growth of radical Islam in Indonesia (LaMoshi 2004), the US now judges that the war on terror necessitates the military's international rehabilitation (Hallinan 2004).

The particular impact of this shift in American priorities as far as Southeast Asia's militaries and political elites are concerned will be explored in greater detail in subsequent chapters. The general point to make at this stage, however, is that the impact of American hegemony generally and military strategy in particular in what is seen as a 'long war' against terrorism (Department of Defense 2006), is likely to bear a striking resemblance to the cold war period. During the cold war what mattered was order and reliability; a commitment to democratic principles, economic openness or human rights was invariably judged to be of less importance than a capacity to maintain social order and promote economic development within a broadly capitalist framework. In such circumstances, not only was there little pressure placed on the region's militaries to reform themselves in line with international 'best practice', but they were also frequently seen as the ultimate, indispensable guarantor of regime stability. If history is, indeed, repeating itself and we are witnessing a return to the priorities of the cold war period in which security concerns trump all others, then the prospects for meaningful SSR look rather dim.

Conclusion

For all the talk of globalisation, convergence and international benchmarking, the reality is that institutional differentiation and variety remain significant markers of national and regional space. True, in some areas of activity – economic cooperation and coordination is the most developed and important example – there are significant instances of cross-border agreements and consensus about how to regulate or facilitate international interaction. Indeed, it is revealing that the area in which the coordination of regional activities has developed furthest in East Asia has been monetary cooperation: the financial crisis demonstrated how necessary such cooperation could be, both in managing specific technical challenges and 'functional' requirements of an increasingly integrated international economy, and in bolstering the region's economic autonomy and political authority (Henning 2002). The transmission and adoption of policy ideas and practices in the economic sphere has been in part, at least, driven by a recognition that this is an increasingly necessary part of 'globalisation', and that there may be direct pay-offs for those economies and economic actors that achieve this successfully. The dynamics at work in the security sector are quite different and suggest that similar processes will be more difficult to replicate.

The central, defining, putative preoccupation of militaries everywhere is the security of the nation and the protection of national borders. Despite the fact that there is now a significant history of internationally based cooperative efforts to achieve this aim – of which ASEAN is the key exemplar in the East Asian region – the underlying logic of military security remains significantly different to other issue areas. For participants in international economic regimes there is the prospect of direct and immediate benefits, and significant potential costs associated with exclusion from international regimes and activity. Consequently, despite all the well-documented disparities of influence and outcomes that characterise organisations like the World Trade Organisation, few nations wish to be excluded from it, even though it has the potential to enforce compliance with its regulatory agenda on individual members. Not only is there no similar organisation in the security sphere, but national sovereignty, autonomy and integrity also remain non-negotiable aspects of the military rationale. In short, despite growing international security cooperation, the attractions of cooperation are often not compelling, and resistance to external pressures for reform can have greater immediate instrumental value.

This is especially true of a Southeast Asian region in which the stability of the state and the integrity of national borders frequently remain uncertain, and where local elites have been highly sensitive about the possible erosion of national sovereignty. Given the pivotal role that regional militaries continue to play in many Southeast Asian countries, we might expect potential challenges to their position, structure and behaviour to be treated with caution at best, outright hostility at worst. An historically informed analysis of regional development and the role of the military within such processes helps to explain why security forces have come to assume the roles they have, why they may be resistant to change, and under what circumstances change is most and least likely. In attempting to assess the prospects for SSR, therefore, we need to consider the following:

- What are the overarching geopolitical circumstances within which SSR is being encouraged, and does the comparative historical record suggest they are likely to prove conducive to change? In other words, are the prospects for successful SSR likely to be determined solely by contingent local circumstances or will the configuration of the wider international order also prove decisive?
- How have national security forces developed institutionally, and how are they embedded in a wider array of social institutions? Is it possible to identify particular arrays of, or intersections between various societal institutions that make the prospects for SSR more or less likely?
- To what extent has the language of SSR been adopted by policy networks and is this adoption the result of coercion, instrumental calculation or belief (Wendt 1999)?
- Is it possible to identify points of access for the introduction of externally generated norms, ideas and practices?
- To what extent is SSR 'owned' by Southeast Asian elites?
- What have been the major obstacles to formulating and implementing the SSR agenda?

It is these questions that we seek to address in the four subsequent case study chapters. We will return to these questions in the conclusion.

4 Malaysia

Constitutionalism corrupted?

In a Southeast Asian region where the military has played a prominent – often anti-democratic and repressive – part, Malaysia is something of an anomaly. Malaysia is the only one of our case studies where the military has not played a major role in either directly running the country, or at least determining the nature of the national government. At the very least, the Malaysian experience suggests there is nothing inevitable about the role the military will play as a consequence of either Southeast Asia's distinct history, the challenges of nation-building, or the nature of the colonial experience (cf. Crouch 1978). Indeed, Malaysia provides something of a counterfactual case in which we have an example of a Southeast Asian nation where the military has not played an overtly prominent role in the political and economic life of the nation. As such it provides an important exception to the general pattern of high-profile military interventionism that has been so typical of the region until relatively recently. Although there may be common security imperatives that confront the governments of all newly independent states and emerging economies – especially in the context of the sort of overarching superpower confrontation we described in the previous chapter – the precise way various national governments address these challenges is not pre-determined, nor simply a function of universal 'structural' constraints, as some theorists such as Michael Desch would have us believe (see Chapter 2). On the contrary, despite some remarkably similar general international pressures and historical circumstances, there is a surprising degree of variation in the experiences of Malaysia, Thailand, the Philippines and Indonesia, and in the role played by their respective militaries.

Even by Southeast Asia's famously heterogeneous standards, the unique role played by Malaysia's military makes it something of an outlier. At first blush it may well be asked whether there is anything that actually requires reform in a country where the military has seemingly subscribed to high standards of professionalism and never looked remotely likely to challenge the authority of civilian authorities. Indeed, it might be supposed that the low-profile and professionalism of the military is indicative of a more 'Western-style' accommodation between civilian power and the security services and in keeping with the constitutional model of civil–military relations we outlined in the introduction. However, we need to keep in mind that the constitutional model is an ideal-type that focuses primarily on the military in particular, and has some inbuilt assumptions about the nature of the security sector more generally. In Malaysia's case, while some of the formal elements of civil–military relations are in keeping with the constitutional model, in practice the operation of the security sector and its relationship with government is rather more complex, particularistic and idiosyncratic. What is of particular importance here is that elements of the security sector – most notably the police in general and Special Branch in particular – are deeply politicised.

In Malaysia, the assumed constitutionalised, legally regulated control of the security sector is at best partial, at worst a travesty of what we might expect from the constitutional model. In reality, both the police and the judiciary have become key components of regime maintenance, rather than the impartial application of the law. Indeed, Malaysia has been just as – if not more – authoritarian as some of its neighbours, and the security forces have played a decisive role in underpinning what has at times been a highly repressive and coercive regime. What distinguishes Malaysia, however, is that the most powerful security agency of the Malaysian state has been the police rather than the army. Consequently, if the ultimate objective of SSR is the promotion of civilian governance, liberal democratic control, and 'the strengthening of norms in relation to the proper relationship between the security sector and society at large' (Chanaa 2002: 29), then the Malaysian case reminds us that we must look beyond the military as a target of reform. Furthermore, this case study also serves as a reminder that processes of security sector reform can work in both directions and that it is not necessarily the case that security sectors in the region are moving in the same direction. In a context where almost no international pressure has been brought to bear in support of security sector reform in Malaysia primarily because of the veneer of constitutionalism, and where there have been few other impetuses for rethinking key elements of the state's security culture, Malaysia's security sector – especially its police – has engaged in a process of 'fine-tuning' that has taken its practices further away from the constitutionalist ideal.

To understand why the military is a comparatively unimportant actor in Malaysian development and unlikely to pose any challenge to civilian (ostensibly democratic) rule, and why we might need to direct our reformist impulses elsewhere, we need to trace the precise circumstances in which the unusual division of labour between the military and the policy force evolved. As we shall see, the military has been preoccupied with its own affairs and is an important expression of Malay identity and vehicle for social mobility. While this may have made the military *per se* a non-threatening force and not in need of the sort of reforms that our other case studies arguably require, this does not mean that there is not a 'problem' to be addressed as far as Malaysia's security services are concerned. On the contrary, the close connections between the police and government, the compliant and politicised nature of the judiciary, and the failure of a number of state agencies to act independently suggests that reform is needed, but not in the usual areas. Malaysia, we suggest, provides a compelling example of why we need to unpack apparently universal organisations like the military or the security forces more generally, and place them in a wider array of social institutions if we wish to understand how coercive state apparatuses actually work and where reform actually needs to occur.

The Malaysian military in historical context

One of the most important long-term influences on the development of, and role played by, the Malaysian military has been British colonialism. Some observers consider the fact that Malaysia is an ex-British (rather than Dutch or French) colony to be the decisive factor in explaining the subsequent role and professionalism of the Malaysian army.[1] While such claims are receiving a surprising amount of support in the currently fashionable revisionist interpretation of the British imperial experience (Ferguson 2003), we shall suggest that there are other important contingent factors that have ultimately been more important determinants of civil–military relations in Malaysia.

Nevertheless, the British *were* a powerful influence on military development. The British established the first Royal Malay Regiment (RMR) Experimental Company in 1933, and have been an 'inseparable' part of 'Malaysian national security conceptions' more generally (Nathan 1998: 514). Keen to retain a monopoly on military power, the British were deeply reluctant to create the RMR, preferring instead to maintain a local constabulary to deal with lawlessness. However, under pressure from local elites Britain consented to the RMR's creation but attempted to make it subordinate to both the local police and the British military.[2] While this may help to account for the particular ideational orientation of the Malay military, other institutional factors help to explain their subsequent low domestic profile. Significantly, both the civil service and the police were established much earlier in the late nineteenth century as part of the apparatus of colonial rule. The comparative longevity of both the police and especially what Zakaria (1985: 120) describes as the 'haughty' civil service in comparison to the army helps to explain the latter's relative institutional inferiority to both the other organisations.[3] The police force, for instance, was formed in 1870 whereas the military – as we noted earlier – had to wait until 1933, by which time many of the core security relationships had already been bedded down.[4] Consequently, the armed forces tended to be regarded as the poor relations in Malaysia's evolving institutional order and not the centre of power and national development that they became in Indonesia.[5]

Significantly, even where we might have expected the Malaysian military to have played a decisive and authoritative role – in the maintenance of domestic security and order, for example – they have generally played second fiddle to the police. Remarkably enough, even during the 'Emergency', or the drawn-out struggle with communist insurgents which began in 1948, it was the police, rather than the army, which took primary responsibility in dealing with the threat to domestic stability. The military, in this case, played a subordinate role to the police.[6] Although the police and the army were considered to be part of the overall 'security forces' under the provisions of the Internal Security Act, there is a clear division of responsibility as far as their respective roles are concerned. In this context, the police have developed a much more significant capacity for intelligence gathering and surveillance, and even have a substantial combat capability. Not only did the police force suffer twice as many casualties as the army during the Emergency, for example, but they also acquired armoured cars for their jungle operations

(Crouch 1991: 133). Before the 1980s, the military's primary role was to assist the police in its anti-insurgency activities. Only in the 1980s, with the permanent demise of the insurgents, did the military confront the task of articulating its own role as a 'regular conventional force'.[7] In Malaysia's case, therefore, expectations about the 'normal' activities of, and division of labour between, the police and the military tend not to be realised, and we need to consider contingent social realities and broader geopolitical imperatives if we hope to understand their distinctive and atypical developmental trajectories.

The socio-economic basis of Malaysian security practice

Paradoxically, the definitive domestic consideration shaping Malaysia's post-independence policies has international origins. The colonial period may have bequeathed the Malay military with a sense of professionalism, but it was also a major influence on the composition and role of the military itself. As we noted in Chapter 2, the major domestic reality post-independence governments have had to deal with in Malaysia has been the multi-ethnic nature of the population. In this regard it is highly significant that the Royal Malay Regiment (RMR) remains just that, and there has been no attempt to rebadge it as the potentially more inclusive, Royal Malaysian Regiment, for example. On the contrary, from its inception the RMR has been self-consciously conceived of as a predominantly Malay organisation and a key component of Malaysia's distinctive ethnic accommodation. The fact that during the Emergency the insurgency movement had been led primarily by ethnic Chinese reinforced the importance of an all Malay military unit at the centre of the fledgling nation's security forces. Although there are significant numbers of Indians and Chinese in the army, since independence the upper echelons of the armed forces have been exclusively Malay or British.[8]

Achieving some sort of racial accommodation, if not harmony, has been a continuing element of Malaysian security perspectives and military development though there is another important contrast with the police in this regard. It is significant that the major expansion of the Malaysian Armed Forces (MAF) did not occur until the racial riots of 1969, which proved to be a defining event in Malaysia's short independent history. Prior to this, the armed forces had been small, frequently commanded by British officers and an almost tokenistic assertion of independent nationhood.[9] In the early post-independence period there was a reliance on British forces for external protection from what were, in truth, remote threats to national security. Even during the confrontation with Indonesia – clearly the most tangible challenge to Malaysia's national integrity – it is revealing that Malaysian strategy was overseen by British officers and relied primarily on the police force rather than the military (Zakaria 1994: 124). It was only the British decision to withdraw its forces from East of Suez in the mid-1960s that caused Malaysian policymakers to consider a more self-reliant posture.[10] Even then, it was domestic threats to security that proved to be decisive factors in the expansion of the military. As a consequence, not only was there an expansion in the size of the conventional military forces, but there was also a major expansion of the paramilitary Police Field Force, reinforcing the latter's position as the pre-eminent domestic security organisation (Crouch 1991). Only after the Vietnamese invasion of Cambodia in 1979 did the MAF's focus turn from supporting the police against internal enemies towards an external focus primarily concerned with stemming the spread of communism from Indochina.

It was not until the 1980s, after this shift in focus, that the Malaysian military began to consolidate a more conventional role, with the army doubling its size to about 100,000 in the period from 1979 to 1983. Britain's withdrawal from the region was rapidly followed by the enunciation of the so-called Nixon Doctrine in the aftermath of the Vietnam War; both factors that encouraged greater self-reliance on the part of regional militaries. Yet despite the increase in the size of the military establishment, there was no similar expansion in the breadth of social inclusiveness in the armed forces. On the contrary, the dominance of Malays in the RMR which was the premier corps in the Infantry, and the latter's dominance of the Army Staff Division at the Ministry of Defence, 'worked effectively to perpetuate the continued lopsidedness in the ethnic composition of the officer corps' (Jeshurun 1988: 261). There is little evidence that this ethnic imbalance has been overcome more recently. On the contrary, there are indications that Malay dominance has consolidated as potential Chinese and Indian recruits come to believe that they will not be able to rise as far as their Malay contemporaries and choose to pursue careers elsewhere (*The Economist* 2004a). Given the importance that is frequently attached to the military as a vehicle for nation-building and overcoming particularistic interests, this is plainly one area in which reform is needed. Similar problems are evident in the police, where the ethnic mix is actually moving further towards Malay domination. Whilst the police was always dominated by ethnic Malays, there was a significant demand for Chinese officers, especially in the Special Branch, during the communist emergency. Following the defeat of the communists the number of ethnic Chinese in the police declined 'drastically'.[11]

The reality of the security sector's ethnic make-up is a salutary reminder of the difference between form and substance. While there may be no formal obstacles to an ethnic Chinese becoming head of the army or defence minister, in practice the prospects are still very limited. Similar caution needs to be exercised when thinking about the relationship between the security forces and civilian government. Although there is little question that the military is subordinate to government (Jeshurun 1999: 230), an over-emphasis of the formal aspects of civil–military relations gives a somewhat misleading picture of the broader role of the security forces. Taken in the narrow sense, the defence forces – here understood as the army, navy and air force – are clearly under civilian government control: there is a formal authority structure in which the armed forces are answerable to the National Security Council, which comes under the purview of the prime minister. However, while the formal structures of defence accountability and responsibility may seem familiar and much like their counterparts elsewhere, in practice the reality is somewhat different. Not only is the broader role of the security services – especially the police – not captured in this picture, but the underlying dynamics of civil–military relations are not apparent either. To gain a clearer picture of this complex and rather opaque structure, we need to consider the wider institutional framework of which the military and the police are a part.

Politics, economics and the security forces

One of the most important background features of Malaysia's post-independence experience has been steadily rising living standards and generally fulfilled expectations about continuing economic development. Of our case studies, Malaysia has by far the highest average income levels, and the success of various governments in overseeing a generally successful process of economic development is clearly part of the explanation for both the stability and legitimacy of successive governments in Malaysia (Case 1995). Unsurprisingly, therefore, economic development is an integral and explicit part of Malaysia's overall security perspective, but one that is refracted through the prism of ethnicity.

In this regard, it cannot be re-emphasised too strongly quite what a defining moment in Malaysia's history the race riots of 1969 were. Although there have been few challenges to the long-term integrity of the state in Malaysia – the confrontation with Indonesia and the Emergency not withstanding – the bloodletting associated with the 'May 13th incident' has been a seminal influence not just on attitudes toward security, but toward economic and social policy as well. In the short-term, this could be seen in future prime minister Mahathir's decisive intervention into domestic politics, when he demanded greater recognition of, and rights for, indigenous Malays, thereby bringing about the downfall of then premier Tunku Abdul Rahman. Although Mahathir was briefly expelled from the United Malays National Organisation (UMNO) – which remains the dominant political force and expression of Malay political power in the country – he was rapidly reinstated by Rahman's successor, Tun Abdul Razak. In the longer-term, Razak's major achievement – and one of the principal political legacies of this period – was to establish the *Barisan Nasional* (BN), which absorbed a number of other, non-Malay political parties into a ruling coalition.

This coalition of forces has dominated Malaysian politics ever since and entrenched the political dominance of the *Bumiputeras*, or indigenous Malays. While the consolidation of Malay power in the political and military fields was achieved relatively easily, a similar transformation in the relative economic importance of Malaysia's various ethnic groups presented a much more formidable challenge. The development of the New Economic Policy (NEP) in the aftermath of the riots was a programme of 'reverse discrimination' with the explicit aim of reducing the economic power and dominance of ethnic Chinese and ' "breeding" Malay capitalists' (Case 2002: 100). What is of greatest significance here is that economic development has been seen as a central part of domestic security and stability, and an integral part of a more comprehensive view of what constitutes a security issue. Even more conventional security threats are what Loh (2005) describes as small 's', and more to do with issues like piracy and illegal immigration, rather than external threats. This is an especially important consideration given the views of the man that came to dominate Malaysian politics for much of its post-independence history. Speaking in 1986, Mohamad Mahathir suggested that:

> ... security is not just a matter of military capability. National security is inseparable from political stability, economic success and social harmony. Without these, all the guns in the world cannot prevent a country from being overcome by its enemies.
>
> (quoted in Nathan 1998: 514)

Such views reflect Mahathir's personal scepticism[12] about the merits of, and necessity for, a powerful military establishment given Malaysia's lack of obvious external threats and the importance of economic development. This helps to explain why there has been a more generalised preoccupation with development issues in the aftermath of the cold war. On the contrary, and perhaps in line with a more widespread international re-prioritising of economic and strategic imperatives, economic issues have become an even more central component of overall policy. As former Minister of Defence, Syed Hamid Albar put it in 1997

> We shall not neglect economic growth in order to concentrate attention on defense, because we feel that economic growth is our first and foremost security line. Without economic growth you will have civil strife and internal instability – and internal instability is even more dangerous to a country's future than external aggression.
>
> (quoted in Tan 2002: 9)

This quotation encapsulates some of the most distinctive security concerns of both Malaysia and the region more generally: not only is there a familiar emphasis on internal rather than external security threats, but also economic development is seen as the central policy concern of government. In a region where democracy is generally incompletely or only recently realised, such priorities are predictable perhaps. What is more surprising, especially in Malaysia's case, is the precise way the developmental project has been realised and the implications this has had for internal political order and stability. Put bluntly, security perspectives have of necessity been 'comprehensive'[13] because at the top of the security agenda has been the maintenance of the political regime itself, rather than simply questions of the conventional strategic integrity of the nation-state. This also helps to explain why core aspects of security governance have remained heavily politicised. For instance, there is a tradition of significant intervention in the procurement process by civilian politicians, a question that has been raised in Malaysia's parliament but with little effect at least partly because of the relative powerlessness of civil society.[14] Furthermore, procurement has also been identified as one of the principal arenas for corruption in the security sector.[15]

The political-economy of domestic security

There is little question about the overall success of economic development in Malaysia. Although there are still some concerns about the quality and depth of the industrialisation process, and the continuing dominance of, and reliance on, multinational capital (Jomo 1997), Malaysian living standards have improved substantially since the inauguration of the NEP. While there are still significant differences between most of Peninsular Malaysia and less developed regions like Sarawak and Sabah, poverty levels have fallen significantly overall. It is also clear that the presence of *Bumiputeras* in Malaysian business has also increased in line with the policies of positive discrimination noted above. But these broadly economic developments have been accompanied by a concomitant reconfiguration of political power that helps to explain the distinctive nature of Malaysian security priorities.

The prioritising of development issues generally and *Bumiputera* economic advancement in particular led to a transformation in the relationship between politics and economics in Malaysia. Economic policy and decision-making became increasingly centralised and concentrated in a few agencies which were dominated in turn by the UMNO. At one level this process was broadly similar to the sort of state-led developmental process that had been so characteristic in other parts of East Asia (Beeson 2006). In Malaysia's case, however, some of the potentially more self-serving aspects of this process were especially prominent. As Peter Searle notes,

> As [a] shift in the Malay elite occurred, from politicians and administocrats (sic) to a combination of politicians and businessmen, so the political system also assumed a more patrimonialist caste. Persons who were politically loyal and committed to the leadership's world view were given authoritative positions, rather than those who were merely technically competent.
>
> (Searle 1999: 47)

Two long-term aspects of this process merit emphasis when thinking about the context from which Malaysia's distinctive approach to security issues emerges. First, the conventional 'Western' assumption about a clear analytical distinction between the political and economic spheres is generally not terribly useful even in a north American or European context; in the case of Malaysia and our other case studies, it is fundamentally misleading and obscures a critical driver of domestic social relations (see Gomez 2002). Public policy aimed at increasing indigenous control of economic activity has meant that 'involvement in politics increasingly came to be viewed by Bumiputeras as a quick means to obtain profitable business opportunities' (Gomez and Jomo 1997: 26). The international fashion for privatising former state assets became, in Malaysia's case, an important mechanism for redistributing economic wealth and – perhaps even more importantly – consolidating the political power of the *Bumiputeras* generally and the UMNO in particular (Searle 1999: 95).

The other noteworthy aspect of the fusion of political and economic power that occurred during the Mahathir era was its direct impact on the military. It has become increasingly commonplace and expected that retired military officers will become chairpersons or directors of major companies, or appointed as figureheads to various company boards (Searle 1999: 83). In this context, it is important to remember that, unlike equivalent political parties elsewhere, the UMNO is a major investor in many Malaysian companies – including key media outlets (Gomez and Jomo 1997: 52; Rodan 2004: 25) – and thus has the capacity to reward loyal public officials and functionaries relatively immune from public criticism.[16] The general point to emphasise here is that, not only did general economic development allow the government to ensure that the military were comparatively well paid while actually in service, but the nexus of political and economic power that dominated Malaysia meant that there was every opportunity for ex-military officers to obtain lucrative, loyalty-inducing positions within that dominant elite upon retirement.

Although there is little doubt that under Mahathir in particular the Malays generally and the UMNO in particular came to dominate the political landscape and profoundly influence the context within which economic development occurred, it is necessary to qualify this picture somewhat and acknowledge the 'contradictions' in Mahathir's hegemony. A good deal of this inherent tension can be attributed to the personality of Mahathir himself. Despite Mahathir's occasional fulminations about the evils of global capitalism, he was concerned about the potentially debilitating impact of a state-protected domestic economy and the lack of entrepreneurship amongst the cosseted *Bumiputera* economic elite (Khoo 1995: 129–136). This potential structural weakness was thrown into sharp relief during the economic crisis of the late 1990s when Mahathir moved to insulate the domestic political-economy from the impact of long-term changes in the global economy and the scrutiny of external agencies like the IMF (Beeson 2000). What is especially significant about this period for our purposes is that it triggered a major political crisis which dramatically illuminated not just the nature of the political process in Malaysia, but the direct involvement of the broadly conceived security services in maintaining it.

The politicised nature of the Malaysian security sector

As we have already seen, in Malaysia the security sector involves a complex division of labour between the armed forces and the police. The police in Malaysia are responsible for a much broader array of security threats than is normally the case and have come to play an especially prominent role in the maintenance of both public order and the ruling regime. As Nathan and Govindasamy (2001: 263) note, what is especially significant about the police is not just that they 'clearly enjoy pre-eminence in domestic security', but that 'their influence is projected via the security apparatus all the way down to the village level'. Interestingly, although the police projects influence, it is also the most politicised section of the security sector with close links between the force and the ruling party.[17] These linkages are especially pronounced in the relationship between the government and the Special

Branch, with the Special Branch's inspector openly reporting directly to the prime minister.[18] As we shall see when we examine the role of the army in Indonesia, this capacity to penetrate the most far-flung elements of domestic society gives the police in Malaysia and the army in Indonesia an added significance as consequence of their institutional reach. It is important to re-emphasise that if we want to understand the nature of the security sector and the areas most in need of reform in Malaysia, we need to focus on the police and not the army, for as Loh (2005) notes

> 'militarization' has occurred in Malaysia without the armed forces assuming a pre-eminent role in politics or in the society writ large. Instead, militarization is by other means: it is derived from the ideology of national security and the consolidation of a national security state led by civilians, but who resort to coercive legalism or 'rule by law'. In such a national security state, it is the police, which acts at the behest of its BN political masters, that plays the critical role.

Given the prominent role the police have played in the maintenance of Malaysian security it is remarkable how little academic attention they have received. In the case of Malaysia's military, which has kept a low-profile and never played a prominent role in Malaysia's security affairs, let alone its political life, the limited scholarly interest in the MAF is understandable perhaps. But given the high-profile and often overtly political role of the police in Malaysia's internal security, the paucity of scholarly literature is noteworthy and may inadvertently contribute to the absence of reformist pressure on Malaysia, despite its very patchy human rights record.[19] In what follows we draw on our own investigations and the limited resources available that actually consider the role of Malaysia's police to highlight two important points. First, the Malaysian police were an integral part of the authoritarian regime of Mahathir in particular, and a key determinant of security practice in Malaysia as a consequence. Second, despite both a series of well-documented human rights abuses and partisan political interventions by the police, and the departure of Mahathir from the Malaysian political stage, thus far the police have remained relatively immune to significant reform. This absence of reform has been at least partly enabled by the absence of foreign pressure. For example, bilateral policing relations with the West have tended to focus on intelligence sharing and the conducting of joint training courses.[20]

This is not to suggest that there has not been significant public concern about their role and behaviour. On the contrary, there has following rising public anger about the extent of police corruption and the deaths of 680 people in police custody between 2001 and 2004 – about which inquests were held in only six cases – a government-appointed commission was established to examine police behaviour. The commission found widespread evidence of corruption and systematic human rights abuse, and brought down no fewer that 125 recommendations designed to address major failings in police practices and behaviour (Cumming-Bruce 2005).

Yet, despite great optimism about the reformist credentials of Abdullah Badawi, Mahathir's replacement as prime minister, it is significant that thus far he has failed to implement any of the recommendations (Kuppusamy 2005). To understand why there is such inertia as far as reforming the most important element of the security forces in Malaysia is concerned, we need to locate the police service within a wider institutional array that includes not just the government but also the judiciary, as the latter institution became closely aligned to the ruling regime during the Mahathir era. The politicisation and compromised nature of the judiciary reinforced the power of Mahathir in particular and the Malays more generally, entrenching the position of a regime that was permeated by patterns of corruption and patronage, which have made it impervious to reform.

The ISA and the judiciary

The formal centre-piece of the coercive apparatus that Mahathir developed while in power was the Internal Security Act (ISA). Introduced in 1960, three years after Malaysia's independence and in the aftermath of the Emergency, the Act allowed the police to arrest anyone suspected of having acted or even being *likely* to act in such a way as to threaten national security. Suspects could be detained indefinitely without evidence or warrant, and without charges actually being laid. Despite the ostensible reason for the Act's extraordinarily sweeping powers having long disappeared – the communist threat associated with the Emergency – the ISA has continued to be a key part of Malaysia's overall security structure and a highly politicised one at that. The arrest of Anwar Ibrahim and his supporters in 1998, for example, occurred under the Act's auspices. Even so, sources close to the government claim that the ISA enjoys popular support because of its perceived contribution to public order.[21] Others, however, argue that support for the police and the ISA are propped up by government sponsored advertising, reminding the people of the role they played during the Emergency.[22] But it is not just the direct impact of the Act in terms of individual arrests that accounts for its importance in Malaysia. As Amnesty International (1999: 7) note

> Beyond the violation of basic rights experienced by particular individuals, the ISA has a wider, intimidating effect on civil society, and a marked influence on the nature of political participation and accountability in Malaysia. The ISA has been used to suppress peaceful political, academic and social activities and legitimate constructive criticism by NGOs and other social pressure groups. It limits the political space for important debates on issues of economic policy, corruption and other social challenges.

These failings and the lack of domestic reformist pressures and voices are exacerbated by the nature of the judicial and political processes. As noted earlier, since the late 1980s the judiciary has been a compliant and non-independent tool of the ruling elite. Although the specific catalyst for the transformation of Malaysia's formerly independent and respected judiciary was a clash with the Mahathir government in

1988, the relationship between the executive, the judiciary, the constitution and the monarchy had already been transformed, allowing greater centralisation of power within the ruling BN. The first step in this process occurred in 1983 when the election of a new 'Agung' (or king) from amongst Malaysia's ruling sultans threatened to install an independently minded figure who might oppose government policy. One of the possible candidates for election to Agung – the Sultan of Johor – was close to senior military officers and rumours circulated about a possible declaration of emergency to counter the power of Mahathir. A Bill to amend the constitution was eventually passed in the midst of a constitutional stand-off and crisis between the sultans and the government, but only after Mahathir manipulated popular opinion and support. The subsequent reforms deprived the Agung of his legislative veto and right to call a state of emergency. Significantly, this was followed by a number of high-profile 'retirements' amongst those military figures deemed too close to the sultans (Milne and Mauzy 1999: 30–36).

The other major incident that helped to consolidate Mahathir's authority and fundamentally compromise the independence of the judiciary in particular, and by extension the domestic security services, had its origins in a political crisis within UMNO. As a consequence of a major split within UMNO ranks, Mahathir's position as president (and thus prime minister) was challenged by former finance minister Tengku Razleigh Hamzah, the leader of the so-called Team B. In a manner that foreshadowed the later clash with Anwar, divisions revolved around policy differences and the competing economic interests Razleigh and Mahathir represented. Although Mahathir narrowly won the leadership contest, what is significant for our purposes is that the losing Razleigh faction decided to challenge the outcome in the courts. In an atmosphere of mounting political crisis, Mahathir used the ISA to launch 'Operation Lalang' in late 1987, arresting more than 100 opposition figures including prominent academics and intellectuals. Shortly afterwards the High Court ruled that while the UMNO election could not be nullified, UMNO itself should be deregistered as a political party. This provided Mahathir with the catalyst to move decisively against a judiciary that was too independent for his taste (Hilley 2001: 87–90).

The dismissal of Supreme Court president Tun Salleh Abbas marked the end of the Malaysian judiciary as an independent body, something that was confirmed by the Supreme Court's subsequent dismissal of the Razleigh faction's legal challenge. In addition to removing some of Malaysia's most experienced Supreme Court judges the BN under Mahathir's leadership amended the constitution to remove the judicial power vested in the courts and bring them under the control of federal law and the legislative body. Parliament could thus enact legislation immune from judicial review. As Hector (2003: 5) points out, 'Mahathir, by removing the head of the judiciary and two Supreme Court judges, had sent a clear message to the judiciary that could be simply stated as "if you do not do things according to my will, then you too will be removed" '. Thus, throughout the latter years of the Mahathir ascendancy, the judiciary became a compliant tool of the regime and provided a crucial part of the overarching context in which the security forces operated and in which abuses occurred. This was achieved because Mahathir was able to 'pack' the judiciary and other key areas of the state with supporters who owed their positions to his continuing patronage. Consequently, as Dan Slater (2003: 89), puts it, Mahathir 'used the packing strategy to transform the Malaysian judiciary from one of the more respected and independent legal bodies in Asia into a powerful fist at the end of his executive arm'.

The potential significance of a compliant judiciary was dramatically highlighted during the trial and subsequent imprisonment of Anwar Ibrahim. Although this episode does not bear directly on the dynamics of security sector reform, it merits brief consideration as it not only highlights the extensive and multidimensional nature of Mahathir's regime, but it also helps to explain the role and significance of Islam in Malaysian society generally and within the military in particular.

Since the 1970s, Islamic activism and consciousness has been a growing part of Malaysia's social and political life. Indeed, Anwar's rise to prominence occurred in conjunction with this wider international trend as a consequence of his ability to provide leadership for Malaysia's disaffected Islamic youth. As Bill Case (2002: 127) points out, 'The government responded to this Islamic revivalism with its trademark combination of coercion and patronage'. On the one hand Anwar was detained for two years under the ISA, on the other hand the principal political expression of this movement – the Pan-Malaysian Islamic Party (PAS) – was absorbed into the dominant BN. Once Mahathir became prime minister, however, he 'cunningly recruited Anwar into the UMNO, then rapidly escorted him up through the party's apparatus and cabinet hierarchy' (Case 2002: 128).

At a more general level, in addition to co-opting its most charismatic figure, Mahathir responded to the potential challenge of Islamic revivalism and the departure of PAS from the BN by initiating his own reformist drive subsumed under the heading of 'Vision Islam'. Two points are worth noting about this period. First, this attempt to accommodate the Islamic impulse had a direct impact on the military and eventually led to a significant change in its internal culture. At one level this was manifest in the fairly trivial, but symbolically telling, banning of alcohol from military establishments. At a more serious level with potentially more important long-term implications, a special religious corps was established with an *ulama* holding the rank of brigadier. It is very difficult to gauge the extent of Islam's influence in the military and the evidence is in any case contradictory. On the one hand, anecdotal evidence suggests that many older members of the services are unhappy about the changes and the transformation in the *esprit de corps*. Indeed, a number of the people we interviewed in academia or with close connections to the military confirmed this emerging generational division between the longer-serving personnel who were imbued with more 'traditional' British-style values, and a younger group of officers and soldiers who are more sympathetic to Islamic values. Furthermore, commentators argue that the military's identity remains dominated by a professional ethos that stands in the way of Islamisation.[23] On the other hand it is revealing that electoral voting patterns suggest that in those constituencies where there is a large military presence, government-supported BN candidates have polled badly in comparison to opposition candidates associated with Anwar (Jeshuran 2004: 340).

The political-economic crisis and its significance

Although the goal of co-opting Islamic leaders and neutralising Islam's political impact had significant long-term consequences, it is important to note that the cause of the rupture between Anwar and Mahathir was not theological but political. The trigger was the external shock of the East Asian economic crisis which had a profound effect on the course of security sector reform in other states in the region. In Malaysia, the manner in which the shock and the subsequent political crisis unfolded serves as an important exemplar of the difficulties of imposing reform and the limited impact external agencies and actors can have when vital political interests are at stake. Furthermore, it demonstrates that external shocks can move strategic and security cultures away from a reformist path.

At the heart of the split between Mahathir and Anwar was a fundamental disagreement about how the crisis should be handled and the role that external agencies should play in its management. Anwar as Minister of Finance was keen to reassure international investors about the continuity of Malaysia's broadly liberal economic policies, and willing to accept IMF advice about how to manage the crisis. Mahathir, by contrast, fulminated against IMF support of 'foreign speculators' that were bringing down the economy (Khoo 2003). Consequently, Mahathir wanted to try and insulate the Malaysian economy from external pressures by experimenting with capital controls. It is not necessary to explore the 'technical' merits of these opposing positions to recognise that Mahathir was concerned about the possible implications that might flow allowing external 'intervention' in and scrutiny of the domestic political-economy. As we have seen, Malaysia's distinctive, highly integrated political and economic relationships, provided the basis for an institutionalised structure of patronage, favouritism and outright corruption. The political and economic crisis in Indonesia, which we consider in Chapter 6, had already provided a salutary illustration of what could happen to a regime that found itself dependent on external agencies for its economic and thus political survival. The rationale for Mahathir's unorthodox and inventive economic policies was, therefore, as much a political response to the threat posed by external regulatory intervention, as it was to changes in the international economy (Beeson 2000).

To understand why the Mahathir regime – and that of Badawi, too, for that matter – might be so sensitive about external scrutiny and reformist pressures, it is important to recognise how pervasive corruption and 'money politics' are. As we shall see, this is a problem that pervades all of our case studies. In Malaysia's case, money politics is central to the operation of UMNO and the Anti-Corruption Agency (ACA) has a 'pathetic' record of combating it, only targeting low level, insignificant figures (Pillai 2004: 1).[24] While corruption is not necessarily an obstacle to economic growth (Kang 2003), it does have implications as far as the operation of the security services are concerned and their role in underwriting the stability of a particular regime. Not only have many senior appointments to pivotal institutions like the judiciary and the bureaucracy been made on the grounds of political loyalty and cronyism rather than professional competence (Slater 2003), but corruption is endemic in the 'normal' operation of the police in particular. One of the reasons why there was significant public pressure to conduct a review of the police in Malaysia, is that routine dealings with the police invariably involve corrupt practices and intimidation at all levels of the organisation. There have been a number of notorious cases where senior policemen have been unable to account for significant personal wealth, while junior colleagues routinely rely on corruption to boost their incomes. The entrenched and systematic nature of corrupt practice is best illustrated, perhaps, by the practice of 'tendering' for promotion or appointment that is a routine part of personnel movements within the police.[25]

Clearly, the fact that the police are presented with greater opportunities for corrupt practices and intimidation as part of their day-to-day activities, makes this an especially significant problem in that organisation. However, it is important to note that the conventional security sector is not immune from corruption either. One of the most distinctive features of the Malaysian armed forces is the highly diverse, often incompatible, array of weapons systems that have been purchased over the years. Although it is difficult to document, there is overwhelming and consistent anecdotal evidence that this rather incoherent pattern is a direct consequence of corruption as a variety of individuals involved in the acquisitions process receive kick-backs from various arms suppliers.[26] A number of our informants emphasised the negative impact this widely held belief had on morale and – more pertinently, perhaps – behaviour within a military institution in which some of its most senior figures appeared to be acting corruptly and not in the overall interest of the services.

When seen against this backdrop Anwar's downfall – and the manner in which it occurred – takes on an added significance. Not only was Anwar a potential threat to Mahathir's own personal position at the top of regime in which personal patronage and corruption was endemic, but Anwar's willingness to align himself to external reform-minded agencies added an additional danger. It is revealing, then, that both the police and the judiciary played crucial roles in the successful prosecution and subsequent imprisonment of Anwar on what were widely regarded as being implausible charges with little evidentiary base. It is also revealing that the government's defenders argue that it was Anwar's decision to 'take to the streets' that landed him in hot water.[27] What is significant when thinking about the possibility of reform in any area of public policy in a country like Malaysia, is that for all the support of the international media, and despite substantial domestic support within Malaysia itself, Anwar was still toppled by Mahathir and the regime over which he presided. The swelling support Anwar received from civil society was incapable of off-setting his abandonment by powerful domestic political and business interests or the more direct intervention of the commandos who took him into police custody.

Despite widespread domestic and international outrage at the, at times farcical, conduct of the trial and the assault Anwar suffered in custody at the hands of the inspector-general of Police, the BN were still able to win the subsequent general election. As a consequence of Mahathir's tight control of the media, outright gerrymandering, and an enduring concern on the part of non-Malay voters about the implications of a PAS dominated government, the BN was returned to power (Khoo 2003: 118). This underlying fear of either social unrest or the Islamisation of Malaysian society helps to entrench the BN's grip on power and makes it very difficult for domestic or international reformist pressures to find points of access that might allow them to be realised.

The other factor that may be working to actually diminish the possibility of encouraging reform within Malaysia's security sector in particular, has been a significant change in the overarching geopolitical situation. Before 9/11, especially under the US' Clinton administration, the Mahathir government had come under sustained pressure for reform. Indeed, vice president Al Gore offered explicit support for the *Reformasi* movement generally and Anwar in particular during a meeting of the Asia Pacific Economic Cooperation (APEC) forum in Kuala Lumpur in 1998. While this intervention may have ultimately done little more than allow Mahathir to play the nationalist card with his typical finesse (Yee 1998), it stands in stark contrast to the current situation. In the immediate aftermath of the attacks on the US, Mahathir was invited to visit the White House, inaugurating a rapprochement with the Bush Administration which saw Mahathir as a crucial part of its evolving 'war on terror' (Nesadurai 2006). In effect, Mahathir was given carte blanche to crack down on 'militants', a task his authoritarian government took to with alacrity (*Straits Times* 2002).

The point to emphasise, therefore, is that if the Mahathir regime was able to ward off unwanted external 'interference' at the height of it most serious post-independence economic crisis, *and* deal decisively with internal sources of opposition and criticism, then the prospects for reform in the present environment are not bright. Indeed, when security issues are once more at the top of the international policy-making agenda, and when Malaysia is seen as a comparatively stable and secular bulwark against Islamic 'extremism', then it is not unreasonable to expect that pressure for reform will actually decrease.

Conclusion

'Money politics' and corruption are alive and well in Malaysia and there has been little serious effort to root them out. Not only has incumbent prime minister Abdullah Badawi failed to fulfil the hopes of reformers inside and outside Malaysia, but it is significant that the deputy prime minister, Najib Razak – who is also defence minister – has described the problems of vote-buying and corruption as 'internal UMNO matters', and not something that needs to be dealt with by the Anti-Corruption Agency (George 2005: 2). What is significant here is that the dramatically reconfigured post-9/11 security environment means external pressure for reform looks set to decrease. This is especially problematic in a Malaysian context because domestic pressure continues to be hamstrung by an ineffective, government-controlled mass media and the continuing threat posed by the ISA. Having said that, it is clearly significant that Anwar has been released from imprisonment since Badawi came to power and there are signs that the judiciary is beginning to take a slightly more independent line.

What is of greatest significance about the Malaysian experience for our purposes is that it alerts us to the importance of casting our conceptual net more widely than is typically the case in much of the existing literature. Not only have notions of security in Malaysia been much more 'comprehensive' and inclusive than is the case in the West, but the actual security apparatus that is in most urgent need of reform is not the military but the police. As we have demonstrated, the security sector in Malaysia – as in other parts of the region – is part of a broader array of historically contingent institutions which help to explain both the precise role of various elements of the security sector, and the reasons that they have proved so resistant to reform. Not only is what Loh describes as the Malaysian security state dominated by the police rather than the army, but they play a crucial role in maintaining the position of the dominant BN regime of which they are a critical part. In such circumstances, the unwillingness of the ruling regime to take the reform process seriously in the way its own investigative commission recommends, is entirely understandable. What is more surprising is that the Commission should have chosen to take a fairly independent and highly critical line when bringing down its recommendation. This is, perhaps, one of the most encouraging recent developments as far as reform is concerned, although one that still awaits effective implementation.

While there are some modest, but in a domestic context, significant indications of change in the post-Mahathir era, there are also troubling indications of continuity and an unwillingness or inability to tackle reform issues. The highly institutionalised patterns of power, patronage and interest that permeate the overlapping political, economic and even security fields, means that any attempt at serious reform necessarily confronts powerful vested interests that are reluctant to overturn the mutually rewarding status quo. When such relationships are further complicated by Malaysia's unique ethnic divisions and tensions, then reform is likely to be even more fiercely resisted on the grounds of national stability and ethnic equality. But even if the prospects for reform remain uncertain, an important first step is to identify more precisely where reform is actually needed and what the obstacles to it may be. In this regard the Malaysian experience reminds us that not only is the security sector a more complex entity than it may seem at first blush, but it may also have a wider political and social significance and role that may render it virtually impervious to reform. Unless pressure can be brought to bear that encourages a much more comprehensive process of political, administrative and judicial reform the most important aspects of the security sector – in Malaysia's case the police – are likely to remain unaffected.

5 Thailand

Military rule, there and back again?

Prologue: the 2006 coup

On the night of 19 September 2006, Thailand experienced its eighteenth coup since the overthrow of the absolute monarchy in 1932. While coups have occurred at regular intervals across the decades, this was the first intervention by the military since 1991–1992. It was also the first coup to take place under the 1997 constitution, which had strengthened civilian authority over the military and purportedly instituted legal safeguards to prevent overt military involvement in politics. The coup removed the controversial Thaksin Shinawatra from power. Thaksin had served as prime minister since 2001 and had presided over a dramatic escalation of the Malay separatist insurgency in the south and political gridlock in Bangkok, whilst simultaneously attempting to control the military through politicisation.

Led by General Sonthi Boonyaratglin, the first Muslim to lead the Royal Thai Army, the military formed the Council for Democratic Reform (CDR). Upon their seizure of power, the CDR suspended the 1997 constitution, dissolved the Constitutional Court, took over public broadcasters, closed down radio stations in regional areas, detained senior politicians from Thaksin's *Thai Rak Thai* party, and sent tanks onto the street. The coup met little or no resistance, and it appears that Sonthi successfully negotiated with military officers loyal to Thaksin to not actively oppose the coup. An opinion poll conducted in the days after the coup suggested that the vast majority of Thais supported the military's intervention. Even rural voters, who provided Thaksin's bedrock support, backed the coup in large numbers (Cumming-Bruce 2006; Crispin 2006a, 2006b).

General Sonthi acknowledged that the military's actions were highly unorthodox, but argued that in launching the coup he had acted on at least three compelling reasons. First, to resolve the insurgency in the three southern provinces that has raged since 2004, which escalated dramatically in 2005–2006, and which precipitated what the military termed a 'national security crisis'. Second, to break the political deadlock that had ensued since the disputed general elections in April 2006 (see Sipress 2006). Third, and unofficially, it was widely rumoured in Bangkok that Thaksin was planning his own 'phoney coup' designed to tighten his grip on the armed forces and parliament. In the second half of 2006, rumours began to circulate suggesting that Thaksin would attempt to suppress anti-government street protests, the last conduit for opposition to his rule. According to this version of events, Thaksin would bus in supporters from the north and set them in conflict with the urban protesters. He would then claim that the security situation in the capital was out of the control of the armed forces, and use this as a pretext to replace Sonthi, the incumbent commander, with a more pliant military officer. It appears that Sonthi supporters gained wind of this plot and acted to prevent Thaksin's gaining complete control over the armed forces.[1] However, because this third justification remains, at the time of writing, unofficial and largely unsubstantiated, we will briefly address the first two.

The insurgency in the south erupted in the wake of Thaksin's harsh response to a law and order crisis in 2004. Critics accused Thaksin of using the US-led 'war on terror' as political cover to ruthlessly suppress the insurgency, a strategy that ultimately backfired. One of the consequences of this strategy was the disruption of social arrangements carefully negotiated by figures close to the monarch and leaders in the country's south, which led to a dramatic increase in violence in 2005 and created significant discord between the government and Privy Council (see McCargo 2006). Thaksin ordered the police, and later the military, to use overwhelming force to crush resistance to the state.[2] After the well-publicised death of almost eighty Muslim youths in 2004, the insurgency escalated. Approximately 1,700 people have died in the past two years. A bomb went off two days prior to the coup in the regional centre and tourist hub. It appears that the fear of the insurgency spreading further north to the main tourist destinations encouraged the military to intervene and adopt a new approach to the insurgency.

However, Thaksin's handling of the insurgency was only one example that the CDR cited as evidence of his misrule. The broader criticism was that Thaksin's government wielded a disproportionate degree of power. Indeed some have argued that Thaksin was more powerful than any previous leader, either civilian or military.[3] Thaksin's accumulation of power gravely concerned the military and (it seems) the monarchy. The 1997 constitution, while intended to enhance the capacity of civilian governments to prevent unlawful interventions and abuse of power, actually empowered Thaksin beyond a level thought acceptable to other sections of the Bangkok elite. In particular the constitution had favoured the executive (prime minister) at the expense of the legislature (Kuhonta 2006).

An unintended by-product, at least in the early part of this decade, was to allow Thaksin to emerge as a 'CEO prime minister' with what was widely viewed as disproportionate power. Thaksin entered politics in 2001 against a backdrop of almost ten years of multiparty democracy. Traditionally it was the Bangkok-based parties that had dominated party politics and competed to form governing majorities in the National Assembly. However the 1997 constitution sought to discourage the defection of entire parties or factions thereof from one coalition to another, a practice referred to as 'party-hopping'. It also sought to remedy the concomitant problem of bribery. Thaksin's electoral strategy was to present himself as a new addition to the political landscape, free of ties with either the military juntas of the past or the traditional urban elites. Instead he opted for a populist stance, promising impoverished rural electorates injections of funds for local development projects, subsidised healthcare and deft relief for farmers in return for their votes (Pasuk and Baker 2004). This strategy proved successful insofar as the populous northern provinces sent large numbers of *Thai Rak Thai* ('Thais love Thais') candidates to the National Assembly. Thaksin was thus able to bypass the urban political elites and voters, who were highly critical of his approach to politics. For the first time in Thai political history, a political party attained a majority in the Assembly.

It was Thaksin's attempts to neuter the power of the military and the monarchy that provided the second key impetus for the 2006 coup. The precise degree to which king Bhumibol Adulyadej influences Thai politics remains unclear, but it is evident that the monarch takes an active and ongoing interest in the affairs of state. The king has worked assiduously to protect the capacity of the throne to maintain a level of prestige and discreet influence over day-to-day politics. In particular the king is known to indirectly communicate with political leaders through the Privy Council, a small group of retired military and political elites. Indeed, the military itself was divided between networks whose primary loyalty was owed to the monarchy through the Privy Council president and contending networks associated with Thaksin (see McCargo 2005). Crucially, the interim prime minister appointed by the CDR in early October, the retired General Surayud Chulanont, was a key member of the Privy Council and the primary instigator of military reform in the 1990s, an issue we will return to later (Tasker 2006). It is also noteworthy that this was not the first coup under the current king, underlining the idea that the Thai military's loyalty has traditionally been to the monarchy rather than to the elected government of the day and that this is a core part of the military's identity and Thai strategic culture. It was for this reason that Thaksin's frequent clashes with Privy Council members in 2006 and his attempts to install loyalists to key positions in the military was such a sensitive issue for the king and senior military commanders. In effect Thaksin was seeking to enter uncharted territory in terms of the authority wielded by a Thai civilian politician – or indeed any Thai political leader. Military and political leaders loyal to the throne viewed Thaksin's accumulation of political power as a case of *lèse-majesté*, as it threatened to reduce the capacity of the incumbent king to influence Thai politics (Crispin 2006b).

The military was also a target for Thaksin's power grab. As we will show later, Surayud, anointed as interim prime minister by General Sonthi, was removed from his position as head of the army in 2002, as part of a move to strengthen support for Thaksin at the top of the military. Thaksin's cousin, Chaisit Shinawatra, assumed the post of army commander in 2003, and several other supporters also moved into prestigious positions. Another reshuffle was planned for later in 2006, and Sonthi feared that more loyalists would enter the upper echelon of the military. In particular Thaksin had planned to promote loyalists and friends from his military cadet class (Class 10) to the command of the First Army Division, which is responsible for the Bangkok region – and the hotbed of opposition to his government. It is reported that on the night of the coup, Thaksin had scheduled a teleconference during which he planned to declare a 'severe state of emergency' and use this as a pretext to remove Sonthi as army commander. Sonthi acted first and the conference did not go ahead (Crispin 2006b).

Thaksin's critics also charge that he had misused his power in a manner that has been highly detrimental to the interests of Thai society. For instance during the past five years Thaksin has used his authority to centralise power in his office, heightening the perception of his acting as a CEO rather than prime minister. Not only has he commanded a majority of seats in the National Assembly and put Cabinet decisions beyond the reach of parliamentary scrutiny, he has also sought to reduce the capacity of other institutions to challenge his power. Notably the Thaksin government has appointed allies to head key institutions such as the police, the judiciary and the electoral commission. Thaksin also marshalled state power to challenge independent sources of media scrutiny, threatening to imprison those who have criticised his government. Another example of Thaksin's misuse of power was the sale of Shin Corp, his family-owned company, to Singapore's Temasek. Thaksin gained a two billion dollar windfall without any tax on the sale. He also established the Thailand Asset Management Corp, which used taxpayers' funds to rescue corporations who had proven loyal to the government. Though not in themselves illegal, these practices became the rallying point for his opponents in early 2006.

Nevertheless, Thaksin won large majorities at the 2001 and 2005 general elections, greatly reducing the capacity of opposition parties to criticise his government through the parliament. As a result street protests were the only effective means for his opponents to draw attention to the misdeeds of the *Thai Rak Thai* (TRT) government. Protestors flooded the streets in the wake of the sale of Shin Corp, rallying the various opponents to Thaksin. In the face of large-scale demonstrations and calls for his ouster, the government agreed to new elections on 2 April 2006. However, opposition parties led by the Democrats boycotted the polls on the grounds that Thaksin's positioning of loyalists in the Electoral Commission and other branches of the state apparatus would not allow for a fair election. The election turned into a farce, with the TRT standing unopposed in many electorates. The party's vast majority was reduced somewhat but it emerged victorious. However, the result went a little way towards reducing the widespread animosity towards Thaksin, especially in Bangkok. On 26 April the king intervened and asked the Constitutional Court to resolve the impasse. The Court subsequently annulled the poll result, and new elections were scheduled for October. Thaksin then agreed to stand down as leader to break the impasse, but later reneged on his promise to step down from politics. With or without Thaksin at the helm, the TRT looked likely to win the October poll.

During the coup's first hours, its military leaders promised to install a civilian as prime minister. After much bargaining, Sonthi convinced his former military colleague, the retired General Surayud Chulanont, to serve as interim prime minister. As we will see later, Surayud was a respected soldier with a track record of advocating democratic military reform. Amongst other things, he was credited with rooting out corruption and also reducing the number of military officers substantially.

The reaction of urban elites to these events was largely positive, with only sporadic violations of the military's ban on public gatherings of five people or more (Crispin 2006a, 2006b). The CDR gained support from retired judges, diplomats, journalists, academics and even human rights activists for the coup against Thaksin. The installation of a Cabinet comprised of technocrats has eased the concerns of foreign investors about the populist signals sent out by some of the new regime. Western governments initially expressed concern about the coup and called for the restoration of civilian rule, but the configuration of the new government appears to have assuaged their concerns. The US, for example, initially suspended $24 million in military assistance, but is widely expected to resume payment of these funds soon (Deen 2006). Nonetheless some commentators are uneasy about the future. The military has claimed that it will not control the interim government, but the Council for National Security (which replaced the CDR) reserves the right to dismiss the prime minister and will set the parameters for the body (the Constitution Drafting Assembly) charged with drafting a new constitution.

The coup and security sector reform

To what extent does the coup demonstrate the absence of security sector reform in Thailand and the continuation of military-led authoritarianism that, as we will demonstrate in the following section, has tended to dominate Thai politics? Apologists for the coup argue that 'this military coup is different' (Tasker 2006). It is different, they argue, because the coup-leaders and the interim prime minister are well known reformists and there is little suggestion that they acted for personal gain. The aim of the coup, according to this account, was to remove a corrupt and authoritarian civilian government and protect the institution of the monarchy (Tasker 2006). Critics of the coup, including many Western governments and especially the US, argued that it is not for militaries to decide when to depose democratically elected governments. It is for the people to decide on the composition of the government and for the judiciary to determine whether the government is acting lawfully or not. Critics also argue that past coups have been justified on broadly similar grounds (defence of the monarchy, defence of democracy).

The purpose of this chapter is not to pass judgement on the coup but to ask what it tells us about the state of security sector reform in Thailand. Clearly, the coup demonstrates only too well that the claim that the military had 'returned to barracks' in 1992 was premature. We argue that this case demonstrates the importance of differentiating between surface level and fundamental reform. That is, after 1992 and under the leadership of General Surayud, the Thai security sector embarked on a process of surface level fine-tuning reforms that tackled specific problems (dealing with insurgents, the size of the officer corps, corruption), but which did not alter fundamental aspects of strategic and bureaucratic culture. As a result, the security sector never lost its self-identity as the guardian of the monarchy and 'Thai style democracy', or its entrenched belief that it had an important part to play in domestic politics.[4] The Thai case illustrates clearly the importance of embedding and internalising reform in this case, civilian and democratic control of the military was a weak rather than embedded norm, violated and undermined – it must be said – partly by the Thaksin government itself through its strategy of politicisation. Furthermore, it suggests that sectors can sustain profound contradictions between the direction and logic of fine-tuning reforms (heading in a distinctly SSR direction in the 1990s) and underlying sets of ideas and values, but that when the two come into direct competition, the latter tend to carry more weight than the former – a further indication of the role of ideas, history and culture.

To address these issues, we proceed in four parts. The first places Thai civil–military relations in historical context by looking at the military's role in politics since its establishment by King Chulalongkorn in 1887 and setting out the infrastructure of civil–military relations in Thailand. The second section focuses on the critical turning point of the failed coup in 1992. The third part of the chapter evaluates the post-1992 reform process and evaluates the extent to which the Thai security sector reformed itself along the lines suggested in the first part of this book. The final part of the chapter identifies critical stumbling blocks to reform during the Thaksin era that acted as a precursor to the 2006 coup. Our central argument is that the Thai military assumed a critical role in the project of national unification and economic development which encouraged, and legitimised, its intervention in politics. This role was made possible by alliances between civilian and military leaders, patron–client relations running in both directions, and significant business support for the military (see, e.g. Pasuk and Baker 1995: 125–130). A combination of factors, including the 'shocks' of the killing of protestors in 1992 and the Asian financial crisis of 1997 and a changing international environment[5] contributed to a crisis of legitimacy that brought about changes in the military's internal role but no fundamental change in its self-identity and strategic culture. Importantly, although bureaucratic politics is a key characterisation of the Thai system so-called extra-bureaucratic forces played a pivotal role in provoking these shocks and forcing change.[6] However, since 1997, the armed forces have resisted further reform and the civilian authorities have been divided amongst themselves between Thaksin loyalists and monarchists centred around the Privy Council. To secure the 'support' of the military, Thaksin has embarked on a policy of politicising the officer class. As a result, the security sector failed to fully internalise and embed values such as democratic control or professionalisation, which ultimately enabled the coup.

The military, polity and society in historical perspective

The military fulfilled a pivotal material and ideational role in fostering the modern Thai state and to this day considers itself to be the 'strength of the nation'.[7] From its creation in 1887, the modern Thai army has had a predominantly internally focused role. Prior to this process of modernisation, which some scholars suggest began in 1868 (Bunbongkarn 2005), there was no centrally orchestrated standing army. Mirroring the European feudal system to some extent, local lords and rulers were permitted by the Siamese king to raise their own armies to settle local disputes and defend the wider kingdom when necessary. Establishing the new army, king Chulalongkorn argued that standing armies were an essential component of modern statehood, because only through the army could the political centre in Bangkok exert its authority over rebellious peripheries (Baker 2004: 61). Thus, whilst the military did not share the colonial origins of most of the region's other states, it was nevertheless a pivotal vanguard of the modern Thai state. In addition, the establishment of the military was heavily influenced by European ideas. According to at least one writer, the origins of the modern Thai military can be found in European military science and the colonial military prowess of Thailand's neighbours (Anderson 1978). Thai kings employed European military advisors and the modernisation process was at least in part a bid to secure European recognition of Thai sovereignty by mimicking ostensibly European practices.[8]

Within this new army, conscription fulfilled two principal purposes. First, it helped fulfil the perceived instrumental need to exert the centre's authority over marginal areas of the kingdom. As in much of Europe, the modern Thai state was as much a product of the forced amalgamation of different peoples as it was an expression of self-determination. This effect was not necessarily accidental. Chulalongkorn sent six of his sons to Europe to receive military and naval education (Bunbongkarn 2005) and the king self-consciously chose to mimic the European precedent because military modernisation brought with it a host of benefits for the state. During the 1880s, military spending rose to account for around 23 per cent of the entire state budget. The centrepiece of modernisation was the establishment of two military academies at which European and Thai instructors educated the new breed of officers along basically Western lines. Military education in the academies included professional ethics and emphasised the importance of civilian control of the military (Ockey 1998: 187).

Second, conscription provided the central authorities with a means of inculcating particular ideas about history and identity among the Thai youth. Historians note that the creation and modernisation of the Thai military went hand-in-glove with the rise of modern Thai nationalism and that, at the turn of the twentieth century, this new nationalist ideology was particularly evident within the officer class (Bunbongkarn 2005). Whilst the military was widely seen as a vanguard of modern Thai nationalism, the new military's principal 'enemies' were commonly identified as non-Thai groups. Such groups were prohibited from establishing associations by the 1897 Secret Society Act and the new security forces were charged with policing that act (Samudavanija 1997: 46). This helped to entrench the role, authority and identity of the military in a number of ways that remain pertinent today. First, the military's role from the outset was understood to be primarily about defending the Thai state from potential and actual internal opponents such as Chinese secret societies. Second, because political associations were banned by the Secret Society Act, the primary forms of mass mobilisation in the new Thai state were those within the formal ambit of the state, chiefly the bureaucracy and military. As Samudavanija (1998: 48) argues, given the Secret Society Act, 'it is not surprising that the only legitimate and legal organisations permitted to engage in organised political action were the military and bureaucracy' though it is important to note that overtly non-political associations were permitted and that some of these proved to be the vanguard of civil society resistance to Thailand's 'bureaucratic polity'.[9] The government's intention to retain tight control of modernisation by severely limiting the extent of legal political association gave the military a domestic role as the vanguard of national identity. Finally, the close linkage between the Thai state, Siamese rule and the suppression of alternative political voices sowed the seeds for armed rebellion and unrest. Between 1909 and 1932, there were a series of uprisings against Siamese rule (Christie 2000: 175). As a result, one of the primary preoccupations of Thailand's security sector was the control of internal unrest amongst those who resisted the propagation of Thai nationalism and Bangkok's hegemony. As the remainder of this chapter attests, this became (and remains) one of the Thai military's primary roles and one of the principal obstacles to security sector reform.

Evolving civil–military dynamics

The key turning point in the military's relationship with the government came with the 1932 coup against the absolutist monarch. There are a number of competing explanations for the coup, largely because several forces, both internal and external, drove political events in Thailand. For our purposes, the 1932 coup is important for two reasons. First, it marked the end of the military's unquestioning subservience to monarchical rule and widened the military's role as guardian of the new constitutional regime, encouraging the military to see itself as the protector of Thai democracy (Ockey 2001: 191). Second, it demonstrated the emergence of a concordant relationship between the two principal sources of political association in Thailand – the bureaucracy and military – and marked out the parameters of the relationship between them. That is, rather than being organised hierarchically with the military controlled by civilian institutions, the military and bureaucracy were organised horizontally as two distinctive sources of coercive and administrative power. To be sure, this relationship did not emerge overnight in 1932, but was formed over the preceding decades and became more prominent after the coup. In the case of the 1932 coup, and for much of the rest of Thai history, alliances within and between the two blocs acted cooperatively on the basis of shared interests and ideology (a mixture of Thai nationalism, anti-communism and, particularly after the Second World War, royalism) but that cooperation was based on consensus politics and shared interests rather than on hierarchical or legally regulated interactions.

There were complex international dynamics behind the 1932 coup but, once again, they revolved around the officer class's commitment to modernisation and Thai nationalism, which combined both liberal and conservative elements. In particular, nationalists objected to the monarch's consistent pattern of ceding hard-won territory outside Siam to Thailand's colonial neighbours, starting with the cession of Lao territories to France in 1893 and continuing until 1909 with the cession of territories to the south, which resulted in Thailand losing approximately one-quarter of its 1880s territory. Tellingly, however, they tended to blame the king's advisors rather than the king himself, enabling them to portray moves against monarchical rule as actually concerned with defending the king's interests. Although Thailand's support for the Western allies in the First World War helped it recover some of the lost territories and secured formal Western recognition of Siamese sovereignty, the territorial disputes provided a source of tension. The more immediate causes of the coup, however, were the economic crisis partly caused by the Wall Street Crash and calls for reform of the absolutist monarchy emanating from a group of civilian bureaucrats and a relatively small number of military officers collectively calling themselves the People's Party. In the economic domain, the king dramatically cut government spending which certainly helped stabilise the economy but at the expense of significantly reducing the size of the bureaucracy and the wages of those who remained. Spending cuts also affected the military but were spread unevenly, favouring nobles (some of whom actually made gains) over commoners who suffered disproportionately. The king's advisors cautioned against radical reform, arguing – among other things – that Thai peasants were not ready for democracy. The slow pace of reform agitated the lower classes, threatening political order and inspiring the coup. The post-coup order was somewhat less than democratic, however, as the People's Party promulgated a permanent written constitution that permitted it to appoint half of the members of parliament and forbade alternative political groups or parties, with the right of free association denied until 1950. The government came to be dominated by military officers who were key members of the People's Party and whose control of the army was entrenched after government forces defeated a regional rebellion led by a former defence minister (Bunbongkarn 1993: 6).

The 1932 coup and period of military rule that followed are interesting because of the paradox they encompass. On the one hand, the People's Party, comprised of civilian bureaucrats and military officers – claiming to represent the national interest – justified its assumption of authority in democratic terms and ushered in a period of unprecedented, though not unfettered, popular participation in politics. On the other hand, in practice it entrenched its own control over the government and limited democratisation. Because it dominated government positions in the new regime, in the immediate aftermath of the coup the military was effectively the only national institution with real capacity. From 1932 onwards the military identified itself as the vanguard of Thai democracy and – along with its bureaucratic allies – took upon itself the role of essentially creating the Thai nation from the disparate ethnic and religious groups that owed affinity to the Siamese king. As Wattanayagorn explains, 'numerous institutions were established to support the military elite's interpretation of "Thainness" ' (Wattanayagorn 1998: 421). This included measures to enforce standards of national dress, the Thai language and a new 'national' new year's day. Such measures were accompanied by bureaucratic centralisation which contributed to acceleration of nationalism and solidified political, cultural and economic power in the hands of the elite (Riggs 1966). As a result of the 1932 coup, therefore, the military assumed political pre-eminence along with its civilian allies and legitimated itself by direct reference to democracy and nationalism, which it had increasingly come to define. As Elliott (1987: 78) put it, 'the 1932 coup resulted in a shift in the power bloc enabling a bureaucratic, mostly military, fraction to take over the state apparatus'.[10]

The consolidation of military power

The military's control of the state continued for several decades though there were also many periods of civilian rule and, typically, military officers usually sought to hand formal power over to civilians within their governing network. The military's role was initially legitimated by the threat of colonial invasion and later by internal revolt. After the Second World War the threat of communism, external interference from China and Vietnam, and more internal unrest had a similar impact. Thus, it is important to distinguish Thailand's brand of military rule from other cases of direct rule, such as Burma, because this has a direct bearing on later attempts to reform the security sector.[11] First of all, from the outset, the Thai military attempted to legitimate its rule by ruling indirectly, through parliamentary processes of one form or another. Only in relatively brief moments of crisis was direct military rule imposed. Second, the different military factions that came to compete for control of the government were broad coalitions comprising soldiers and civilians – mostly bureaucrats, professional politicians and business people. Although these features of Thai military rule may have saved the country from some of the worst excesses of military government endured in Burma, Latin America and elsewhere, it makes the contemporary task of reforming the security sector that much more difficult because of the interconnectedness of military and civilian institutions and elites.

During this time, the use of force became the ultimate arbiter of political disputes between rival factions within the military elite and between the military elite and civilian politicians. Although the next coup was not until 1947, there were two 'unconstitutional' changes of government in the interim. In 1933, the prime minister, Phraya Mano, used the military to forcibly close parliament in response to a cabinet quarrel over the state budget. This prompted the military wing of the People's Party to overthrow Mano later that year. At the same time, the military was continuing to suppress rebellions such as the Bowerdet rebellion (1933) and Songsuradet rebellion (1939). Moreover, prime minister Phibun, responsible for Thailand's acquiescence with the Japanese in World War Two before he was forced to resign in 1944, began using military means such as special military courts and summary executions in order to suppress dissent.

Like these earlier confrontations, the coups in 1947 and 1958 were primarily related to transitions of power within the military in a context where military control of the government and bureaucracy remained deeply entrenched but where the military sought to legitimate its rule through the chimera of parliamentary politics. The Second World War caused something of a legitimacy crisis for the military as it cooperated with Japanese troops, but resistance to Japan was being led by the civilian 'Free Thai-Movement' (Bunbongkarn 2004: 48). This legitimacy crisis was manifested in the 1947 coup. Ostensibly a reaction to the promulgation of a new constitution in 1946 which replaced a unicameral parliament with a bicameral system comprising an upper house of elders, the coup can also be understood as a changing of the guard and re-legitimisation within the military elite because it involved the replacement of the wartime elite with a new group of officers not previously involved in the political fray (Samudavanija and Bunbongkarn 1985: 83).

According to Bunbongkarn (2004: 48), the conspirators lacked a clear political vision and were primarily motivated by an intention to weaken the tentative civilian grip on political power (granted by the 1946 constitution) and to re-legitimise military rule in the wake of the legitimacy crisis caused by the military's wartime record.

After the 1947 coup, Thailand's militarised politics took on the character of the 1930s, as the military–civilian elites divided into factions and competed for power. There were, however, notable similarities between the different factions especially a determined anti-communism, anti-regionalism and a common view that democratisation was a second-order priority behind national security and economic development. Although there were frequent coups and violent changes of government between 1947 and 1958 (four successful forced changes of government in 1947, 1951, 1957 and 1958 and two failed rebellions – the 'Grand Palace Coup' (1949) and the 'Manhattan Coup' (1951)) (Aphornsuvan 2005: 2), it is important to bear in mind that these disputes were confined to a relatively small section of the political and military elite who shared much in the way of a strategic culture. As in the 1930s, moreover, there was no readily discernible battle-line between military and civilian actors. The government's advocates and political opponents consisted of military and civilian elites (Aphornsuvan 2005: 2). Moreover, civil society agitators for democratic change in Thailand were peripheral figures, limited to a handful of civilians, politicians and academics (Bunbongkarn 2004: 49). To be sure, most civilian and military leaders advocated democracy as the most modern and legitimate form of government. The problem lay in turning this rhetorical commitment into practical reform in the face of arguments that national security and economic growth demanded 'responsible government' and curbs upon individual liberties.

The subsequent 1957 coup, which brought the ambitious senior soldier, Sarit Thanarat, to power only served to reinforce these trends. Under Sarit, government figures turned away from a rhetorical commitment to constitutionalism to favour a new paternalistic system justified by reference to the monarchy. Whereas earlier governments had maintained the appearance of a separation of powers, the Sarit government privileged the executive, creating a system whereby the Constituent Assembly (dominated by Sarit loyalists) played the role of both legislator and constitutional overseer. Instituting what he called 'Thai-style democracy', measures were taken to curtail the activities of civil society groups and the media. Sarit argued that his new form of paternalistic government eschewed the privileging of Western precepts that had shaped Thai politics since the end of the nineteenth century and returned to earlier patterns of monarchical rule, establishing a direct relationship between the government and the people. In short, therefore, the Sarit government established itself as a benign dictatorship under the king which ruled directly in the interests of the people. This 'ideology of reverence for the king' allowed the military to legitimate playing a leading role in government (Elliott 1978: 137). As Thanat Khoman, Sarit's foreign minister explained: 'the fundamental cause of our political instability in the past lies in the sudden transplantation of alien institutions to our soil…if we look at our national history, we can see very well that this country works better and prospers under an authority, not a tyrannical authority, but a unifying authority around which all the elements of the nation can rally' (in Baker 2005: 177).

This consensus was aided by the external environment and specific political actors. In relation to the former, the perceived threat of communism helped solidify domestic opinion around a national security first agenda. What is more, significant portions of Thailand's capitalist and middle classes actively supported the authoritarian regimes because their social position, access to resources and protection from other social forces was attached to the coercive power of the state (see Hewison *et al.* 1993). The civil–military alliances that these shared interests forged provided the basis for strong and pervasive patterns of patron–client relations (Hewison 1997: 4).

In relation to external actors, the United States was increasingly generous in its diplomatic, military and economic support to the region's non-communist states. From as early as the 1950s, the US provided material support to the ruling elite, providing finance for the rural development programmes described below and direct military assistance that the government used to suppress communist and other opposition groups (Morell and Samudavanija 1981: 91). Furthermore, the US actively promoted the relationship between security and development, tacitly encouraging the deepening of the military's involvement in economic development in alliance with an increasingly powerful class of development technocrats, establishing a bilateral relationship that would persist beyond the cold war (Connors 2006). However, this patron–client relationship did not extend to the US being able to dictate the ebb and flow of military and civilian factionalism in Thailand (Girling 1981: 91–92). At the very least, though, these external conditions militated against democratic challenges to military rule; they might also have helped reinforce and legitimise that rule.

For our purposes, the period of Sarit's rule is important for two reasons. First, (a point we will return to later), by removing the veneer of constitutionalism and thereby weakening the civil–military coalitions that had earlier characterised government, Sarit created the conditions for a confrontation between the military and civil society, including some civilian elites. Second, in order to legitimise his rule, in the late 1950s Sarit shifted the government's social bases of legitimacy away from nationalism and anti-communism (both of which remained important nevertheless) towards economic development and monarchism. As the state's principal bureaucratic arm, the military was given the task of spearheading national economic development with a special focus on Thailand's poverty stricken regions which continued to give rise to communist opposition. For the government, which labelled the programme 'development for security', the overarching aim of the turn to state-led developmentalism was to legitimise military rule and encourage the regions to turn their backs on communism (Bunbongkarn 1987: 49–76). Amongst military officers there was a broad consensus which held not only that economic development was pivotal to the preservation of internal security but also that the military was particularly well placed to deliver economic development to rural areas (Bunbongkarn 1988: 153). To accomplish this task, a number of new institutions were created including the National Security Council (a cross-institutional body), Accelerated Rural Development Agency and the Internal Security Operations Command (Bunbongkarn and Sukapanich-Kantaprab 1987: 27–59) which expanded the military's influence in the national economy. Through locally based organisations like the National Defence Volunteers, the military directed and coordinated projects which aimed to foster economic development in rural regions susceptible to communism. In so doing, of course, such initiatives also widened and deepened the military's control of these thought to be vulnerable areas. During this period military spending (which included 'development' spending) accounted for around 27 per cent of the state budget (Chai-Anan 1998: 50). These two factors – the relationship between government, army and society and the centrality of economic development to the state's legitimacy – continued to shape civil–military relations in Thailand over the next few decades.

The decline of military authority

The 1970s proved to be particularly paradoxical for the military. On the one hand, it was given more freedom of manoeuvre to tackle the internal threat of communism as well as a greater role in economic development. In 1976, for instance, the government went as far as to legally recognise the military's 'special role' in economic development (Wattanayagorn 1998: 422). This was reinforced in the early 1980s by orders granting the military the right to autonomously use the country's resources to prosecute the fight against communist insurgents in the northeast of the country, who were now receiving foreign assistance from Chinese, Laotian and Vietnamese communists. Most infamously, this involved timber trading with the notorious Khmer Rouge in Cambodia, providing the *genocidaires* with money to continue their resistance to Vietnamese occupation. On the other hand, the division between government and people created by the imposition of direct rule was manifested in 1973 when a student-led revolt which started as a protest against Japanese imports and turned into a full-scale revolt against military rule, brought down the government and forced some of its leaders into exile. The king then appointed a new assembly which would serve as a pathway to democratic government.

When this transition to democracy failed to materialise, primarily because the new civilian government was divided amongst itself and was unable to win sufficient support from the military to suppress ongoing sporadic violence (though some commentators concluded that the military continued to direct government during this brief period of civilian rule (see, Morrell and Samudavanija 1981: 95)), the regime collapsed amongst violence and student protests. In October 1976, military forces opened fire on protesting students and Maoists at Thammasat University (see Chai-Anan 1985). According to one former defence minister, this incident caused something of a crisis of legitimacy within the Thai military.[12] It also helped to further divide the military and Thai civil society. But this only tells part of the story. First, many members of the 'old guard' (supporters of Sarit's ideology of direct rule) were forced into exile. Second, brief civilian control of military promotions permitted the partial politicisation of the officer corps, increasing the number of democratically minded officers in key positions.[13] The government's inability to restore order or build an effective governing coalition enabled the military to oust the civilian government in 1976 and it was left to a group of reform-minded officers – elevated into key positions by civilian bureaucrats – to take the lead by launching a further coup in 1977.

According to Bunbongkarn (2004: 49), however, the 1977 coup was fundamentally different in quality from earlier coups. The 1977 coup was instigated by a group of young officers espousing a democratic ideology. For these 'young Turks', themselves divided amongst those who supported the generals who ruled for the next decade and those who joined two attempted coups against them, the principal political role of the military was to ready the country for a transition to democratic rule. Under Prime Ministerial order 66/2523 (1980), the government declared that the best way to defeat communism was through democratisation. This order was informed by another grouping within the military, collectively labelled 'Democratic Soldiers' who espoused a version of democracy that saw the military acting on behalf of the 'general will'. Furthermore, it formally set out the military's need for a new basis of legitimacy, which was to be found in developing and widening its role in 'national development' (Ukrist 2001: 24). It is important to note that this push for liberalisation (though importantly not 'democratisation' as understood in the West) and re-legitimisation was also necessitated by a significant drawing down of US patronage to the military elite, which accompanied the withdrawal of US bases from Thailand in 1976.

After the 1977 coup, Thailand enjoyed almost twelve years of parliamentary rule, albeit closely supervised by the military leadership. The communist threat dwindled significantly and evaporated altogether in the late 1980s, and liberal political parties gained significant support from civil society and especially from the business community. As civilian control of the military became more entrenched, however, relations between them became more troubled. Between 1985–1987, members of parliament criticised the size and secrecy of the defence budget. The military countered by trying to invoke constitutional clauses that afforded the institution a formal role in political decision-making. Parliament responded by passing laws that curtailed that role and handing down budgets that began to significantly cut military expenditure. Between 1985 and 1996, for example, the military's share of the state budget declined from 22 per cent (down from 27 per cent in the late 1970s) to 13 per cent (Baker 2005: 246). However, structural reform of the military sector remained elusive. The military itself remained deeply divided between reformists and traditionalists, with the latter keen to protect what they saw as the military's role as the principal authority in Thai government.

Matters came to a head in the early 1990s. First, prime minister Chatichai appointed the reform-minded former army chief, General Kamlangek, as deputy defence minister with a mandate to tighten civilian control of the military (Bunbongkarn 1993: 132–133). Second, the government embarked on a policy of military restructuring which involved significant spending cuts and reductions in the number of senior military officers. Furthermore, the long-term size of the military was to be trimmed by reductions in recruitment (see Hewison 1993;

Ukrist 2001). The traditionalists responded by launching a coup. As with previous coups, the military justified itself by pointing to weakness and corruption in the civilian government. These justifications were initially well-received by the urban middle class, but the coup-leaders failed to solicit nationwide support and failed to legitimate the return to military rule, causing an ebbing away of middle-class support (Panaspornprasit 2003: 2). The military leadership attempted to re-legitimate its rule by calling elections in March 1992 and backing one of the parties, but General Suchinda Kraprayoon reneged on an earlier promise not to serve as an unelected prime minister, provoking a mass civilian uprising.

Suchinda responded with a violent crackdown, in which 52 people were killed and 39 went missing, now presumed dead. The crackdown only served to intensify the protests and attract foreign criticism, forcing the military government to step down and bringing about the end of military rule in Thailand. According to Connors (1999: 202), 'Black May' as it came to be known, was a 'defining moment' in terminating the military's leadership role in politics. The crisis of legitimacy inspired by the killings forced the military to return to barracks prompting one prominent commentator to insist, rather optimistically, that 'any effort by the military to defy civilian authority and intervene in politics to protect its own corporate and personal interests is now out of the question. The public, especially the urban middle classes and civil society organisations, will not allow that to happen' (Bunbongkarn 1999: 58). Such assessments, however, proved to be premature because the shocks of 1991–1992 did not elicit fundamental changes in the military's sense of identity, purpose and strategic culture. Tellingly, the temporary return to the barracks was forced upon the military by the crisis of legitimacy, not entered into willingly.[14]

Summary: the structure of civil–military relations

From this historical narrative, it is clear that the nature of Thailand's security sector is structurally different to that of the West, despite early attempts to emulate Western military ideas. Most significantly, for the bulk of its history the Royal Thai Army has been the pre-eminent state institution and has seen its primary role as that of a nation-builder. Thus, in addition to expanding the Siamese kingdom, suppressing nationalist and communist revolts and protecting Thailand's borders from external threats, the military has also actively promoted a particular vision of Thai national identity and taken on a lead role in economic development. It would be wrong, however, to see the military as a homogenous bloc with a single collective interest. Throughout the twentieth century, military officers have established networks and coalitions with civilian figures, including politicians and, more recently, business leaders. Almost every military regime has sought to legitimate itself through civilianisation either by direct appeal to the authority of the king or by invoking the rhetoric of democracy and handing over to civilian allies. Furthermore, the military itself was deeply divided and most, if not all, of the coups pitted military factions against one another. As a result, appointments and promotions remain highly politicised as historically they tended to determine the outcome of political squabbles and character of the Thai government. Although formal civilian control of the military was established in 1992, this structure of civil–military relations caused a number of entrenched problems: there was no tradition of civilian *or* democratic control of the military; the military was heavily politicised; the military was a determinant of national political struggles; there was no tradition of merit-based and transparent promotion; the military's role has traditionally been inward looking and has tended to conflate regime security and national security.

Political reform and the military: defence spending and the 1997 constitution

This section charts the extent of security sector reform in Thailand after the military's temporary 'return to barracks' in 1992. Our central claim here is that although the Thai military played a less overt role in politics, there was very little – if any – formal restructuring of the security sector and wider political reforms have not fully reoriented military–civilian relations along democratic lines. What reform there has been was best described as fine-tuning which did not tackle the fundamental problems made evident by the 2006 coup. The military's formal legal and bureaucratic structure, for example, has not changed since it was reformed in 1960 by the Sarit administration. Neither has there been any discernible shift in the way the military defines its role. Although the precise targets have changed (i.e. there is no longer a communist threat) and new roles have been added, the military's primary role remains engaged with internal threats associated with minorities, nowadays principally Muslim minorities in the south. Moreover, the military retained a significant role in economic development although to a much lesser extent than in the 1970s and 1980s.

The most significant problem, however, was the continuing relationship between politics and the military. Although the decade before 2006 witnessed an ostensible demilitarising of politics and the spread of democratic ideas among the officer class – often imbued by periods of military education in the West – there was no concomitant process of depoliticisation within the military. On the contrary, military leaders continued to see a significant internal role for the military, and military appointments and promotions were awarded primarily for political reasons in the knowledge that control of certain key elements of the military arm (such as the 1st Army, based in Bangkok) were critical political assets. This section begins by charting attempts to reform the security sector, culminating in the stalled reform process initiated by General Surayud under the Chuan government in 1998. Where reforms occurred, most notably in professional military education and subtle changes to the role of the military, these have been incremental, military-led and essentially fine-tuning.

Reasserting political authority?

In the immediate aftermath of May 1992, Thailand's new civilian government was reluctant to embark on a process of wholesale security sector reform for fear of inciting another coup. Uniquely, Chuan served as both prime minister and defence minister and was the first civilian to hold the latter position. Until Chuan's reform proposals in 1998, reform was limited to a protracted debate about military spending and adjustments to the processes of promotions and appointments which attempted to instil civilian oversight. As we noted earlier, the size of the military budget had been one of the key sources of civil–military discord prior to the 1991 coup. In 1985, the secretary-general of the National Economic and Social Development Board, and deputy governor of the central bank, warned that continuing high levels of military spending could lead to 'national bankruptcy' if left unchecked (in Huxley 2001: 30). Shortly after the 1991 coup, Anand Panyarachun, the interim prime minister, rejected military requests for additional funding (Huxley 2001: 30). The military responded to what it saw as an assault on its finances by agitating for extra resources to fund future major procurement. Unwilling to tackle the issue head-on for fear of inciting a new coup, the Chuan government instead issued a directive that permitted the army to use its continuing role in economic development to raise procurement funds by entering into agreements to sell agricultural products. Senior military officers responded by sharply criticising the initiative (Huxley 2001: 31). The following year, in 1995, the most senior army commander insisted that the army general staff, not the ostensibly civilian defence ministry, was 'in charge' of military procurement. Other evidence, however, suggests that despite this claim – which illustrates the sensitivity attached to procurement and finance – the ministry was able to gradually assert civilian control over procurement spending at least. In 1995, the government suspended plans to acquire submarines when the Budget Bureau found that the cost exceeded annual procurement spending ceilings (Huxley 2001: 31). A year later, Chuan's successor, Banharn, deferred the submarine project once again and shelved a military satellite project.

The 1997 Asian financial crisis assisted the government in establishing its authority over procurement and enabling it to reduce military spending. Moreover, the 1997 constitution, described as a 'watershed' (Suwannathat-Pian 2003: 10), purported to entrench two principles critical to the democratic control of the military: the idea of the constitution (rather than monarch) as the foundation of law and, for the first time, parliamentary scrutiny of defence spending. With the economy spiralling downwards and the government budget significantly reduced, the Chavalit government's insistence that military procurement would bear the brunt of spending cuts was widely applauded outside military circles as a way of restoring economic stability. Thus, the government cancelled the purchase of F-18 aircraft for a saving of $390 million and pegged spending at the actual pre-crisis level. Given the rapid devaluation of the *baht* during the financial crisis, this amounted to a US dollar decrease in spending from around $4 billion per year to $2.25 billion, a reduction of 43.75 per cent (US Senate 1999: 18).

Why didn't these deep cuts provoke a coup? First, in November 1996 the Banharn government – widely seen as corrupt and ineffective – was removed by peaceful election. Second, the government that replaced Banharn was headed by Chavalit, a former senior officer. Given this, it would have been difficult to portray defence cuts as an assault on the military. Third, the defence cuts came in the context of economic crisis and evident need to reduce government spending across the board. Because cuts to military spending have less direct and discernible social impacts than cuts in other areas of government spending, they enjoyed a high level of public support and that made armed opposition to them unfeasible. Finally, the defence cuts received external support most notably from the US. According to the State Department, the US took 'concrete action to assist Thailand in reducing its defence spending' (US Senate 1999: 18). Such actions included permitting Thailand's release from the contract to buy F-18s, the provision of IMET (International Military Education and Training) funds to enable Thai officers to receive military education in the US and an insistence that Thailand not be permitted to purchase weapons from the US that were not already held by other states in the region. Though perhaps not amounting to much in themselves, such measures sent a clear message of support to both the government and a warning to any potential coup-plotters.

The heightened level of control that the Ministry of Defence asserted over military procurement and reduced overall level of defence spending prompted by the financial crisis continued once economic stability had been restored. Chuan, returned to government in November 1997, cut defence spending by 30 per cent after the stabilisation of the *baht* to set a new benchmark for defence spending commensurate with that established during the crisis. Significantly, other government ministries did not suffer similar fates (Huxley 2001: 32). These spending cuts had significant consequences for the military in at least three important areas. First, it has put pressure on the military to supplement its income through business activities. Some army units in less well-off areas were so poorly funded that they resorted to growing vegetables and raising livestock for subsistence whilst other units reportedly developed commercial interests, including the development of tourist resorts (Huxley 2001: 32). Furthermore, many, if not most, senior military commanders have 'side businesses' and use their military titles and status to win business.[15] The military's key commercial interests, however, lie in banking (Thai Military Bank) and in particular in the media, with the military owning commercial TV stations (Channels 5 and 7) and almost half the country's radio stations (130 of 300) (Lewis 1998). In the immediate aftermath of the 1997 crisis, the military's television stations were given a much easier ride in their bid to secure new licences than other commercial stations but on the other hand it was forced to recapitalise the bank, reducing the military's ownership from 43 per cent to 25 per cent (Ukrist 2001: 28).

Although they may deliver short term financial gains to ameliorate some of the negative consequences of sharp defence cuts, the development of these commercial activities is problematic for a number of reasons. On the one hand, the US State Department noted that such activities make the defence budget less transparent and therefore less open to democratic scrutiny; an important obstacle to one of the key components of security sector reform. On the other hand, the development of business interests undermines efforts to develop new roles for the military based on the premise that it should serve the democratically elected government (see Chapter 1). Instead, significant portions of the military's activities are directed toward income generation and the promotion of its corporate interests. This is particularly problematic given that the military's business portfolio includes important media outlets, affording it a continuing role in influencing politics.

The second consequence of the funding decline was a changed attitude towards procurement which, among other things, became a major obstacle to General Surayud's proposed reforms. Rather than buy new equipment, the military leadership instead opted to procure second-hand weapons systems. The military has also been more creative in the way it funds procurement projects, sometimes eliciting criticism. For instance, in 2000 the defence ministry used a legal loophole surrounding monies paid to the US for a subsequently cancelled order of F-18 aircraft to purchase second-hand F-16 fighters without subjecting the deal to parliamentary scrutiny (Huxley 2001: 32). Over the past few years, the air force has commissioned an Israeli company (Elbit systems) to upgrade its T5 Tiger fighters, the army has bought 160 second-hand tanks from Switzerland and the navy has purchased two off-shore patrol vessels from China (Tan 2004: 15). More recently, the army has turned to the US for helicopters. Although each of these decisions might make sense in themselves, they create serious problems of interoperability within the armed forces making it more difficult for the security sector to restructure itself in order to adopt new roles (see below).

Finally, the decline in funding was accompanied by only a moderate decline in the size of the armed forces from around 301,000 to approximately 280,000, with recent figures suggesting that this has climbed once again to a total of 306,000 (IISS: 2004). As a result, individual commanders have been forced to make what money they do have stretch further. This has had the effect of heightening inter-service competition for scarce funds, with one general commenting that 'the internal struggle in the armed forces is much tougher than war with the enemy' (in Tan 2004: 13). Such discord also aids politicisation and militates against professionalisation (see Chapter 2).

The second key transformation of 1997 came with the promulgation of a new constitution which, according to its advocates, altered the relationship between parliament and the military in favour of the former. During the process of constitution-writing there were credible claims that sections of the military elite were contemplating a coup in response to demonstrations against the proposed constitution: 10,000 village heads protested against measures to strip them of *ex officio* membership of local council, the interior minister Sanoh Thiethong warned that the proposed constitution was a 'communist plot'; and deputy supreme commander of the armed forces, Preecha Rojansen, argued that the military had serious problems with the proposals because they did not set out the role of the military clearly enough (Klein 1998: 13). In response to these attacks on the proposed constitution, civil society and student groups organised massive pro-constitution demonstrations in central Bangkok, provoking rumours of an impending military coup. However, the army's chief of staff, General Chettha Thanajaro publicly insisted that the army would not interfere in the political dispute and, indeed, it is rumoured that the army rejected a request from the Chavalit government to step in and permit the creation of a government of national unity (Klein 1998: 13).

According to its advocates, the constitution itself dealt two severe blows to the military's formal influence on politics. First, the constitution asserted its own primacy. The 1997 constitution left open no loopholes for potential coup-plotters. It insisted that 'the constitution is the highest law of the country. The provision of any law, act or decree which is contrary to or inconsistent with this constitution shall be unenforceable' (Article 6). Moreover, Article 27 placed a legal obligation on the parliament, cabinet, courts and other government agencies to protect the rights set out in the constitution. Effectively, this rule prohibited future military coups and purportedly denied the military one of its core sources of legitimacy for past coups – the idea that by acting against a corrupt, divisive or ineffective government the military was in fact upholding the country's supreme law. However, the constitutional provisions are only as powerful as the institutions that police them and although the constitution grants the courts the power of judicial oversight, in practice the military has retained its ability to get its own way. In particular, critics point to the 2005 'emergency decree' which gave the security sector wide authority to use force against and detain suspected Islamic insurgents in three southern regions (Narathiwat, Pattani and Yala) and significantly limit individuals' constitutional rights (see International Crisis Group 2005a). Furthermore, the constitution did nothing to prevent military leaders from seeking royal blessing for anti-constitutional behaviour, thereby short-circuiting the system. It is worth bearing in mind in this context, that most previous constitutions had similar clauses. Throughout this period, the military leadership clung onto the view that the constitution regulated politics but that the king protected democracy and sat above the political realm and was therefore not regulated by the constitution.[16] This, of course, provided an avenue for justifying intervention in politics.

The second set of provisions in the 1997 constitution that appeared to signal an important formal shift in the relationship between military and civilian agencies was its insistence on parliamentary scrutiny of budgetary matters and the replacement of the formerly appointed senate with a democratically elected senate. The proviso significantly strengthened the hand of the Ministry of Defence vis-à-vis the general staff by formalising the idea that all military expenditure had to be authorised by civilians and formally instituted parliamentary scrutiny of defence spending and policy, an important prerequisite for democratic control of the armed forces. The other element of parliamentary reform to significantly affect the military's role in politics was reform of the senate, the upper house of parliament. After 1932, the senate was an appointed body, giving the executive the power to control the legislature through the appointment of allies to the senate. As a result, even during periods of civilian rule, the military enjoyed a high degree of influence, if not outright control, in the senate. Moreover, this arrangement provided the catalyst for the establishment of the alliances between military and civilian elites described in the first part of the chapter. For the reformers in 1997, correcting this was a fundamental element of removing the military from politics and democratising the political system. In its place, the constitution established an elected senate.

However, it was prescribed that the senators must be over forty years of age, must hold an undergraduate degree and must represent a constituency. Together, these provisos meant that only members of the elite could seek election to the senate.

To summarise this section, following the 1992 coup there was a protracted struggle to wrench control of defence spending from the military and place it under civilian control and an associated push to bring the military under civilian control by asserting the primacy of the constitution and formalising the idea of parliamentary scrutiny. Although the military leadership acquiesced in these reforms, they in no way 'owned' the process and have attempted to manipulate the process at every opportunity to serve its institutional interests. By this, we mean that none of the reforms described above were initiated or supported by senior military leaders on the grounds that they contributed towards the modernisation and professionalisation of the armed forces. That the armed forces chose not to respond by toppling the government was more a consequence of their relative weakness – the legacy of the 1992 killings made military involvement in politics deeply unpopular; and there was significant external pressure from both overseas governments (the US) and transnational business groups mitigating against a coup – than a product of ideational change within the military. As a result, a gap emerged between formal politics and actual practice in the military. That is, the changes instituted in the constitution and the altered balance of power between the defence ministry and general staff on the subject of spending did not translate into behavioural or cultural change within the military. The following section looks at this problem in more detail by considering the stalled attempt to institute wholesale reform of the military and associated reforms connected to professionalisation, anti-corruption, military education and the role of the armed forces.

Reforming the military

Stalled proposals for reform

This section briefly considers proposals for the restructuring of the armed forces since 1997. We find that attempts at major reform have stalled and were replaced by two tracks of fine-tuning. On the one hand, there were moves to strengthen civilian control of defence policy under the Thaksin government, but there are good reasons for thinking that the primary driver of reform in this direction was the government's intention to politicise the military in order to serve the ruling party's interests. This contributed an important impetus to the 2006 coup. On the other hand, there was limited restructuring of the military itself but no moves towards the establishment of a 'joint' framework of operations and although there has been much talk of downsizing by as much as 70,000 (including 10,000 senior officers), in practice downsizing has been marginal if it has taken place at all.[17]

A combination of the financial crisis and new constitution created an impetus for wholesale military reform including the restructuring of the armed forces at the end of the 1990s and spurred the generation of a raft of reform proposals. According to one Thai commentator, the proposals amounted to 'the most sweeping revamp [of the armed forces] in over 100 years' (in Huxley 2001: 31). The reform-minded General Surayud, appointed to head the army by the Chuan government in 1998 to push for reform, insisted that the military needed restructuring to better reflect the changed budgetary situation, the military's legitimacy crisis at home and the emergence of so-called non-traditional security threats. Chuan and Surayud's plan involved reducing the overall size of the armed forces in order to cut the amount of the defence budget expended on personnel from around 65 per cent of the total to 45–50 per cent. The money saved would be invested in procurement, education and training, aimed at developing a more professional and better equipped and trained armed force (Huxley 2001: 31). This plan never won the wholehearted support of the individual service chiefs and both the prime minister and defence ministry proved reluctant to force the issue of personnel cuts without the military chiefs' consent. As a result, although military spending plateau'd at post-1997 levels, there were no significant reductions in the number of military personnel. Indeed, according to at least one report, Surayud's reform programme was so popular that it inspired a flood of new volunteers into the armed forces, leading to a slight increase of personnel overall (BICC 2004: 161). Surayud genuinely recognised both the necessity of cuts and the problems associated with putting them into practice. As he told journalists, 'we admit that we have too much personnel, especially generals. We have to lay out a new manpower structure in the form of a pyramid. There should be fewer people at the top administrative level and a proportionate base of manpower, however' he continued, 'it will take time, about ten years, and we will be able to cut our forces by 25 per cent' (in Suriya 1998: 2). Reflecting on the potential consequences of the proposed cuts, Surayud acknowledged that 'we can't just sack a whole lot of people, otherwise my subordinates will shoot me' (in Suriya 1998: 2).

The structural reform programme also included an initiative to reduce the military's role in politics by weakening the army's stranglehold on military policy in general and strengthening the role of the navy and air force which had traditionally played much smaller roles in politics. The plan involved empowering a 'supreme commander' with authority over the commanders-in-chief of the three services. Following the American model, the supreme commander would chair a committee of the joint chiefs of staff which would determine military policy, ending the army's dominance. The committee would be appointed by the prime minister in consultation with parliament, a mechanism aimed at entrenching civilian control over the military by buttressing the defence ministry's role with direct civilian control of the general staff hierarchy. In practice, however, this reform did little to alter the way that the armed forces organised themselves and the office of the supreme commander remained that of a figurehead. Thus, when Thaksin moved Surayud himself to this position in 2002 it was widely seen as a move aimed at ending the reform process as a prelude to the politicisation of the military hierarchy through the appointment of Thaksin loyalists (discussed below, see Funston 2002). In light of this opposition, it is not surprising that Surayud's most pronounced reform successes were those that involved subtle but important changes of behaviour in matters such as the army's participation in politics, its business interests and the roles that it envisaged for itself (discussed below). Before charting Surayud's demise in 2002 and the politicisation of the military under Thaksin under the rubric of 'administrative reform' it is worth considering the different types of reforms that were introduced.

Fine-tuning reform and behaviour change

To structure this brief discussion we will focus first on issues to do with the 'control' of the armed force, then on questions of 'capacity' and professionalisation and finally briefly chart the changing role of the armed forces. The key point to note here, and this is why we have marked this subsection out from the preceding discussion, is that these changes were *ad hoc*, piecemeal fine-tuning reforms, and often led by Surayud himself. Thus, although taking place in a general context of reformism, they were not necessarily part of a broader process of fundamental reform and as such tackled none of the structural problems identified earlier in the chapter. Indeed, sceptics might suggest that the reform process was mainly window dressing aimed at improving the military's image in the wake of the crisis of legitimacy sparked by the 1992 crackdown. To that extent, the reforms have been relatively successful. According to the father of one of the military's victims in 1992, 'he made people trust and believe in the army…because of Surayud, we no longer fear our own soldiers' (in Horn 2003: 2).

Control. Following the 1997 constitution, the key 'control' problem as far as the reformists were concerned involved the myriad ways in which armed forces personnel continued to fill political roles. With the subjugation of the defence chiefs to parliament and the ministry of defence, one of the most visible forms of political activity was direct military involvement in elections. Such involvement included fairly innocuous activities such as political canvassing by military officers but extended, in some cases, to the use of threats, bribes and coercion in support of preferred candidates (Suriya 1998: 2). Surayud ordered regional commanders to prohibit soldiers from playing any part in elections, insisting that 'soldiers must support the democratic system of government. They have to cast their ballots and take part in politics. The military will allow all political parties to campaign in military areas. But soldiers cannot get involved in politics, they cannot become canvassers' (in Suriya 1998: 3). However, there were no further substantive reforms to the relationship between the military, government and parliament until Thaksin introduced an Administrative Reform Bill in 2002 that formed part of the government's broader strategy of politicisation (discussed in the next section).

Capacity. In relation to the capacity of the armed forces, Surayud's vision, outlined earlier, was for a smaller but more capable (better trained and equipped) and professional military. With that in mind, Surayud succeeded in pushing through small but important changes in the army's composition. For example, he created rapid-response units to deal with border incursions and insurgency threats. As we noted earlier, although there has long been talk about the need to reduce the size of the armed forces the government has lacked the political will to force personnel cuts on the military and the military leadership itself – riven with inter-service rivalry – has refused to take the initiative. As a result, a greater proportion of Thailand's shrunken defence budget was spent on personnel costs. There have therefore been relatively few changes to the fundamentals of Thai military capacity. What reforms were introduced were generally limited to two areas connected with professionalisation – anti-corruption measures and measures to internationalise professional military education. In relation to the former, the 1997 constitution gave new powers to the National Counter Corruption Commission and attempted to depoliticise it by granting the senate the authority to oversee appointments to the commission. Under the constitution, prominent military figures were obliged to declare their assets and sources of income. To mirror these processes, Surayud set up his own anti-corruption unit within the armed forces. Corrupt officers were transferred or dismissed (Marhsall 2001: 3). In one high-profile case in 2001, which seemed to demonstrate the security sector's anti-corruption drive, forces intercepted an election campaign convoy which contained money stuffed in envelopes bound for local politicians. To add to the controversy and further give the impression of a military clampdown on corruption, the convoy was associated with former prime minister Chavalit who, according to reports, continued to wield significant influence over both the police and army (Horn 2001). However, despite high-profile cases such as this, anti-corruption watchdogs in Thailand argued that corruption remained endemic in the military sector. The key problem, according to Abhisit Vejjajiva, was that corrupt practices were part of military and political culture. Thus, 'it is very hard to make people realise that what they've done all their lives is in fact illegal and can land them in court', adding that in order to stamp out corruption 'you have to change the political culture' (Sreshthaputra 2000).

There was more discernable progress in the field of professional military education and Western ideas about the need for professional armed forces were incorporated to a limited extent (Sucharat 2002: 6). Although the basic military education curriculum remained heavily dependent on the 1950s American curriculum and focused almost entirely on military issues, there were some notable changes.[18] After 1997, education in democratic principles has become a feature of basic military training with civilians invited to participate in the provision of military education for the first time. Indeed, princess Maha Chakri Siridhorn played a key role in revising the curriculum for officer cadets. This new education programme was initiated by Surayud and won the support of several other senior military figures and included significant collaborations with Thammasat and Chulalongkorn universities, with the universities providing academic services to the military colleges. Most recently, in 2006 the programme was further developed to permit officer cadets to attend classes at Chulalongkorn University, a significant reform in that it is the first time that officer cadets have been permitted to educate themselves outside the military system. Although early indications suggested enthusiasm for this broader style of military education that attempted to inculcate cadets with democratic and professional values, the impact of such reforms were limited by the fact that attendance at classes was voluntary and not a core requirement for cadet graduation. Thus, such education was offered in addition to the traditional programme not as a component of the programme.[19] It did not represent a fundamental change in values.

Role. Nowhere, arguably, was the tendency towards *ad hoc* fine-tuning more apparent than in the subtle changes to the military's role under Surayud's command. As late as 1994, the Royal Thai Army was continuing to publicly insist that it had a significant role to play in national development (Royal Thai Army 1994). Subsequent role changes involved two elements. First, the military took on new roles that reflected wider global shifts in military roles. Second, Surayud attempted to articulate new and more effective ways of fulfilling well-established roles such as border protection. In relation to new roles, the Thai military began making a significant contribution to UN peacekeeping, especially in East Timor and also undertook peace monitoring roles in Aceh and provided troops for humanitarian and security assistance in Afghanistan (Horn 2003). More recently, after September 11, various parts of the military have contributed to the global 'war on terror', for instance the aforementioned contribution to the multinational force in Afghanistan, the navy's contribution to the US 'Proliferation Security Initiative' and a contribution to the ongoing occupation in Iraq (Connors 2006). In addition to the articulation of new roles, Surayud also brought a new way of thinking about how to respond to old problems. Most prominently, perhaps, he implemented a raft of new ways of dealing with Muslim–Malay separatists in the south of country. Engaging with the Bangkok consensus view that there was no centrally orchestrated separatist movement, just a group of criminals and terrorists numbering fewer than five hundred, Surayud ran educational schemes for Muslim youths aimed at improving their economic welfare and introducing them to less radical forms of Islam by providing youths with the means to stay with Muslim families in Bangkok.[20] The objective, Surayud argued, was to 'win hearts and minds' and 'show the kids from the south that we – Thais of all religions – can live in peace' (in Marshall 2001). Likewise along the Thai–Burma border, whilst Surayud's rapid reaction units were used against illegal border crossings by Karen rebels among others, they were also instructed to cease the practice of forcing refugees (to the point of killing them) back across the border and into the hands of the Burmese military (see Horn 2003; Davies 2005).

During the Surayud period, therefore, the military engaged in *ad hoc* fine-tuning reform that moderated its role in politics and moved in the direction of professionalisation but without fundamentally changing the way that the sector was structured or its overall ethos. As we mentioned earlier, Surayud was removed from office in 2002 by the new prime minister, Thaksin Shinawatra, who from the outset embarked on a strategy of renegotiating civilian control of the armed forces through politicisation. As a result, not only did the reform process stall, it went into reverse, culminating in the 2006 coup.

Limits of reform: Thaksin's politicisation; Thailand's Thaksinisation

As we demonstrated in the previous section, what reform there was in the period between 1997 and 2002 was *ad hoc* fine-tuning largely initiated by the military command itself. At the national level, further reforms aimed at entrenching civilian control of the military were slow and tended towards facilitating the politicisation of the military hierarchy, a trend especially apparent under the Thaksin premiership. It is perhaps worth noting in this regard that Thaksin himself studied at the police college and fostered close and direct ties with friends in the police, arguably trying to emulate the relative marginalisation of the military evident in Malaysia (see Chapter 4).[21] Indeed, the Thaksin administration embarked on a strategy of politicisation by installing allies into key bureaucratic positions across the whole of government (see Panaspornprasit 2004). In 2003, the government introduced an Administrative Reform Bill which created the innocuous sounding Office of the Public Sector Commission (OPDC) to drive further administrative reform ostensibly along the lines set out in the 1997 constitution. In practice, however, far from decentralising authority as envisaged by the constitution, the OPDC became a vehicle for centralisation and politicisation. The Commission, directly appointed by the prime minister, was chaired by his deputy, Visanu Kruengam and contains hand-picked representatives from the ministries, armed forces, and legal and academic fraternities. Working committees forwarded proposals to the OPDC which made policy recommendations which are adopted by the cabinet and passed in parliament. Because the OPDC played a critical role in shaping policy and funding decisions and because its members were hand picked, this structure has effectively permitted Thaksin to place his political allies in key positions within the military and civilian bureaucracy.[22] More importantly, perhaps, the OPDC was used to systematically weaken department heads within the civil service and thereby strengthen the prime minister's position (see Painter 2006: 35).

Specifically, the OPDC was given four primary areas of reform to work on: budget reform, implementing the 'CEO-governor' scheme, bureaucratic restructuring and personnel management reform. In the words of one commentator, 'implementation of these programmes has been strategic and selective. Little concrete action took place with respect to measures concerned with customer satisfaction, public participation, empowering employers or improving the citizen-government interface. Instead, the emphasis has been on internal reforms aimed at undermining the traditional bureaucratic power centres (Painter 2006: 35). For example, in the field of budget reform, Thaksin preferred a system that would permit the government to rapidly transfer resources to priority areas with the priorities, of course, being determined by political considerations. As such, Thaksin implemented a proposed reform to create a Budget Commission, chaired by himself and consisting entirely of prime ministerial appointees (ministers and experts), which took upon itself the authority to determine budget allocations. In a system made operative largely by executive order (thus bypassing parliamentary scrutiny) the Commission reached funding and performance agreements with individual departments and allocated recourses accordingly. In practice, however, the World Bank has noted that the performance measures have remained inoperative (World Bank 2003: 6). What is clear, as Martin Painter (2006: 36) argues, is that 'selective implementation of the budget reforms' were 'thus aimed first and foremost at top-down politicisation of the budgetary process'. Painter points to similar practices across the whole gamut of administrative reform.

Thaksin has used the appointments and promotions system to fill the senior military cadre with loyalists. Thaksin appointed his cousin as defence minister, but he was later forced to stand down on the grounds of incompetence.[23] He replaced Surayud with General Somthat Attantat, a well known Thaksin loyalist and relative of the defence minister. At that time General Shinawatra, Thaksin's cousin, was installed as Somthat's deputy and took over command in 2003 (see Pongsudhirak 2003: 4). By 2004, Thaksin's allies and family members occupied many, though not all, of the meaningful senior military and police command positions.

As we mentioned earlier, there was a long-standing recognition among some members of the military elite of the need for restructuring in order to reduce personnel costs and free-up money for major procurement initiatives. Taking up this challenge, a group of experts was commissioned to provide recommendations about the types of reform that were needed. Those recommendations were adopted by the OPDC and referred upwards to the cabinet. Primary amongst them was the call to establish a joint command, by empowering the office of the upreme commander and awarding it budgetary authority. This recommendation reflected global changes in the military whereby an emphasis on single services was replaced by the idea that joint operations (i.e. integrated operations involving all the services) were much more effective. Furthermore, the 'joint' option provided a conceptual justification for personnel cuts based, as it is, on effects rather than inputs.

Unsurprisingly, perhaps, the proposals were stalled at the cabinet level for at least two reasons. First, the idea of empowering the supreme commander won little support amongst the single service chiefs. The navy and air force chiefs in particular feared that this was a backhanded way of re-imposing the army's supremacy over the military. Furthermore, the single service chiefs worried about where the personnel cuts would fall and were reluctant to lose control of their portion of the procurement budget to the supreme commander. Second, the fact that the reform proposals came from the OPDC suggested that they had Thaksin's support. Given what we know about Thaksin's security policies, it would not be out of place to suggest that the prime minister supported the reform because it would have enabled him to place an ally as supreme commander and further entrench politicisation. However, as we noted in Chapter 2, according to Huntington, politicisation can produce hostility towards civilian authorities within the military and encourage military intervention in politics. Therefore, as a result of the hostility to the reform plan from senior military officers, the plan has been quietly dropped and replaced by more subtle forms of politicisation.[24] Nevertheless, the broader trend of politicisation continued, creating hostility within sections of the military elite.

Politicisation also involved a number of measures designed, not to infiltrate the armed forces with Thaksin supporters from the outside, but rather to permit

Thaksin supporters within the military to come to the fore. Moreover, politicisation involved the use of the military for the narrow political or economic interests of the government. Thus, Thaksin installed 53 sympathetic 'inactive' army officers as advisers across the government. According to commentators, their precise role was unclear but two specific responsibilities were identified. First, these advisers monitored a programme to turn provincial governors into chief executive officers and they have been assisting in the implementation of a controversial gas pipeline venture with Malaysia's Petronas (Funston 2002). In other words, Thaksin sought to reward certain 'loyal' sectors of the military by encouraging them to resume economic activities. Second, to support this broadening of the military's economic role, the advisers played key roles in pushing through controversial procurement decisions. For instance, the air force recently purchased six C-130 heavy lift aircraft. According to Thaksin, their primary function will be to transport agricultural products to foreign countries, the military being the preferred method because they are 'more efficient' than the private sector (Funston 2002). Furthermore, the Thaksin government installed allies in most of the key military positions. In early 2006 this caused a political dispute with the king, who remained formally responsible for military appointments and promotions. The crisis came to a head, of course, over the future of General Sonthi.

One of the principal reasons why Thaksin was able to circumvent parliamentary scrutiny on these matters was that parliament itself lacked military expertise.[25] Paradoxically, this also permitted the military to avoid proper subjugation to civilian and democratic scrutiny. As we observed earlier, military education remained largely the preserve of the military and the military command is only indirectly accountable to parliament. As a result, Thailand has only a handful of military experts in the civilian sector and – as in other countries where this is the case – most of them have been at some time co-opted into or by the government. This lack of expertise means that although parliament may have had the formal right to scrutinise defence policy, it lacked the capacity to do so.[26] As Sucharat Bamrungsuk put it in 2002 (2002: 1–2)

> the Thai parliament has not yet taken any steps to empower itself to be an informed and authoritative actor concerning military affairs. Both houses have an 'Armed Forces Committee', but they are not institutionalized. Moreover, they do not have the technical capacity in military and security affairs. As a result, the parliament is lacking competence to conduct debate on military affairs. Military affairs are left out of the legislative branch.

According to Sucharat, this problem also reflects the fact that military matters were not widely discussed by civil society, once again primarily because civil society lacked the technical expertise necessary to conduct such debate. In addition, it has long been recognised that Thailand lacks strong participatory institutions more generally (Bunbongkarn 1987), a tendency only strengthened by the 1997 constitution's regulations on candidature. As a result, Sucharat (2002: 2) argues that

Thai civil society failed to create a normative context conducive to military professionalisation because the absence of informed public debate encouraged the military to maintain its practical autonomy. Moreover, the absence of public scrutiny also enabled the government to pursue its policy of military control through politicisation. What this meant is that although the military 'returned to barracks', it was unwise to be 'optimistic … that they will not come out again' (Sucharat 2002: 2).

Conclusion

There have clearly been important shifts in Thai civil–military relations over the past two decades. However, fundamental reforms have been slow to emerge, replaced instead by a limited amount of fine-tuning initiated by a group of reformists around Surayud. In this brief conclusion we reflect on the drivers of reform to date and the obstacles to further reform, in order to suggest that some of the obstacles are deeply entrenched in the cultural, political and economic structures of civil–military relations. Thailand's historical legacy means that future reform will have to be incremental rather than dramatic and will only happen with proactive external support. Given that the West's strategic priorities have shifted from democracy promotion to waging a war on terrorism, such support and close attention is unlikely to emerge. These problems became manifest in the 2006 coup.

The principal drivers of the withdrawal of the military from Thai politics were a combination of external shocks (the 1992 killings and 1997 financial crisis) and the creation of a less benign environment for military rule brought about by the end of the cold war. The military's response to the uprisings of the early 1990s, which turned violent in 1992, caused a crisis of legitimacy which made its key justifications – that military rule was sometimes necessary for economic development and national unity – untenable. In other words, after 1992, protracted military rule would have required a fundamental shift away from the pattern of elite alliances that had characterised earlier military governments towards more direct rule based on military force. Such a move was always unlikely in part because it ran counter to the military's way of thinking about government and partly because of the external environment. That crisis of legitimacy persisted, however, and mitigated against military action against the government when it used the 1997 financial crisis as a pretext for dramatically cutting military spending. It is debatable, however, whether these shocks alone would have produced reform were it not for two important contextual changes. First, the period of civilian government prior to 1991 enabled the rise of civilian business and economic elites whose cooperation was essential for national economic development. Second, the end of the cold war caused the US to rethink its military assistance to non-communist states and to pursue a new pro-democracy agenda in its foreign and security policy.

The subsequent 'fine-tuning' reforms of the late 1990s, up to Thaksin's election, also tell us important things about the drivers and limits to reform. On the one hand, they demonstrated the role that epistemic communities can play in reshaping authoritative knowledge about what constitutes 'good practice' in a particular area. On the other hand, however, they also showed their limits when they come up against well entrenched political and economic structures – in this case a government intent on politicising the military in order to insure itself against future coups and making use of the military for its own purposes. When the military is structurally predisposed towards 'turf protection', the challenges to reform become even more acute.

The Thai case is instructive in calling us to think more carefully about the relationship between military and civilian entities. During periods of so-called military rule, the military leadership actually forged alliances with groups of key civilians in the state bureaucracy. Indeed, those alliances sustained the military. Amongst other things, they were crucial for maintaining the military's budget. In more recent times, military leaders themselves have driven the reform agenda though some of the key opponents to reform were also in the military. This study also highlights the fact that security sector reform is not concerned with only establishing civilian control of the military and that conceptualising civil–military relations in this way creates as many problems as it solves. Finally, this chapter demonstrates that external actors can play a role in fostering security sector reform. External conditions went a long way towards setting the normative context for Thai civil–military relations both in terms of helping to legitimise military rule during the cold war and making it harder to legitimise and more costly to sustain thereafter.

Overall, however, the principal lesson of the 2006 coup is that it is important to distinguish between surface level fine-tuning and fundamental reform. The pre-2006 consensus that the Thai military had 'returned to barracks' was a product of the conflation of these two types of reform. On reflection, it is clear that very few of the fundamentals of Thailand's strategic culture or the military's sense of itself were transformed. It is also clear that when the underlying structures, identities and cultures collide with surface level rhetoric, the former prove stronger than the latter. This suggests that those interested in furthering SSR need to pay more attention to the embedding and internalising of its basic ideas within the relevant sectors.

6   Indonesia

From concordance to constitutionalism?

If Malaysia represents an approximation – albeit a rather corrupted one – of the constitutional model, Indonesia lies at the other end of the spectrum of civil–military relations. From its inception as an independent nation, the military has played a major, sometimes pivotal, role in the political life of the country. Indeed, much of the authority and standing of the military was derived from the role it played in bringing about Indonesia's political independence. This historical role and the relative paucity of other effective national institutions – even in the contemporary period – helps to explain both the centrality of the Indonesian armed forces in Indonesia's political life, and their consequent fit with the concordance model of civil–military relations. And yet, the most remarkable thing about contemporary Indonesia is that, despite the central role the Tentara Nasional Indonesia (TNI)[1] has played in Indonesia's post-independence history, the country has embarked on a bold process of political reform that has the potential not only to diminish the importance of the military, but also to place Indonesia in the ranks of the constitutionalists. As we shall see, however, while much of the reformist rhetoric draws on the basic ideas of security sector reform, the prospects for actually achieving some of the reformers' goals look far from certain.

In order to identify possible obstacles to the reform process we need to begin by placing the Indonesian experience in the specific historical context from which it emerged. The particular contingent circumstances that surrounded Indonesia's initial independence struggle and subsequent nation-building efforts meant that the armed forces inevitably assumed a pivotal, path-dependent position (see Chapters 2 and 3). As we shall see, this centrality was reinforced by the Suharto regime, when the then general placed himself – and subsequently his family and the army – at the centre of Indonesia's political and economic life, as well as its more conventional security affairs. But while this chapter's primary analytical focus may be orthodox enough – in that it is the army rather than the police that will be of principal concern – as in Malaysia and Thailand, the precise way the security sector is institutionally embedded in a wider complex of social relations bears little resemblance to some of the more conventional or idealised accounts of civil–military relations described in Chapter 2. On the contrary, not only is the definition of 'security' in Indonesia a lot broader and reflective of contingent circumstances than elsewhere, but the manner in which it is pursued and the activities of the military forces themselves often bear little resemblance to the activities of comparable forces elsewhere.

For our purposes this is especially significant because it means that any possible reform of the military must confront a much wider set of institutionalised obstacles to change than we might 'normally' expect. Certainly there are issues of internal governance, organisational restructuring, accountability and the like that need to be addressed, but in some ways these are less important and potentially easier to deal with than the more fundamental issues that flow from Indonesia's distinctive civil–military relations. In short, the success of the reformist endeavour will depend in large part on other political and economic developments in Indonesia: until the economy has the wherewithal and stability to underpin a fundamental transformation in the way the military is funded, and unless Indonesia's political class can implement effective legislation to ensure civilian control of the security sector and its operations, then fundamental reform is unlikely. While there are some promising signs and well-intentioned initiatives, there are still some formidable hurdles to be overcome that are a direct consequence of Indonesia's distinctive historical trajectory.

The historical origins of military domination

Like so many other 'developing countries', the military has played a crucial role in Indonesia's emergence and consolidation as an independent nation-state. In this context, the military was seen as a critical force of stability and potential agency of modernity. The preoccupation with internal security in the context of nation-building and economic development helps to explain the potential for the coercive application of military force that often follows as a consequence. We might even be forgiven for thinking that there is something inevitable about both the dominance of the military and the possibility of state-sponsored repression in the difficult period after independence. But as we have already seen in Malaysia's case, the transition period can be relatively smooth, and the military may not necessarily play a prominent role in maintaining order. The other possibility that needs to be considered, therefore, which is dramatically highlighted in the Indonesian case, is that the roots of military dominance in general and the prospect of violent coercion in particular may be found in the specific colonial experience, rather than the general independence struggle.

Dutch colonialism played a large part in establishing the idea that coercion and violence are effective parts of regime maintenance. As Nordholt (2002: 36) points out, in the last decades of the nineteenth century and the first years of the twentieth, the Dutch violently imposed their will across the archipelago, conducting more than 30 colonial wars and killing perhaps 100,000 people in Aceh alone. The colonial period, in which organised violence became an instrument of social repression and economic expansion, had an enduring impact on what would become modern Indonesia in ways that merit spelling out:

> The post-colonial states have inherited more from their predecessors than their nationalist rhetoric would suggest. As such, they retain an intense distrust

toward their own subjects, as well as a strong concentration of power in the centre because of the fear that the delegation of power could lead to disloyalty and separatism. First and foremost, the army – supported by the various intelligence services, each of which controls the other – has the task of protecting the interests of the state within its own national borders . . . The Indonesians have inherited a repressive government apparatus that was chiefly designed to effectively exploit the territory and control the people.

(Nordholt 2002: 42)

The point to emphasise at the outset is that the propensity for the application of organised violence, state repression and centralised authority that would become such a distinctive part of the Suharto regime, had noteworthy parallels in the colonial state established by the Dutch (Anderson 1990). Put differently, there is nothing particularly 'Indonesian' about the utilisation of coercion and violence to maintain order, as the relatively peaceful period immediately after independence reminds us. However, we also need to remember that, unlike the Malaysian experience, the decolonisation process in Indonesia was violently opposed by the colonial power, a reality that gave a particular intensity to the independence struggle and a concomitant authority to the ultimately victorious indigenous forces as a consequence.

It would, however, be incorrect to assume that the Indonesian armed forces were a coherent and unified whole as a direct consequence of a common, collective experience during the independence struggle. In reality, the personnel that would eventually comprise independent Indonesia's armed forces had a more disparate heritage. Some members of the early officer corps had been trained by the Dutch as part of the Royal Netherlands Indies Army (KNIL) and actually fought alongside the Dutch against the early republican government that proclaimed independence – somewhat prematurely, as it turned out – in August 1945 (Pauker 1962: 188). Other members of what would become *Angkatan Bersenjata Republik Indonesia* (ABRI), which was established shortly afterwards, were either trained by the Japanese occupation forces during the Second World War, or began their military careers as part of the independence struggle between 1945 and 1949. Indeed, a number of the key figures of the revolutionary struggle were trained by the Japanese, including future president Suharto and the first commander of the armed forces, General Sudirman. Japanese training and encouragement of the nationalist forces toward the end of the war were important parts of the independence struggle, efforts that reinforced the more general desire to be free of European colonial powers that gripped much of the region (Pauker 1962: 193; Beeson 2007).

Not only did the personnel of the putative national army have different military histories, and concomitantly different views about the role of the armed forces,[2] but they also came from a variety of ethnic and class backgrounds. The nature of the guerrilla warfare waged against the Dutch further fragmented the Indonesian army during this revolutionary period. More important, perhaps, many military figures viewed their political counterparts with disdain as a consequence of what they saw as their accommodating attitude toward the Dutch; such attitudes remained pervasive in the post-independence period (Robinson 2001). Indeed, the armed forces became politicised as a direct consequence of their prominent role in a guerrilla struggle in which 'military and political aspects were inextricably inter-twined' (Crouch 1985: 53). Following the capture of the political leadership by the Dutch, the military found themselves responsible for civil administration in addi-tion to their more customary role. As a consequence of their overall contribution to the independence struggle, army officers felt they had earned the right to play a prominent role in the life of independent Indonesia.

Important as the efforts of the military were in dislodging their colonial mas-ters, of even greater importance in encouraging the departure of the better trained and equipped Dutch forces was the dramatically reconfigured international environment discussed in Chapter 3. The pivotal change in this context was a trans-formation in the foreign policy preferences of the United States, which became increasingly hostile toward the continuing imperial ambitions of the European powers (McMahon 1999). Without this change in the international environment, it is likely the Dutch would have hung on for longer than they did. When they did finally admit defeat, however, indigenous military forces unsurprisingly occupied a large place in the post-colonial order.

Many of the distinctive structures, attitudes and doctrines that continue to charac-terise military thinking in Indonesia have their origins in the revolutionary period – or so many in the military like to claim. Not only did the army come to see itself as a central component of Indonesian society and politics, in addition to its more conventional military role, but the very organisational structure of the army itself reflects the nature of the guerrilla warfare that was waged against the Dutch. One innovation with major, path-dependent consequences which was consolidated during this period, was the division of the countryside into defence areas called *wehrkreise* (MacFarling 1996: 41). As we shall see, these became the basis for the territorial command structure, which is such a defining feature of the mili-tary's wider role in Indonesia, a major source of its power, and which remains a major obstacle to thoroughgoing reform to this day. Before examining this in any detail, however, it is important to say something about the way in which post-independence politics evolved, as this period ultimately allowed the military to consolidate its position at the centre of the Indonesia's politics and economy, as well as its security.

Post-independence politics

For the first two decades of its post-independence existence, the Republic of Indonesia was marked by social, political and economic turbulence. The com-mon problems of nation-building and economic development that confronted all such newly independent countries were compounded in Indonesia's case by major divisions within the national political elite. On the one hand were those who wanted to concentrate on domestic consolidation and good governance, on the other, were those who thought the revolution was incomplete because of the con-tested status of West Irian in particular (Feith 1962; Anwar 1998). The latter faction was led by president Sukarno. His mercurial personality and strident anti-colonial rhetoric would come to dominate Indonesia's political landscape, but there was comparatively little sign of this in the early years of independence. Significantly, in the immediate post-independence period the army accepted its subordinate position under the constitution of 1950, mainly as a consequence of its own lack of coherence, competence and a common identity (Crouch 1978: 28). However, when technocratically minded army officers attempted to reduce the size of the army they were fiercely resisted by other elements within the army itself, and by members of Indonesia's political opposition. This unstable period highlighted divisions within the military, as well as the ineffectiveness of the parliamentary government, and culminated in the introduction of martial law in 1957 following outbreaks of regional rebellion. Paradoxically, as Crouch (1978: 32), points out, 'the continued factionalism within the army both prevented the army leadership from moving against the civilian government and created the conditions leading to the substantial enhancement of the army's political role'. As we shall see, factionalism has been a continuing feature of the military's internal politics and helps to account for the fact that they have not assumed a more prominent position on the national political stage.

With the development of 'guided democracy' in 1959, the military became complicit in ending electoral contests and installing Sukarno as 'president for life'. This was possible, in part, because of the relationship that Sukarno established with the army, in which the latter maintained order, especially in the more far-flung parts of the archipelago, underpinning the stability of the overall regime. At the same time, however, Sukarno sought to diminish the military's importance by encouraging the development of the Indonesian Communist Party (PKI). The rivalry between the PKI and the military was one of the central dynamics of the Sukarno period, until its bloody unravelling in 1965, when the PKI was destroyed and the army was instrumental in helping Suharto seize power. Yet even before this unambiguous manifestation of the military's potential power, it had already become an increasingly central part of Indonesian political life, and its own doctrines reflected this reality. Army Chief of staff Nasution articulated the doctrine of the 'middle way', which suggested that army officers ought to participate in government, but not seek to dominate it. This active involvement in political life would eventually be given its most complete expression in the doctrine of *dwifungsi* or dual function.

The emergence of the *dwifungsi* doctrine cannot be disentangled from the political upheaval which marked the downfall of Sukarno and the military's rise to prominence under Suharto. Even now the events surrounding this period are murkier than we might like, but the central facts relevant for our purposes are clear enough. Many in the military were increasingly concerned about the possible threat posed by the PKI and its links with an increasingly erratic Sukarno. The apparent attempted coup by the PKI and its supporters in the military was thwarted by the decisive actions of Suharto, who mobilised elements of the army against the plotters and assumed control once order was restored. In the aftermath of the coup attempt, Suharto moved to nullify the threat posed by the communists by ordering the army to round up PKI sympathisers. The military in turn allowed civilian opponents of the PKI and their sympathisers to unleash a bloody rampage that resulted in the deaths of some half a million people. Robinson (2001: 232) argues that the brutal manner in which Suharto came to power helped to establish a 'culture of violence' within the army and the state that helps to account for many subsequent actions. While this ruthless brutality may have proved effective in eliminating prominent political opponents, Suharto's ascension to power was not without its tensions and difficulties even then: Suharto had to unite the deeply factionalised armed forces, especially the pro-nationalist Sukarno supporters, and reassure those worried about their career prospects in a Suharto-dominated regime (Elson 2001: 127).

For the military as a whole, one of the defining moments as far as its role in the new Suharto regime was concerned occurred at the Army Seminar in 1966 (MacFarling 1996). At this seminar the key elements of what became known as the New Order, and the military's role within it, were outlined. Two aspects of this process would prove to be especially important in retrospect: from the outset, the army was seen as being a central part of the political process and guarantor of internal social stability. In addition, however, the military under Suharto was to be directly involved in economic activities. As Elson (2001: 151) points out, 'Suharto's own track record demonstrated an enthusiasm for the military to embed themselves in business activity, and a proclivity to allow close associates who demonstrated energy and entrepreneurial flair to have their heads'. In other words, the prominent position occupied by Suharto in particular and the military more generally in Indonesia's economy – which has subsequently proven to be such an obstacle to reform – was there from the outset. Consequently, the deeply institutionalised and entrenched networks of power and patronage that have effectively blurred the boundaries between political, economic and military power were integral and defining parts of the evolving, increasingly 'corporatist' Suharto regime.[3]

The most important innovation at the political level to emerge from this period as far as the military was concerned was that it was given corporate representation in the parliament, and members of the military – both active and retired – were given key positions in the cabinet, the civil administration and state-owned corporations (Rabasa and Haseman 2002). This was entirely in keeping with the new doctrine of *dwifungsi* and the wider 'socio-political' function envisaged for the army. As part of the emerging structure of 'Pancasila democracy' the army was primarily concerned with internal security and national development, rather than the more customary military role of protecting the nation from external threats. The five principles of the ideology of Pancasila were initially propounded by Sukarno,[4] but under Suharto they were turned into 'the basic credo to which all Indonesians had to adhere' (Liddle 1999: 40). As far as Suharto himself was concerned, his own ruling idea had 'become that of development, with security its necessary condition and expected result' (Elson 2001: 175).

Two points are worth emphasising about this early phase of the Suharto era in which the role of the military moved even further from the sort of concerns we might expect from a 'professional' military until it became 'a political instrument of authoritarian rule' (Kristiadi 2001: 101). The first point to stress is that Suharto's New Order put great emphasis on economic development as the cornerstone of a more encompassing political regime that was underpinned by military power. As in Thailand, therefore, goals such as democratisation and liberalisation played second fiddle to economic development. The second point to highlight is that the world generally and American policymakers in particular acquiesced with, and sometimes actively supported, this order and the military's central role within it – because it suited their wider geopolitical purposes to do so. Not only was Suharto seen as more ideologically reliable, stable and sympathetic to the West than his predecessor, but economic development was pursued in line with the nostrums of Western liberal economics and with the active assistance of the increasingly influential international financial institutions (Beeson 2006). As Jeffrey Winters (1996: 53) points out, one of the first acts of the newly installed Suharto regime was to invite the International Monetary Fund and the World Bank into the country to help restructure the economy. At the height of the cold war, American support for such a potentially stalwart capitalistically is entirely unsurprising, despite the flagrant human rights violations that were associated with the rise and consolidation of the Suharto regime.[5]

As we shall see, the intersecting structures of political, economic and military power and influence that emerged as a consequence during the Suharto era persist to this day and present major obstacles to reform. But before considering them in any detail, it is important to say something about the formal organisational structures of the Indonesian military.

Military organisation and the New Order

The organisational logic and internal structure of Indonesia's armed forces reflects its history and its geography. As we have seen, one important consequence of Indonesian history has been to imbue the military with a sense of its own importance in the creation of modern Indonesia as a functioning, independent entity. But the very nature of the Indonesian archipelago and the diverse ethnic and social groups it embraces presents particularly acute potential problems of order maintenance and internal security. This underlying geophysical reality led directly to the development of the doctrine of *Wawasan Nusantara* or Archipelagic Outlook, which emphasised the potentially integrative role that the military could play in forging national unity (Lowry 1996: 8). One of the most distinctive organisational features of the Indonesian military that emerged from this sort of thinking built upon the territorial system that developed during the war against the Dutch. In the post-independence period, this underlying structure has been refined and taken on more formal qualities with the creation of ten Regional Military Commands or *Komando Daerah Militer* (Kodam). These regional commands are further subdivided into smaller geographically based units, right down to the village level, giving the army a unique capacity to extend its institutional reach into every part of the archipelago. Within this system, and in line with the doctrine of 'total people's defence' that developed during the independence struggle, some two-thirds of army personnel are dispersed throughout the country (Robinson 2001).

There is a further distinction to be made between these territorial commands where the bulk of the forces are deployed, and the 'tactical' forces, which constitute a more conventional military capacity. The tactical forces are divided between Kostrad, with around 27,000 personnel, and the elite, but rather infamous Special Forces Command (Kopassus), which has about 5,000 members. Kostrad has two divisions based in Java, with a separate brigade in Sulawesi. The divisions have both infantry and airborne brigades and are used primarily as a rapid-reaction force against civil unrest and guerrilla threats in East Timor and Aceh. Kopassus is also based on Java, but deployed more frequently than Kostrad to deal with a wider range of security threats, including combating guerrilla forces through undercover and intelligence gathering operations. As Rabasa and Haseman (2002) point out, Kopassus troops tend to develop personal loyalty to charismatic commanders and have been associated with frequent human rights abuses in the course of their operations. Significantly, however, they have enjoyed virtual immunity from prosecution.

The army is by far the dominant service in Indonesia, but the Republic does have naval and air forces, too. Both services suffer from out-dated equipment and a lack of funding – a problem the East Asian financial crisis exacerbated. This highlights an issue that both explains the way in which some elements of the army in particular operate and why reform is so problematic: the over-riding structural constraint faced by all Indonesian governments, but especially the post-Suharto leaders, has been the parlous state of the economy. And yet, the reality is that the Indonesian army is perhaps the only institution that allows the state to penetrate the entire archipelago and thus offers a potentially useful arm of internal governance, in addition to its more obvious, conventional security function. The problem faced by the Indonesian state is that it simply does not have the capacity to fund the military in its present condition, let alone a re-equipped force. To maintain and modernise the military would cost an estimated US$6 billion, or about 25 per cent of the Indonesian state's annual budget. In reality, military spending in 2001 was about US$1 billion, with the gap between the 'optimal' and actual figures representing 'an impossible leap', according to the International Crisis Group (ICG 2001: 12). In the absence of sufficient government funding, the military has of necessity become involved in an array of business ventures to make up for the shortfall. Similar drives were also evident in Thailand (see Chapter 5). However, in Indonesia, so extensive and institutionalised have such activities become that they represent a potentially immovable obstacle to reform, and thus one that merits more detailed consideration.

Money and the military

By some estimates 60–65 per cent of the military's actual operating expenses come from 'off-budget sources' rather than the government (Cochrane 2002). This is a euphemism for a host of legal and illegal practices that include legitimate involvement in state-owned and private business, as well as a range of activities in the 'black economy'. Indeed, of the government's already limited and insufficient contribution to military funding, an estimated 30 per cent is 'lost through corruption in the process of buying military equipment and supplies' (ICG 2001: 13). In such circumstances, there is a certain inevitability, perhaps, about the military involvement in business activities as a way of plugging the funding gap. What is more surprising is the extent of these activities and the way they have become regularised, deeply institutionalised parts of civil–military relations in Indonesia. Although there is some debate about the competence of the military as economic managers[6] there is, nevertheless, one critically important consequence that flows directly from the military's involvement in the economy which has major implications for the overall reform agenda:

> The more a military's revenue and spending are outside civilian control, gov-
> ernment control, and the more funds it raises itself, the harder it is for civil
> authorities to engage in meaningful oversight of the military. The result is
> a government that lacks the power to demand accountability from its armed
> forces and to implement needed reforms.
>
> (Human Rights Watch 2006: 1)

The military's extensive business interests date back to the revolutionary period. In the early post-independence period, the central government was simply incapable of adequately funding the military, and regional commanders were forced to find ways of financing personnel and general operating costs from non-government sources. The key moment in cementing the military's role in business came in late 1957, with the nationalisation of former Dutch economic assets. During this period, the military assumed responsibility for running large-scale commercial enterprises – often in collaboration with Chinese business figures who had established themselves as a powerful economic force throughout much of Southeast Asia.[7] Indeed, one expert argues that the Chinese business community played a critical role in helping the military establish its business interests, especially in regions far from Jakarta.[8] Suharto's own career reflects this overall paradigm to some extent. Vatikiotis (1998: 36) claims that in the late 1950s Suharto developed a close relationship with Liem Sioe Long while a divisional commander in Central Java, although Elson claims that the relationship with Bob Hasan was more important.[9] Either way, Suharto established important connections with people who would go on to become some of Indonesia's wealthiest and most successful ethnic Chinese business figures. As in Malaysia, the nexus between political and economic power would not only become deeply entrenched in Indonesia, but would also consolidate the position of otherwise vulnerable major Chinese capitalists (Robison 1986: 267). The point to emphasise once more is that the symbiotic relationship that developed between Suharto and Liem was emblematic of the wider array of patrimonial relationships that would consolidate during the New Order.

The TNI's business activities can be divided into four main types

> cooperatives which focus mainly on troop welfare; unit business; businesses
> run by non-profit foundations, known as *yayasan*, to support charitable,

educational or welfare objectives; and 'influence and facilitation', which may take place outside the formal business structure.

(Lowry 1996: 137)

The cooperatives were primarily established by the Department of Defence and Security in conjunction with (what was then) ABRI.[10] They were intended to provide members of the armed forces with basic goods at low cost – a potentially vital service given the military's low pay rates – and provide additional funding for personnel and infrastructure costs. Significantly, there was a good deal of autonomy for individual commanders about how the cooperatives operated and the sorts of projects they are designed to support. The cooperatives are financed in part by compulsory member subscriptions, but primarily from the holding companies or *yayasan* which the cooperatives run. These independent foundations have become especially significant since 1974 when they were exempt from taxation and 'represent one of the most important formal mechanisms through which the Indonesian military participates in business activities' (Singh 2001: 15–16).

Each branch of the security sector – army, navy, air force and the police – has its own foundation. The army actually has a number of foundations, with Kostrad, Kopassus and the TNI headquarters having individual *yayasan*, while the Ministry of Defence has another two. The foundations operate business operations through various holding companies. As Bilveer Singh (2001: 16) points out in his detailed analysis of the military's business activities, the army's foundation – Yayasan Kartika Eka Paksi (YKEP) – usefully illustrates the way in which the military is involved in business. The army foundation is managed by PT Tri Usaha Bhakti, which in turn oversees more than 20 further subsidiaries. These subsidiaries are engaged in an array of commercial activities throughout the Indonesian economy, including financial sector activities, the travel industry, manufacturing and resource extraction – especially logging. This is particularly significant as the logging industry in Indonesia is notoriously corrupt and seemingly immune to effective regulation and governmental control. The military have been conspicuously successful in obtaining logging concessions, and have used them to establish joint ventures with local Chinese business figures or foreign companies (Robison 1986: 256). As Robison and Hadiz (2004: 54) point out, the military have frequently lacked the entrepreneurial and management skills to successfully develop the assets they controlled, and consequently became reliant on figures like Liem and Suharto's other notorious crony, Bob Hasan.

Under the New Order regime connections with Suharto were vital for business success – be it the more orthodox private sector variety, or military controlled enterprises. Kostrad's business ventures, for example, were originally established by Suharto and flourished under his patronage. The blurred lines between political, military and business interests were particularly apparent in the operation of state-owned corporations like Bulog (the State Logistics Agency – *Badan Urusan Logistik*) and Pertamina, the national oil company. Both companies were dominated by military personnel and became major sources of funding for the military in general, and a lucrative source of income for privileged insiders in particular.

Bulog had a particular strategic importance as it decided which companies were granted control over, or access to, monopoly positions in the domestic economy. Key areas like the distribution of sugar, flour, wheat and rice became lucrative sources of revenue and vehicles for patronage and corruption. Pertamina had even greater significance in that it was a crucial source of wealth creation and foreign exchange, a pivotal part of the overall process of economic development in Indonesia and – of most importance for our purposes – a critical source of funding for the military (Robison 1986: 239).

It is worth dwelling for a moment on the overall position of Pertamina and the windfall oil revenues it controlled as it offers an insight into both the dynamics of Indonesia's wider domestic political-economy, and into the prospects for externally driven reform initiatives. There has been a long-standing tension in the Indonesian polity between rival technocratic and nationalist factions. On the one hand there is a group of Western-oriented technocrats who have tried to implement the sort of market-conforming reforms that have been urged upon Indonesia by the likes of the World Bank and the IMF. On the other hand, however, there has been a powerful group of economic nationalists that were not only unconvinced by the intellectual merit of such ideas, but were keen to protect networks of power, patronage and privilege that rested on their continuing control of key domestic resources. As Jeffrey Winters (1996: 96) notes, when oil prices were high and the Indonesian state was less reliant on foreign assistance and less susceptible to foreign pressure, the technocrats influence was sharply reduced. In short, rising oil prices reinforced patronage politics and the influence of Indonesia's indigenous *pribumi* investors. When oil process fell, by contrast, the influence of the technocrats – and their external backers – rose accordingly. In this regard, it is also noteworthy that the greatest leverage obtained by external agencies over Indonesia's economic policies occurred in the aftermath of the Asian financial crisis when the government's dependency on foreign lenders made it highly susceptible to reformist pressure; ultimately leading, of course, to the downfall of the Suharto regime (Beeson 1998).

Although the Asian crisis was primarily a political-economic phenomenon, rather than a strictly military issue, the nature of the military's involvement in the economy, the all-encompassing notion of security that prevails in Indonesia and the dynamics of the 'economic'[11] reform process suggest some important lessons for those interested in military reform. Clearly, the central role the military continues to play in commercial activities means that it is exposed to changes in the overall health of the national economy that may influence its behaviour. However, it is important to recognise that the military is not necessarily vulnerable to reformist pressure as a direct consequence of deteriorating economic performance in the same way that the national government is. After all, the military's historical role in economic activity might be seen as something of an aberration brought about by the underdevelopment of the national economy and governmental failure. Consequently, political and military institutions may be vulnerable to reformist pressures for very different reasons: unlike the political class, military elites may remain relatively immune to such pressures if the economy is seen to be incapable of adequately supporting them. In other words, unless and until the economy improves, the military's role in extra-curricular activities is unlikely to be challenged; a possibility that the complex and opaque nature of the military's involvement in such activities makes even more likely.

As we noted earlier, one of the most distinctive organisational features of the Indonesian military, and one of the biggest obstacles to possible reform, is the territorial command system. For our purposes, what is of most significance about this structure is that from its inception, regional military commands have been responsible for the bulk of their operational fund-raising. Of even greater importance as far as potential reformist efforts are concerned, perhaps, is the fact that regional commanders have, over time, 'developed their own power base by acquiring economic power' (Singh 2001: 25). In other words, the same sorts of networks of patronage that built up around Suharto and his control of key economic assets, were replicated at the regional level as individual commanders created virtual fiefdoms and became deeply entrenched parts of regional political-economies. As Mietzner (2002a: 77) points out, the military is especially resistant to attempts to reform the territorial structure because its power and independence 'is based on a politically negotiated and supported network of territorial units that secure financial independence of TNI from civilian control mechanisms'. Somewhat ironically, the sort of reformist initiatives that have been encouraged upon Indonesia under the guise of decentralisation in the aftermath of Suharto's downfall may actually have consolidated such localised networks of patronage and rent-seeking as corruption has become more decentralised, too (Hadiz 2004).

The point to emphasise is that while the justification for the territorial command structure may be ostensibly lodged in a strategic culture predicated on the assumption that the military will be primarily engaged with fighting decentralised guerrilla campaigns, occasionally against a militarily superior enemy, in reality its major significance has become political and economic. Consequently, as the ICG point out:

> The army will fight a strong rearguard action to retain the territorial commands for a number of reasons: fear of separatism, the economic advantage flowing from access to resources nationally, institutional ambivalence about democracy, and contempt for the governing capacity of many civilian politicians.
>
> (ICG 2004: 8)

This latter point is especially salient when thinking about the capacity of Indonesia's political class either to initiate military reform, or more importantly, to see such reformist efforts through to completion. For this reason, the relationship between the military and Indonesia's political system merits closer attention.

Power and the armed forces

Indonesia's military occupies a central place in the country's economic activities – albeit one that is frequently informal and not as widely recognised as we might expect. The military's place in Indonesia's political life, by contrast, has – until recently, at least – been governed by institutionalised checks and balances and has widely been considered legitimate. Indeed, as with the military's participation in the economy, there was a certain inevitability about this: in the absence of effective state capacity and bureaucratic infrastructure, the army became a central component of national governance and regime stability. What is most striking about the corporatist-style polity that was consolidated during the New Order, however, was that the military's pivotal role was formally enshrined within Indonesia's political structures. In other words, the New Order established a concordant pattern of civil–military relations that made overt military intervention in politics unnecessary.

As part of its wider socio-political function, and in keeping with the logic of the *dwifungsi* doctrine, the military had been guaranteed representation in the country's main legislative bodies, the House of Representatives (DPR) and the People's Consultative Assembly (MPR), and exercised effective control over both institutions by 'both direct and indirect means'. In the lower level DPR the military was – until 1997 – guaranteed 100 of the 500 DPR seats. The MPR included both the DPR, as well as regional and functional representatives, in both of which categories the military was represented. As a consequence, during the New Order period about one-third of the MPR was controlled by unelected military delegates (Anwar 2001: 13). In addition to these formally allocated positions – which had been reduced to 75 in the DPR at the end of the New Order period – the military also had numerous other non-elected seats on various national, regional and sub-regional legislatures, as well as exercising influence through the retired officers who obtained seats on various bodies as members of Golkar (Robinson 2001: 234).

Golkar had been established in 1964 and eventually became the Suharto government's principal electoral vehicle, and from its inception it was the army's preferred 'functional group' in the overall concordant and corporatist framework (Schwarz 1994: 31). However, relations between Golkar and the military became tense as a consequence of the 'civilianisation' of the Golkar chairmanship in 1993. The nature of the relationship between – and relative seniority of – ABRI and Golkar became caught up in a wider debate about the role of the military that unfolded in the 1990s. At issue was the nature and continuing legitimacy of *dwifungsi*. Two points are worth emphasising about this period: first, much of the – often heated – debate occurred within the military itself and raised important doctrinal questions which are still in play, as we explain later. The second point to note is that, while these debates were ostensibly doctrinal and philosophical, they were overlaid with wider political and even sectarian struggles: the top three ABRI officers in the mid-1990s – Feisal Tanjung, Raden Hartono and Syarwan Hamid – were seen by some as part of the 'Islamisation of ABRI'. One of the more significant consequences of this debate and the eventual rapprochement between Golkar and ABRI was to undermine ABRI's claimed neutrality and role as protector of the 'national interest'. As Jun Honna (2003: 30–35) points out in his definitive analysis of military politics in Indonesia, the net effect of this period was to intensify divisions within ABRI between Islamic and secular forces, and to reinforce the perception that ABRI was a tool of Suharto; all of which fuelled the continuing debate about the military's overall role.

Military influence and power, therefore, is difficult to gauge because of its contradictory nature. At one level, the military was deeply institutionalised and socially embedded, giving it an unparalleled capacity to penetrate Indonesian society. In addition to its roles in the DPR and MPR, for example, the military's influence and power in the overall system of governance was consolidated with the appointment of active and retired military officers as cabinet members, top civil servants, diplomats and provincial governors. Consequently, it was the structural core of the New Order regime. At another level, however, it is also important to recognise that long before Suharto fell and undermined the legitimacy of a regime in which the military had been such a central part, the relationship between ABRI and Suharto was complex and often tense. As early as 1988, Suharto had demonstrated his desire and capacity to frustrate military objectives. ABRI's nomination for the position of vice president, for example, was overruled by Suharto who installed his own preferred candidate, Sudharmono, then chairman of Golkar. As Vatikiotis (1998: 40) observes,

> ABRI was overruled. By demonstrating so openly his disregard for ABRI's advice, and insisting on Sudharmono becoming vice president, Suharto demonstrated that he no longer needed ABRI as a prop to sustain his power. The political fallout made a deep impression on the military and triggered introspection on ABRI's role in politics and its relationship with the national leadership on one side, and the people on the other.

One of the ways that Suharto attempted to consolidate his own position and power was by assuming a much more direct, personal role in senior military appointments. By the 1980s, other key figures from the '1945 Generation' that had been involved in the independence struggle against the Dutch, like Ali Murtopo and Adam Malik, were dead. Suharto was forced to recruit military leaders from the ranks of younger generations of academy-trained officers who were less ideologically oriented and more concerned with personal advancement (Kristiadi 1999: 108). His choice of Benny Murdani for the position of ABRI commander in 1983 marked the beginning of a new style of appointment in which Suharto 'took to appointing men below the topmost ranks of seniority, progressing them rapidly, and thereby *binding them to him personally*' (Elson 2001: 2444 [emphasis added]). In many ways, this practice of politicisation was simply a continuation of the pattern of patronage politics that had come to characterise the regime more generally. It was a strategy that was fraught with potential difficulties, however, as it threatened to create resentment and discontent within the senior ranks of the military.[12]

There are two aspects to these tensions that are especially noteworthy. On the one hand, despite his own military background, Suharto was concerned about the possible independence and power of the military; consequently, it was Suharto who, as Challis (2001: 187) puts it, was the 'architect of its decline'. It was also Suharto who began the process of reducing military representation in the

DPR, and who oversaw a reduction in the military's share of the overall national budget. Equally significantly, Suharto had encouraged the development of the Association of Indonesian Muslim Intellectuals (ICMI) under the leadership of his protégé B.J. Habibie – who would subsequently inherit the presidency following Suharto's demise – as a counterweight to the military (Rabasa and Haseman 2002: 37). This move also had the effect of further heightening tensions within ABRI between Islamists, reformists and secular nationalists (Honna 1999: 107). Thus, even before the traumatic events associated with Suharto's downfall unfolded, his politicking, the creation of potential centres of influence that might counter military power, and – most immediately, perhaps – the appointment of senior officers on the basis of their connections with Suharto himself, rather than any strictly military credentials, had created major tensions among senior officers. To understand why the appointment of figures like Suharto's son-in-law, Prabowo Subianto, should have been especially controversial, it is necessary to say something about the nature of the military hierarchy and the way careers develop within it.

Chandra and Kammen (2002) have persuasively argued that the behaviour of the senior ranks of the military in Indonesia, especially during periods of democratic consolidation and transition, can be at least partly explained by the internal organisation of the military. One of the distinguishing features of the TNI has been the increasing supply of senior officers as a consequence of the growing numbers of graduates from the National Military Academy. In the 1960s and 1970s in particular, larger groups of officers graduated, and they have subsequently risen through the ranks, with the result that there is a large pool of officers competing for a limited number of senior appointments. When combined with a tendency for 'class solidarity' to develop within specific cohorts of graduates, it becomes easier to account for the fact that some graduate classes have managed to dominate particular positions, and why there is frustration amongst those whose ambitions remain unrealised as a consequence. Chandra and Kammen (2002) demonstrate a strong correlation between particular groups of graduating officers in the 1970s and their support for, or opposition to, military reforms. For those groups of officers who found their career progress blocked by earlier graduate classes that had successfully monopolised senior positions, the attractions of reform were more compelling. Incumbents were predictably less enthusiastic about changes to the status quo.

Post-Suharto civil–military relations

Such intra-institutional dynamics are especially important in the context of post-Suharto politics. It might have been expected that, despite Suharto's own efforts to limit the power of the military, his close association with the army and the TNI's historical importance in underpinning the stability of the overall regime, would have meant that pressures for reform would have inevitably intensified following his downfall. And while there have, indeed, been some important attempts to change the formal role of the military, the picture is more complex than it appears at first glance. One of the most important innovations as far as the military is concerned has been a reassertion of control over its internal affairs – especially as far as promotions and appointments is concerned (Chandra and Kammen 2002: 116). In this regard it is important to recognise that the extremely fluid political situation that developed in the aftermath of the Suharto era offered the military – despite widespread calls for its reform and unprecedented criticism of its history of human rights abuses (Bourchier 1999) – significantly enhanced leverage vis-à-vis their ostensible political masters. Rivalries between political and religious forces in Indonesia, which had been kept in check during the Suharto era, came to the fore following his demise. In the somewhat chaotic atmosphere and political jockeying that ensued, the military positioned itself as a mediator between competing social forces (Mietzner 2002b: 24).

In this regard, the manner of Suharto's downfall, and the anarchic, divided nature of the political opposition meant that post-Suharto politics were not as different from the old authoritarian order as we might have expected. On the contrary, the military was able to ensure a high degree of continuity with the former regime and their powerful position within it by effectively excluding oppositional forces from the first post-Suharto government and the decision-making processes associated with it (Mietzner 2004: 137). Moreover, political divisions within Indonesia's Muslim communities, which might have been expected to provide an effective and coherent opposition, allowed the military to maintain its institutionalised authority. The armed forces were, in fact, able to preserve and protect their fundamental corporate interests by rapidly adapting to the merging democratic political framework. Indeed, it is important to recognise that a preoccupation with the form rather than the substance of institutional change had unwanted consequences. As Mietzner, points out

> the heavy emphasis on terminating military engagement in civilian institutions distracted the attention of the public and political elite from other, more consequential areas of reform. Most importantly, the territorial command structure, the backbone of the military presence in socio-political life in the regions, was left untouched for the entirety of Habibie's interregnum.

And yet despite the importance of the territorial command structure to the military as a whole, the military itself did not have a single, coherent set of interests, nor was it immune from the divisions that opened up in Indonesian society. Even before Suharto's departure the army was split between factions loyal to Prabowo and those who supported General Wiranto; a division that was resolved in favour of the latter when he became ABRI's chief of staff in 1998. Wiranto would also become a key figure in the post-Suharto transition; but it is important to remember that he was appointed by, and close to, Suharto and did not represent a major break with the past. Perhaps the greatest significance of Wiranto's appointment as chief of staff was that he was what Crouch (1999: 128) describes as a middle of the road figure, in that he was seen as something of a compromise between the so-called green (Islamic) and the 'red and white' (nationalist) factions within ABRI ranks. However, Wiranto's personal loyalty to Suharto made him ambivalent about an eventual succession that had been canvassed in military circles even before the events of 1998. Consequently, Wiranto's behaviour during this transition phase has been aptly described as 'consistent hesitancy' (The Editors 2000: 125).

To understand both Wiranto's hesitancy and the fact that he ultimately came to play a major role in 'restoring stability and facilitating regime change' (Honna 2003: 162), we need to recognise just how important internal military politics have been and how influential they can be on the wider polity – especially at moments of epochal change – as the events of 1966 and 1998 remind us. For Wiranto, the rivalry with Prabowo was as important as the end of the New Order, particularly given the latter's role in actively fermenting chaos and instability in Indonesian society more generally.[13] Eventually Wiranto was able to enlist Suharto in the downfall of Probowo and distance ABRI as an institution from the activities of destabilising internal forces.[14] The 'de-Probowo-isation' of the army, which involved the purging of many of his supporters, allowed Wiranto to achieve greater unity in ABRI, as other officers recognised that their careers depended on loyalty to him as much as to the institution itself. It also allowed Wiranto to rethink the role of the military in the post-Suharto era when it was increasingly subject to criticism. He did this, in part, by surrounding himself with 'intellectual officers' like Agus Widjojo, Agus Wirahadikusumah and future president, Susilo Bambang Yudhoyono (Honna 2003: 164). This triggered yet another significant bout of introspection on the military's part about its role, purpose and relationship with society, which would rapidly lead to a major doctrinal shift and the development of a 'New Paradigm'. But before we consider this in any detail, it is important to say something about changes in the more explicitly political system as they helped to shape military thinking and determine its subsequent role.

Perhaps the most important characteristic of post-Suharto politics was that, as the country groped its way toward new and genuinely democratic political structures and practises, the military remained a pivotally important and capable institution. This period had one crucial consequence, both as far as both the nature of the new political process and the prospects for reform and control of the military was concerned. As Mietzner (2002a: 75) points out, because Indonesia's emergent political parties 'tried to recruit the military as a partner in the upcoming battle for the presidency. The goal of outmanoeuvring traditional rivals ranked higher than the interest in reforming Indonesia's Armed Forces'. Consequently, there was generally little political pressure on the military; something that allowed it to play its own, sometimes decisive role in the political sphere.

It is widely believed, for example, that Wiranto's private interview with Suharto was the final factor that caused Suharto to resign (see Eklöf 1999: 212). What is clear, is that during the short leadership period of Suharto's successor, Habibie, Wiranto took the opportunity to continue overhauling the military leadership, primarily by purging 'green' officers associated with Habibie's ICMI-oriented supporters. Wiranto's failure to support Habibie's candidature for the subsequent presidential election led to the latter's withdrawal and the eventual election – after much infighting and deal-making[15] – of Abdurrahman Wahid, more commonly known as Gus Dur. One of the most significant consequences of the unexpectedly brief Wahid administration as far as the military was concerned, was that it was distinguished by a significant reformist effort that included the marginalisation and then dismissal of Wiranto. Gus Dur had already displayed an ability to out-manoeuvre both Wiranto and his political rivals during the presidential elections, but his dismissal of Wiranto was something of a surprise, richly symbolic, and a genuine attempt to impose effective civilian control over the military.

However, in a revealing cameo of the limits of civilian power, Wahid was forced to abandon an attempt to appoint the reform-minded lieutenant General Wirahadikusumah as chief of staff in the face of a threatened mass resignation by 46 army generals. Even more significantly, when, in 2001, the parliament moved to censure Wahid over his alleged involvement in a number of financial scandals, the remaining army and police representatives joined the vote and were 'a key element in his political downfall' (Rabasa and Haseman 2002: 43). What is of most significance about the Wahid administration for our purposes is its impact on his successor, Megawati Sukarnoputri. Unsurprisingly, perhaps, Megawati's attitude toward the military was noticeably more circumspect: not only were her own, militarily supported, ascension to power and Wahid's demise salutary reminders of the continuing power of the army, but it would have been remarkable if the memory of her father's downfall and the military's role in it were not also in the back of her mind.

Megawati's more accommodating relationship with the military had been established while she was Gus Dur's vice president, when the military was instrumental in shifting day-to-day power in her direction (Honna 2003: 185). The rise of the 'security first' generals, who sought to refocus the military on core strategic concerns, coincided with this period and was manifest in the much more hard-line attitude toward trouble spots like Aceh. In the context of intra-army struggles about the future role of the military, attitudes toward Aceh 'greatly empowered those TNI officers who had demanded that the military take a larger role in internal security' (The Editors 2005: 123). It needs to remembered that following the 'loss' of East Timor in 1999, the concomitant decline in military prestige, and the rising tide of public criticism, there were many in the army who wished to re-establish its authority; some appeared to think Aceh offered an opportunity to accomplish this. It is also important to recognise that, once again, these events were in large part a consequence of internal manoeuvring and designed to undermine the position of Yudhoyono, who would ultimately defeat Megawati in a presidential election, but who was then her coordinating minister for Political and Security Affairs and thus in charge of the peace process in Aceh.

Yudhoyono has, of course, become a pivotal figure in Indonesia's general political process and in military reform in particular. But before we consider the impact that his own presidency has had on military reform, it is useful to consider his role in the emergence of the so-called New Paradigm. At the very least it helps us to understand the challenges facing the military and its capacity to reinvent itself, as well as shedding some light on the person who is potentially best placed to influence its future development and role.

The 'New Paradigm'

Given the convulsive and rapid nature of the changes that have re-shaped the formal political system, it is worth recapping their general features. It was this wider political context, after all, which effectively constituted the environment within which the military had to rethink its role, and come to terms with a political and economic system that was increasingly under civilian and ostensibly democratic control. For all the tensions that existed between Suharto and the military as a consequence of Suharto's efforts to bring it under his control and neutralise it as a potential site of opposition to his rule, there was relatively little questioning of its dual purpose and centrality in Indonesia's domestic affairs. All of that changed with the downfall of Suharto; political liberalism and freedom of speech became increasingly powerful forces with which ABRI – by now re-badged as the TNI – had to come to terms. It also had to deal with the reality that for many in Indonesia, the military were irrevocably associated with the – frequently brutal, always authoritarian – Suharto regime, which could no longer even claim to deliver economic development (Bourchier 1999).

The military's new vision of itself in a post-Suharto era was initially developed in 1998, following the downfall of Suharto himself and – from the perspective of internal military politics, at least – the highly significant 'de-Prabowo-isation' of ABRI. The 'intellectual' generals, especially Yudhoyono and Wirahadikusumah, were behind the development of the so-called New Paradigm that emerged as a consequence. Significantly, there was acknowledgement of the damage that the army's role in human rights abuse cases had done to its institutional standing. The widespread criticism of the military that ensued centred on the role of *dwifingsi* and openly called for it to be abandoned (Rinakit 2005: 100). It was from within this novel, rather febrile atmosphere that the New Paradigm emerged. Its key principles were:

- ABRI's withdrawal from its traditional position at the 'forefront' of politics;
- a concomitant shift from political control to political influence, involving the ending of military appointments in 'civilian' posts;
- an associated shift from a direct to an indirect role in society that involved the diminution of ABRI's 'socio-political' role;
- power-sharing with civilians in a more inter-dependent, integrated national system.[16]

Sukardi Rinakit (2005: 102–104) argues that the military felt compelled to rethink its role and develop a new doctrine for three reasons: first the changed geopolitical situation meant that an interventionist, non-democratic and occasionally brutal military was at odds with prevalent international norms. As we shall see, this is an especially important consideration when we think about the overarching geopolitical situation that has changed yet again in the aftermath of September 11. The second reason, Rinakit argues, was the inherent difficulty of running complex business operations in an increasingly 'globalised' economy: the military was simply compelled to rely on civilian specialists. As we shall see this is also a factor that has constrained the military in the Philippines. Finally, growing pressure from an increasingly politicised domestic civil society was undercutting the authority and legitimacy of the military and compelling a rethink of civil–military relations.

While some of these proposed reforms might seem unremarkable, appropriate and/or overdue to many outside observers, as far as the military was concerned they fuelled internal divisions. Rinakit (2005: 109) distinguishes between status quo, moderate and radical groups – divisions that undid much of the coherence that had been achieved following Probowo's demotion. Interestingly, Rinakit argues that factional cleavages were not determined primarily by officers' graduation classes, but by 'the social status of their family, their overseas training and education, and the speed of their military career'. If this claim is accurate, it suggests that officer exchange and training programmes that involve overseas exposure may be effective means of inculcating vales and attitudes conducive to military reform. Although given the importance that has been attached by the US in particular to re-establishing close ties with Indonesia's military – even to Kopassus – then we cannot be certain that such initiatives will be linked to a wider agenda of reform (LaMoshi 2004a). Nevertheless, there have been some unambiguous outcomes of the TNI's own reform agenda promoted under the rubric of the New Paradigm, one of the most significant of which was that it paved the way for a formal separation of the military from the police.

As we saw in the case of Malaysia, under certain circumstances, the police can play an extremely influential role in security issues in particular and regime maintenance more generally. It was potentially highly significant, therefore, that the military was prepared to give up part of its internal policing and intelligence gathering role; not least because it potentially created a more independent institution with which to scrutinise the military itself and its extensive – frequently illegal – economic activities. In reality, part of the historical, institutionalised tension and competition between the police and the military had flowed from 'competition for legal and illegal business opportunities, and conflicts over women, gambling debts and ego' (ICG 2001: 19). Indeed, it is important to re-emphasise just how important extra-curricular economic activities actually are to the army and – to a lesser extent – the police. There is consequently great sensitivity about scrutiny of, and control over such activities – tensions that have, on occasion, actually resulted in violent confrontations between rival elements of the police and army as they vie for control of illegal activities (see Roosa 2003).

The potential for counterproductive institutional rivalry between the police and the army was highlighted by the latter's reluctance to cooperate with the police as it assumed greater responsibility for internal policing. The potential significance of the divisions within Indonesia's security services went beyond simple questions of institutional efficiency, however. It is strongly suspected that elements of the Indonesian military were either directly responsible for, or gave tacit encouragement to, a number of Indonesia's recent high profile outbreaks of inter-communal violence and 'terrorist' outrages in a strategy designed to reinforce their importance in the maintenance of national stability (LaMoshi 2004b). Two members of

Kopassus were convicted of bombing the Jakarta stock exchange, and the army was linked to political assassinations in Aceh, West Papua, as well as the widespread militia violence in East Timor (Fawthrop 2002). Some observers – including ex-president Wahid – have even suggested that the military may have been involved in some way in the bombings in Bali (LaMoshi 2004b). The veracity of such claims is difficult to establish – especially when the military has primary responsibility for intelligence gathering and internal security; a consideration that makes it easier to understand why Wahid moved to expand the role of the police. Significantly, the police now have primary responsibility for anti-terrorism operations (ICG 2004: 5).

Given the economically and politically sensitive nature of intelligence gathering, formal responsibility for such operations is a potentially important part of both domestic security arrangements and for prospective reform processes. The military's record of overt and covert intervention into the political process at crucial moments in Indonesia's history means that the capacity to identify and punish the perpetrators of such activities takes on a much greater importance than in comparable Western polities.[17] Unfortunately, there is no reason to suppose that the police – who are also inadequately funded and forced to rely on non-official sources of funding – are any more likely to prove incorruptible or professional in their expanded role than the military were. Inter-service rivalries and the protection of lucrative economic interests seem certain to further undermine their potential. As the ICG's authoritative report notes, the Indonesian government needs

> to reclaim government policy leadership and affirm the lead role of the police in internal security, clearly define the ongoing role of the military in internal security, resolve the 'grey areas', and institute appropriate mechanisms for political direction and parliamentary and judicial oversight mechanisms.
>
> (ICG 2004: 22)

Given that one of the architects of the New Paradigm is the current president of Indonesia, then the prospects for continuing reform might be expected to be bright. But the very fact that Yudhoyono is an ex-military man may make him reluctant to implement some of the reform initiatives as enthusiastically as he might. Before attempting to assess the overall prospects for SSR in Indonesia, therefore, it is worth examining how the reform process has progressed under Yudhoyono thus far.

The Yudhoyono era

At the outset, it is important to note that Yudhoyono has publicly committed himself to reforming Indonesia's security sector and, according to his spokesman, has committed to pursue the reform agenda within five years.[18] The focus of the reform endeavour is purported to be threefold. First, entrench the military's withdrawal from politics – a cornerstone of the New Paradigm. Second, reduce the military's role in business. Finally, work towards the professionalisation of the military.[19]

As this final section demonstrates, however, in practice the government has been less than willing to pursue its reform agenda.

There are a number of domestic and international dynamics that exert a powerful influence on the Yudhoyono presidency and create pressure on the government to establish a reform agenda. At the international level, it is difficult to overstate the importance of the 'war on terror' and the profoundly reconfigured geopolitical context with which the Yudhoyono administration must contend. As far as the US is concerned, the overwhelming priority it has given to combating global terrorism has meant that the entire Southeast Asian region is now seen in a very different light (Beeson 2004; Glassman 2006).[20] Of late, Indonesia is considered as a 'voice of moderation in the Islamic world', and one that must be nurtured and supported if it is not to succumb to radical, anti-American fundamentalism. Consequently, Washington has decided to resume full cooperation with the Indonesia military, including defence funding and vital re-equipping of the TNI (Guerin 2005). This attitude has been mirrored by Australia which, in 2006, signed a bilateral agreement with Indonesia (the 'Treaty of Lombok') which enhanced security cooperation without demanding moves towards security sector reform or improvements in the Indonesian security forces' human rights record. Indeed, Australia went as far as to renounce support or sympathy with Indonesia's various separatist movements (especially West Papuans), effectively giving a green light for Indonesia to use whatever means it deems necessary to quash resistance. In short, one of the principal potential sources of reformist pressure on Indonesia and its armed forces has been significantly reduced, if not eliminated altogether. Thus, one regional analyst has argued that the 'war on terror' has provided an opening for the TNI to reassert itself and maintain its autonomy.[21]

This problem is compounded by the fact that Western donors have been reluctant to engage directly with the TNI, at least in part because of its poor human rights record. USAID, for example, runs programmes supporting SSR in Indonesia but does not directly work with the TNI, operating through and funding local NGOs instead. It goes without saying that this significantly limits the potential for externally driven reform of the TNI and creates a gap between those actors and agencies involved in the SSR process and the TNI, arguably the most significant actor in the Indonesian security sector.[22]

Nevertheless, Indonesia now has an increasingly vociferous civil society, and a continuing democratisation process that has evinced much admiration and optimism.[23] According to Lex Rieffel, for example, Indonesia's 'democratic system has been overhauled quietly but brilliantly, and the foundations for a better system of governance have been put in place' (Rieffel 2004: 98). Certainly there have been improvements, of which Yudhoyono's own direct election by the Indonesian people is, perhaps, the most important and impressive. Likewise, the steady reduction of the military's formal participation and presence in the political system that Suharto initiated has continued, to a point where they have entirely lost their reserved seats in parliament (Asmarani 2004). Yet, as remarkable as this apparent consolidation of democratic rule may be, at the more mundane levels of day-to-day administration and governance the picture is less rosy. Not only does much of the patrimonialism, corruption and patronage that became the leitmotif of the Suharto era remain in place, but so, too, do many of individuals that constituted it (Robison and Hadiz 2004). Corruption is still pervasive and it is noteworthy that the legal system has been consistently unwilling to prosecute members of the military for notorious human rights abuses in places like Timor (Rusli 2004).[24] Equally significantly, the fact that the current president and one of his former presidential rivals (Wiranto) are both military men serves as a powerful reminder of just how influential the armed forces remain in Indonesia.

Given this continuing prominence, the TNI Reform Bill of 2004 assumes an added significance. The bill is ostensibly designed to limit the military's involvement in political and economic affairs and was at least in part a reaction to external pressure for reform from the IMF especially, which lobbied for the abandonment of the territorial system.[25] But while the bill contains potentially important initiatives, the reality is likely to prove disappointing. One of the bill's key provisions calls for the military to relinquish its business interests by 2009. However, the success of this proposal will hinge, in part, on the ability of the government to make-up the shortfall in funding, which is similarly dependent on the health of the economy. There is nothing to suggest that – absent a dramatic reduction in the size and thus the cost of the military – such an outcome is likely. More worryingly, there seems to be an implicit recognition of this possibility within the bill itself, for there is no provision to do away with the territorial command structure and its underpinning patterns of economic activity and political patronage. As we noted earlier, the TNI's territorial structure is the basis of its pervasive presence in, and influence over, Indonesian society. Unsurprisingly, therefore, there was large scale opposition among senior officers to reforming the system which forced the government to think twice.[26] In the absence of an attempt to reform this basic structure 'the creation of new legislative frameworks for the armed forces is unlikely to have a significant impact on politics at the local level' (Mietzner 2002b: 26). In other words, as currently configured, doubt remains about the capacity of the proposed reforms to actually address the most fundamental aspects of the military's role.

In addition, it is not at all clear how the government will persuade the military to reduce its role in business, which remains one of the military's primary sources of income and provides a significant proportion of the defence budget. By the government's own admission, agreement on this thorny issue depends upon the government's ability to substitute government money for lost earnings from business in order to retain current levels of defence spending.[27] Given the strictures placed on the Indonesian budget, however, it remains unclear precisely how this would be funded. Several experts, for example, have argued that the principle barrier to professionalisation within the TNI is the absence of funds.[28]

Similarly, major doubts remain about Yudhoyono's own capacity – and even desire, perhaps – to rein in the institution of which he was for so long a part. Two consequences flow from this possibility: On the one hand, as the bill stands the president does not have the final say on the deployment of the military. Despite the TNI nominally being placed under the president's direct control, the military does not have to seek permission before deployment, and is accountable to the president only after the fact (Langit 2004). On the other hand, a potentially even more formidable constraint on Yudhoyono's ability to reform the military, which remains the most coherent and potent institution in the country, is the fact that he remains dependent on its support as a consequence of his limited authority in the parliament.[29] This helps to explain Yudhoyono's unequivocal opposition to the dismantling of the territorial system (*The Economist* 2004a: 28), without which any serious attempt at reform is not possible. The seemingly non-negotiable nature of the territorial command structure's status also helps to explain the widespread scepticism that greeted the TNI bill. Indeed, the purported necessity of fighting terrorism has been invoked by Yudhoyono and the TNI as a pretext for actually reviving the territorial structure (Scarpello 2005).

There have, however, been some encouraging signs since Yudhoyono came to power. In addition to a sense that he is personally more able and politically astute than his immediate predecessors, his appointment of the moderate figure of Djoko Santoso as chief of staff in place of Rymizard Ryacudu was widely welcomed (Burrell 2005). And yet the fact remains that many of the proposed reforms either look incapable of implementation or are actually not intended to bring about fundamental change at all. In such circumstances, it is difficult to be optimistic about the prospects for the reform process in general.

Conclusion

Indonesia presents formidable, institutionalised obstacles to security sector reform. Indeed, in some ways the very conceptions that inform much of the SSR literature are ill-suited to, or at odds with, the Indonesian experience. The idea that reform might involve encouraging the Indonesian army to 'return to barracks' and behave in a 'normal', professional manner that is exclusively focused on security issues is profoundly misconceived. As one of the most astute observers of the military's role in Indonesia has pointed out, the expectation that such an outcome would inevitably follow the downfall of Suharto was unfulfilled because 'there were no barracks to return to; TNI [had been] sitting in government-like offices in the middle of cities, small towns, and villages since the mid-1940s' (Mietzner 2002: 75). In other words, the military has become a deeply embedded, and – thus far, at least – indispensable and institutionalised part of Indonesia's broader structures of governance, not simply a security agency. Indeed, it makes little sense to consider questions of security and governance as separate activities at all in Indonesia's case in particular, or in much of the rest of East Asia either for that matter (Alagappa 1998). Even if the TNI were prepared to withdraw from its wider socio-political role it is unlikely such a move would be universally welcomed or indeed feasible as there is often nothing to replace it. In short, the historical role of the TNI in Indonesia confirms Alagappa's (2001: 453) contention that an effective, expanding military presence in all areas of society can 'crowd out' civilian institutions, reinforcing the power of the military.

The centrality of the TNI in Indonesia's structures of governance is, therefore, enough to make the idea of its simple withdrawal from its socio-political role problematic, despite all the criticism that has been levelled at *dwifungsi*. But when combined with the fact that the government simply does not have the capacity to fund the military in a way that would actually allow it to relinquish its pervasive presence in the Indonesian economy, then the prospects for reform are remote, even supposing the desire is genuine. In reality, of course, it is far from clear how genuine the reformist impulse actually is. While there has been much talk of reform, there has not been anything like as much action – the military's formal and significant withdrawal from parliamentary politics notwithstanding. While we have no wish to minimise the scale of the achievement that the consolidation of Indonesia's competitive electoral process and the election of Yudhoyono represent, we also need to be realistic about what this may imply. As we have seen, Yudhoyono has shown little enthusiasm for tackling the most fundamental obstacle to security sector reform in Indonesia: the territorial command structure and the networks of power, patronage and profit it encompasses. However, in the longer term, the declining legitimacy of the military and its wider socio-political role may be entrenching attitudes and expectations that will encourage the continuing decline of its socio-political role.

Thus, our sobering conclusion as far as SSR in an Indonesian context is concerned is that it will be slow, piecemeal, and highly dependent on the state of the economy. Having said that, the great paradox of Indonesia's independent history is that whenever Indonesia's economy has been strongest, its ruling elites have been least susceptible to external reformist pressures. For real change to occur in Indonesia, therefore, it would seem we will have to wait for the Indonesians themselves to take charge of the reform process, something that recent events suggest is beginning to happen despite some continuing impediments. In short, the reform process would seem to depend, in large part, on the consolidation of democracy and the resilience of Indonesia's emergent civil society. For as Alagappa concludes in his path-breaking analysis of security and governance systems in Asia:

> The deepening of democratic civilian control hinges on the continuation and strengthening of the pro-democracy forces and deploying such power to construct strong democratic institutions, including those necessary to exercise oversight of the military. Concurrent development of the state's non-coercive capacity to address the many internal and international challenges confronting these countries is essential so that reliance on state coercion can be reduced.
>
> (Alagappa 2001: 489)

7 The Philippines
The politics of polyarchy

Until the recent coup in Thailand, the Philippines had seemed to face the gravest challenges of any of our case studies – and not just in the area of civil–military relations. Most immediately, perhaps, the under-performance of the Philippine economy stands in marked contrast to most of its neighbours and helps to explain many of the underlying problems that contribute to social discontent and instability. Within this environment, the military has occupied a somewhat contradictory position, instigating the high profile coup attempts that have punctuated the recent history of the Philippines, but also, on occasions, supporting democratic forces. At the time of writing, rumours of new plots to assassinate the president, potentially explosive factionalism within military ranks, and the possibility of a full-scale military take-over fill the pages of Manila's vibrant and independent press. Although these events have been given particular momentum by a number of recent political scandals, the situation is not unprecedented. On the contrary, the Philippine military has not always been a force for stability, despite a familiar Southeast Asian preoccupation with internal rather than external security. On occasion it has been a major source of domestic violence and instability. Moreover, some of the most fundamental relationships between coercive and political power remain fluid and unresolved in the Philippines, contributing to an overall sense of uncertainty and dysfunction.

That the Philippines should have become a byword for ineffective governance, corruption, under-achievement and instability is rather surprising, given its historical trajectory. The Philippines, more than any of Southeast Asia's newly independent nations, seemed to have the most promise in the aftermath of the Second World War when it finally achieved independence. After all, as an English-speaking, ex-American colony, it seemed that the Philippines was uniquely placed to take advantage of the economic transformation that was about to gather pace throughout East Asia. And yet, despite some initial promise, the economic performance of the Philippines has fallen far short of that of Malaysia, Thailand and even Indonesia; its government has been conspicuously ineffective, and its military has been associated with political opportunism and self-aggrandisement, rather than the security of the nation. As we shall see, all of the these factors are interconnected and their origins can be traced to the pre-independence period and the malign influence of American colonialism in particular. Indeed, the Philippine experience gives strong support to two of the main themes and arguments of this book. First, path-dependency has exerted a powerful influence over the course of civil–military relations in the Philippines. Second, the dynamics and evolution of the relationship between civilian and military institutions need to be placed in a wider context that goes beyond the narrow confines of military culture or even civil–military relations, to embrace the overarching, historically determined social, political and economic setting in which such relationships are embedded.

One of the key arguments that we make in relation to the Philippines, therefore, is that the propensity for military interventionism can be traced to factors that extend far beyond the security sector itself. The colonial relationship, the course of economic development this engendered and – above all – the concomitant evolution of social and state structures this encouraged, have given a distinctive character and role to the military. Since the Marcos era in particular, this has given the military the opportunity and – in its eyes, at least – the right to play a major part in the political life of the nation. In the Philippines, therefore, we have seen a form of polyarchy in which separate centres of civilian and military power have developed, often operating in a state of tension. Occasionally such tensions have been resolved, but primarily because an ex-military figure has assumed the political leadership of the nation. This sort of instrumental civil–military accord reached its apogee under Marcos, when a form of authoritarian concordance took hold. In general, however, the underlying, unresolved tension between civil and military power remains one of the defining dynamics of the Philippine polity. Within this context there has been limited internal impetus for security sector reform and external drivers have been inconsistent.

We begin this chapter like the others, by spelling out the specific historical circumstances out of which both the military and the Philippines' distinctive social relations emerged. As we shall see, repression and violence have figured as prominently in Philippine history as they have in Indonesia's – something that helps to account for the military's poor human rights record and willingness to flout civilian authority. But the Philippines has faced even greater challenges than Indonesia in imposing its authority within the colonial borders it inherited from the Spanish and the Americans – a situation that remains unresolved and contributes to the both internal instability and the prominent role of the military. In short, the Philippines remains uniquely disadvantaged and the prospects for achieving the sort of social, economic or strategic stability that might underpin a form of constitutional order, appear remote.

The colonial legacy

Paradoxically, the Philippines has something in common with the very different colonial experiences of Indonesia and Malaysia. This anomaly is explained by the fact that the Philippines was unfortunate enough to have had two colonial masters rather than one, and both have left problematic legacies. On the one hand, Filipinos initially struggled for their independence against the Spanish (with some success), and subsequently against the Americans. Whilst such violent independence movements might seem to parallel the Indonesian experience, the Philippine struggle was unsuccessful, and independence was ultimately granted to the Philippines, rather than occurring as a consequence of an indigenous independence movement that would ultimately help to constitute the post-independence army. As in Malaysia, the prospect of a peaceful transition from the imperial power was a central part of more recent movements toward independence. Both the violent and peaceful periods of Philippine history have had long-term consequences which merit explanation if we are to understand the nature of the military and its subsequent role.

From the outset, contact between the Philippines and European powers has been characterised by an uneasy tension between resistance and collaboration. While there were those who were fiercely independent and resentful of external intrusion, there were also many who were prepared to cooperate with imperial powers of one sort or another. What distinguished Spanish colonialism, of course, was the centrality of Catholicism and the enduring Christian legacy that this conferred upon the Philippines. Consequently, in addition to all its other formidable developmental problems, the Philippines has had to contend with the being the sole substantial outpost of Christianity in an otherwise predominantly Islamic region. As we explain in more detail below, the potential for religious friction has added yet another level of complexity to the Philippines' post-independence history. The failure of the Spanish to either develop the Philippines economically or to establish complete control throughout the archipelago left a residue of religious difference and political independence that continues to undermine the capacity and authority of the central government in Manila to this day.

The failure of the Spanish to establish effective hegemony also led to the development of another enduring feature of Philippine society: the growth of an elite *mestizo* strata of landholders descended from Spanish colonisers who were able to consolidate a grip on economic and political power. As in the rest of Southeast Asia, Chinese merchants played a pivotal role in the Philippines' emerging trade with the rest of the world (Goodno 1991). Significantly, the Spanish were instrumental in actively creating an indigenous elite recruited from traditional chieftains who served the Spanish as tax collectors and providers of labour. Although the Spanish attempted to retain the more important positions in the governmental bureaucracy for themselves, it was inevitable that as incomes and education levels rose among the indigenous population, a sense of separate Filipino identity and a concomitant desire for independence emerged. However, it is important to recognise that even in the nineteenth century there was an 'ambivalence' in the position of the rising agrarian elite who did not want to endanger their privileged economic position through too radical a political transformation (Hawes 1987: 23).

If the principal legacies of Spanish colonialism were the creation of a new class structure, an underdeveloped economy that was skewed toward agriculture, and the dominance of Christianity as the principal religion, the main impact of American imperialism was the consolidation of a new political and institutional order. This is especially important when thinking about the contemporary Philippine polity and the prominent role the military has played within it. For as Hedman and Sidel (2000: 7) observe, 'the broad contours of recent Philippine history are best understood not against the backdrop of "traditional" Filipino culture or Hispanicised society, but rather in the context of the state structures erected and imposed in the course of the American colonial era'. Unlike its counterparts in Southeast Asia, the Philippine state has been notoriously ineffective and incapable of playing the sort of developmental role that has occurred throughout much of the East Asian region (Beeson 2007). This striking difference in the institutional capacities and competence of the Philippine state not only helps to explain the significantly inferior levels of economic development compared to our other case studies and East Asia more generally, but it also helps to explain the state's vulnerability to military influence or even take-over.

A number of aspects of American imperialism are worth highlighting. First, the US had never intended to become an imperial power and acquired the Philippines inadvertently as a consequence of its victory in the Spanish-American War. Given America's own anti-imperial origins and its normative support for independence, it is perhaps surprising that it took up the imperial burden. But in some ways the Philippines provided a template for a more generalised pattern of violent American foreign intervention, invariably on behalf of domestic business interests (Kinzer 2006). The tactics adapted by the Americans in the face of surprisingly fierce and well-organised opposition to their unwelcome intrusion was an extension of those employed against the native American populations decimated by the US own internal expansion, and were consequently just as brutal and bloody. America's military superiority assured that it would eventually triumph, but not before losing more than 4,000 of its own troops and killing about ten times that number of Filipino guerrillas and civilians (Kinzer 2006: 55).

The idea that the Americans might not be accomplished imperialists, is evident in a second, even more important, legacy of their rule. The political model that the Americans attempted to impose upon the Philippines, and which much of the indigenous political elite enthusiastically embraced, was arguably especially unsuited to the challenges of independence. In many ways, American colonialism reinforced the worst aspects of Spain's and overlaid them with an additional layer of ineffectiveness. On the one hand, American policy reinforced the influence of the landed elites by decentralising power relations and structures throughout the country. This had the effect of entrenching a form of 'bossism', in which the central state apparatus was subordinated to local strong men – a pattern that would be replicated at the national level during the Marcos era (Sidel 1999). On the other hand, this fragmentation of power and authority was exacerbated by the Americans' normative rejection of the sort of 'strong' state that would prove such a pivotal part of development elsewhere in the region. Indeed, the Philippine state is much closer to the sort of 'predatory' state found in sub-Saharan Africa, than it is to East Asia's developmental states.[1] In short, the Philippines has inherited the worst of all possible worlds. The net effect of all this, Paul Hutchcroft (1998: 23) argues, is that 'the Philippine state [is] incapable of guiding the process of late, late industrialisation via the statist model; it is, even more fundamentally, incapable of providing the administrative and legal apparatus necessary for the development of free-market capitalism'.

State failure and the associated vulnerability to military pressure have constrained political elites in the Philippines, despite the fact that the political class has often benefited from military activities. We need to recognise that the origins of inadequate state capacity and political impotence can be traced directly to the American colonial period and the failure to create robust institutions of governance. What was important as far as American colonialism was concerned, was 'untrammelled access to Philippine markets and productive resources' (Boudreau 2003: 257), not necessarily effective domestic government in the interests of the indigenous population. Consequently, America's direct involvement in the Philippines was dramatically scaled back following the initial imposition of its colonial rule. A special Philippine Constabulary (PC) was established under American auspices in early 1901 with responsibility for maintaining domestic order with the specific intent of suppressing the indigenous independence movement (Pobre 2000: 98). The PC would provide the nucleolus for the Philippine army when it was subsequently established; the police would also play a surprisingly prominent role in such processes in the immediate, unsettled aftermath of the Second World War. For despite the decline in America's overt presence, it is important to stress just how powerful an effect the general incorporation of the Philippines into a US-dominated international order proved to be in the longer-term: simply put, the introduction of capitalist social relations undercut and destabilised traditional patron–client ties in rural areas, triggering a protracted and bloody 'Huk Rebellion' in Central Luzon in the late 1940s and early 1950s as a result (Kerkvliet 1977).

A number of points about this period are significant for our purposes. First, the Huk Rebellion occurred in the context of the emerging cold war and America's concern about possible communist infiltration. Consequently, the US provided material support to the Philippine military in suppressing the rebellion. This helped establish a pattern of US-Philippine relations that endures to this day, as we shall see when we consider the impact of the 'war on terror'. Indeed, we need to remember that some of the first acts of the independent Philippine government in 1947 were to sign on to both the Military Bases Agreement and the Military Assistance Agreement – the former giving the US de facto responsibility for ensuring the Philippines' external security, while the latter gave it a say over its internal security (Goodno 1991: 42). The net effect of both was to extend the prevalent pattern of patron–client relations to the international sphere, and give the US a long-term strategic stake in the fate of the Philippines. The second point to emphasise is that once domestic stability had been assured, the other long-term impacts of American colonialism came to the fore: a commitment to free trade between the US and the Philippines, and the development of a democratic polity – albeit one dominated by the landholding elite and of 'low quality' (Hawes 1987: 25; Case 2002). These were factors that would exert a continuing influence on the trajectory and nature of post-independence development in the Philippines.

Thus, as the Philippines prepared to take up its long-promised and ultimately peacefully realised independence, it did so with some of the superficial trappings of modernity, but also with a number of unresolved social tensions and institutional inadequacies that would leave it chronically unstable and susceptible to military politicisation.

The development of the military

The principal institutional change in the early period of security sector reorganisation following independence was the formal separation of the PC from the military, which was renamed the Armed Forces of the Philippines (AFP) in 1947. The AFP was also separated into three major commands: the Philippine Ground Force, the Philippine Air Force, and the Philippine Naval Patrol. The Philippine Army was officially designated as the major service with its own separate command structure. Predictably, perhaps, another major innovation was an increased stress on intelligence gathering operations, primarily as a response to the intensification of the Huk rebellion and unrest in the south of the country. In a move that had echoes of Indonesia's dual function, during the Marcos era the military attempted to legitimise its special role within the state and society by playing a wider developmentalist role in the building of a 'New Society', in which the 'political, economic, social and psychological aspects of military operations' were given greater rhetorical emphasis (Pobre 2000: 560). In reality, however, such initiatives were occurring as part of Marcos' attempts to politicise and dominate the military and bind it to him personally (de Quiros 1997: 369–373). As a consequence, the military became an increasingly compromised and discredited institution.

Compromised or not, the military has always played a prominent role in the life of the Philippine nation. This was an entirely predictable consequence of Philippine history. After all, the Philippines, like other parts of the region, is a nation whose development and character has been, at times, powerfully shaped by violence. In this regard, the Second World War, which involved the invasion and subsequent expulsion of the Japanese, added a further layer of trauma to the earlier independence struggles. Many of the local elites who had cooperated with the Japanese subsequently assumed senior positions in the newly independent government and military. The army of the Philippines had actually been established before the war in 1935, with the assistance of General Douglas MacArthur, who was hailed by the then commonwealth president Manuel Quezon as 'the creator of the Philippine Army' (Pobre 2000: 268). The military that MacArthur helped develop became increasingly significant following independence in 1946, despite the fact that up to 80 per cent of Filipino officers were believed to have collaborated with the Japanese. Although such personnel were supposed to be barred from the army, enforcement of this provision was left up to the military hierarchy and not a single person was convicted of collaboration or removed from the services (Shalom 1981: 18). From the outset, therefore, there has been a noteworthy willingness to overlook misbehaviour by military personnel, a concomitant failure to punish disloyalty, and a lack of military discipline driven primarily by the military's own chronic weakness.

But although military indiscipline and an indulgent view of disloyalty have become increasingly entrenched, such attitudes have not always been entirely prevalent. The pivotal moment in independent Philippine history that entrenched and institutionalised a dominant, more politically interventionist, less disciplined role for the military was the declaration of martial law by Ferdinand Marcos in 1972. Prior to this, the Philippines was regarded by some well-informed observers as 'one of the last strongholds of civilian control over the military in the Third World' (Hernandez 1986: 262). Indeed, we need to acknowledge that in some ways American influence during the early independence period had the effect of cultivating a quite professional and well-disciplined military. We also need to recognise that the Philippine military has, from its earliest moments as apart of an independent, but impoverished Philippine Republic, been highly dependent on the continuing support of the United States (Pobre 2000).

From 1935 to 1946, when the Philippines was given limited self-government as a Commonwealth, the establishment of a small, professional indigenous army was envisaged as a major stepping stone on the road to full-independence. Alfred McCoy (1995: 692) emphasises that the first full class to be inducted into the Philippine Military Academy in 1940 'played a seminal role by inventing traditions'. A country that was not even formally independent plainly had little in the way of indigenous *national* custom to draw on, and was forced to adapt and improvise. Significantly, the new officer corps was modelled on West Point and this helps to explain the subsequent determination to remain an apolitical force that emerged within the original Philippine military elite – a culture that survived for some twenty years or so. Somewhat ironically, it was the achievement of independence that, in McCoy's (1995: 712) view, undermined the 'atavistic American influence' and 'opened the armed forces to greater political influence'. Crucially, however, the attempt to retain a sense of military professionalism and political neutrality became a potentially fatal obstacle to the professional progress of the Class of 1940 and its immediate successors, as the new currency of social and economic advancement became political patronage.

The consolidation of structures of patronage, cronyism and corruption had a predictably corrosive impact on Philippine society and its structures of governance. The Philippine state bureaucracy was notoriously riddled with corruption and patronage even before the Marcos era (Kang 2002: 75), but such relationships were potentially even more pernicious in the military where ideas of discipline and loyalty to the state might be expected to be paramount. In reality, some commentators consider that 'Philippine military society is where the traditional culture of patron-client ties…works best' (Kessler 1989: 105). Moreover, Kessler (1989: 106) further argues that 'in moments of crisis – indeed, in the moments in which most military men instinctively obey superior authority – the informal command structure controls behaviour'. As we shall see, this is a potentially important explanation of the dynamics that have underpinned some of the numerous recent coups attempts that have been instigated by the military. Before considering them in any detail, however, it is necessary to explain the influence of Ferdinand Marcos on the development of the military, as his administration had a greater impact on the sheer size, as well as the role and identity of the military, than any other factor in the post-independence period.

The impact of the Marcos era

While the rise of Ferdinand Marcos is rightly considered to be a pivotal moment in the history of the Philippine military in particular and the country's polity more generally, it was not unheralded. The counter-insurgency measures taken against the Huks by the 'corrupt, landlord dominated, and repressive' (Bello 1987: 13) administration of President Elpidio Quirino prefigured the authoritarian approach of the Marcos era. In addition, a growing domestic division between a broadly modernising, urban faction on the one hand and a traditional agrarian one on the other, were fuelling domestic unrest and political militancy. An increase in guerrilla activity on the part of the Maoist-inspired New People's Army (NPA), which was established in 1968, added to a general sense of crisis. While a series of bombings and political assassinations provided the trigger for Marcos to impose martial law, it is important to note that American business interests in the Philippines remained highly profitable, but were jeopardised by continuing instability. When combined with the prospect of political militancy and communist insurgency there was a subsequent willingness on the part of the US to attach a low priority to democratic reform. Indeed, for our purposes, what is of greatest significance is not just that there was predictable support for martial law from the ruling elite and Manila's American community, but also that it enjoyed widespread support within the ranks of the military (Goodno 1991: 67).

Although the imposition of martial law and the AFP's role in it further undermined the legitimacy of a military institution that commanded little authority amongst the mass of the population, it had tangible short-term benefits for the military itself. Marcos recognised that the military was both a source of power – inevitably so under martial law – and a potential threat. Consequently, he 'built a political career by currying the military's favour' (Kessler 1988: 218). Marcos himself initially served a Secretary of Defence and oversaw a major reorganisation and expansion of the military in the process. Between the declaration of martial law in September 1972 and his downfall in 1986, the AFP's personnel expanded from 60,000 to 250,000 (Goodno 1991: 71). All of the services benefited, including the Philippine Constabulary, which roughly doubled in size to 43,500 by the early 1980s (Berry 1986). At the beginning of the Marcos era, and in a direct effort to retain the loyalty of the military, all senior officers were promoted one grade, pay was increased, the military became more involved in economic activities, and positions were found in government corporations for senior military figures (Kessler 1989: 124). Much of the money for this largesse and patronage was provided by the Americans who funnelled additional support to a strategically crucial cold war ally, an importance that was underscored by the Philippines' proximity to Vietnam.

Marcos managed to manipulate the promotion and appointment process within the military to ensure that key senior officers were personally loyal to him.

Politicisation involved handing out perks and promotions to favoured officers, subverting the military's own promotion system.[2] The most egregious example of this was the rapid promotion of his cousin and former chauffeur, Fabian C. Ver, who advanced from captain to brigadier general within the space of five years. Even more ominously, Ver was eventually put in charge of an enlarged National Intelligence and Security Agency (NISA), which reported directly to the president. The relative institutional importance of the AFP was diminished as a consequence of these manoeuvres, sowing the seeds for Marcos' eventual downfall: increasing numbers of junior officers were either not enamoured of his methods or not recipients of his favours. Yet for much of his period in power 'the AFP evolved into Marcos's "praetorian guard" rather than a professional military institution' (Hedman and Sidel 2000: 47). The military was complicit in a process that undermined democratic institutions and accountable government, with the consequence that:

> The destruction of political institutions and processes during the Marcos dictatorship and the resulting military role expansion beyond defense and security and law and order provided the environment for the politicization of a significant number of officers in the AFP. The supremacy of civilian authority over the military, secured by various institutional controls was transformed into one secured primarily by the person of Marcos.
>
> (Davide *et al.* 1990: 475–476)

Eventually, however, disenchantment with Marcos and his methods within the ranks of junior officers culminated in the formation of 'RAM', or the Reform the Armed Forces of the Philippines Movement. The so-called RAM boys continued to play a prominent role in shaping the role of the military and in the conduct of the numerous coup attempts that took place in the late 1980s. As such, they are emblematic of a major transformation in the military elite's self-identity, culture and sense of purpose that occurred between the Class of 1940, which adhered to a comparatively strict code of honour and professionalism, and the Class of 1971, which was the prime mover behind the instigation of RAM. McCoy (1999: 258) argues that the transformation in the values and behaviour of the military can be accounted for by the fact that

> The RAM colonels, liberated from their military socialization, were single-minded in their reach for power, exploiting their position inside the military to mobilize coup after coup. Their attempts drew support, passive and active, from an officer corps clinging to privilege won under martial rule and trying, above all, to avoid prosecution for human rights violations done in service to the dictatorship.

Put differently, the military was transformed under Marcos from an institution that was under the command of, and responsive to, civilian authorities, to one bent on its own diverse purposes and absorbed with the protection of its own welfare.

Coups became a familiar, frequently employed mechanism with which to ensure the political acquiescence and impotence of civilian governments. The government of Corazon 'Cory' Aquino, which eventually took over from Marcos following the assassination of her husband on his return from exile, existed in a condition of continual tension and uncertainty as a direct consequence of the very institution that was nominally responsible for ensuring domestic security. The upshot of this 'season of coups' was that, as McCoy (1999: 260) wryly observes, 'six years and nine coup attempts later, a shaken civil state would abandon any attempt at prosecution [of human rights violations] and instead try to placate a rebellious officer corps'.

The evolution of civil–military relations after Marcos

The 'people power' revolution that brought about the downfall of Marcos and the eventual installation of Cory Aquino attracted world-wide attention and appeared to mark a return to civilian rule and the unambiguous restoration of democracy. Although the formal structures of the democratic process remain largely in place, the authority of civilian governments has been frequently challenged by the military. Indeed, the only period in which the military has not represented a direct or indirect challenge to popular sovereignty was during the administration of Fidel Ramos, who was himself a former military officer. It is somewhat surprisingly, therefore, that, as in Thailand (see Chapter 5) elements of the military leadership are currently attempting to position themselves as protectors of democracy and bastions of national stability. However, before we can assess current developments and the military's continuing challenge to civilian authorities, we need to look more closely at the evolution of civil–military relations in the post-Marcos period. We shall demonstrate that continuing tensions in the political field cannot be separated from the disappointing performance of the economy, which has undermined the authority of the political class and frustrated the military's desire to modernise and re-equip itself.

Managing the military

The so-called EDSA revolution[3] that brought Cory Aquino to power did not resolve the issue of the military's relationship with the civilian government. On the contrary, as a consequence of its integral role in the Marcos administration, the military came to believe that, not only were civilian authorities actually reliant on the military to govern and maintain order, but it had a right to be part of the political process as a consequence. This was underlined by their support for the democratic transition during 'EDSA 1'.[4] Rather than necessarily seeing the restoration of civilian rule as a return to normality, many in the military considered the post-Marcos transformation to be indicative of restraint and magnanimity on the military's part (Selochan 1989: 7–12). In other words, far from believing that the military ought necessarily to be subordinate to a democratic government, some in the senior ranks of the AFP believed that it was the most powerful institution in the country and that civilian authority enjoyed supremacy only as a result of military acquiescence.

In an environment in which the military considered itself to be both more powerful and often more competent than its notional civilian masters, the Aquino government further inflamed the military's wounded sense of dignity by concentrating on more broadly based developmental processes and allowing military salaries to fall. Exacerbating this economic decline was what can only be described as more broadly based blows to the military's self-esteem: on the one hand, the AFP no longer enjoyed the privileged access to the president it had under the discredited Marcos era. On the other, the fact that the new president was a woman had a major psychological impact on the military and its self-image and standing – a factor that was noted by the Davide Commission's (1990: 476) inquiry into the proliferation of coups during the Aquino administration. The Commission also highlighted the fact that the perpetrators of the coup attempts in the 1980s were not subsequently disciplined, establishing a pattern of behaviour that has been followed subsequently, with disastrous consequence as far as coup-deterrence is concerned (Davide *et al.* 1990: 479).

Difficult to quantify though it may be, the significance of 'machismo' and a culture of aggressive masculinity has been a prominent part of both military culture and of Philippine society more generally (McCoy 1999). As such, it is something that sets the Philippines apart from our other examples, and a potentially important part of any explanation of the Philippines' particular problems and social dynamics. The fact that former action movie hero Joseph 'Erap' Estrada managed to become president with no experience in political office and few obvious qualifications other than a mass following is indicative of this possibility.[5] Likewise, it is no coincidence that one of the most prominent and consistent of the coup plotters – Colonel Gregorio 'Gringo' Honasan – was able to use his personal charisma to not only cultivate a loyal coterie of junior officers to assist him in his multiple attempts to overthrow the government, but also to create a much wider public personae; something that appeared to render him immune from prosecution and punishment despite being associated with most of the attempted coups that continue to plague various administrations to this day.[6]

In this context, it is important to note another anomaly in the Philippine situation. It might be supposed, for example, that the existence of a vibrant and largely independent press might be expected to act as a constraint on the anti-democratic excesses of the military. Indeed, the existence of such a media is widely considered a precondition for democratisation. Although the press frequently has played an important role in exposing military activities, plots and internal struggles – often at great personal risk[7] – it has also been used by members of the military for self-promotion and to undermine the civil authorities. The 'RAM boys' were able to use the media to project themselves as a modernising force operating in defence of the nation, despite their destabilising and insubordinate role. Many of them continued to promote themselves when they chose to shift from the military to undertake more conventional political careers within the democratic process.[8]

As for the coup attempts themselves, they were frequently almost comically incompetent and reflective of both indiscipline and hubris, as well as the factionalism and lack of professionalism within the military itself. But even the most farcical, like the 'Manila Hotel coup', which collapsed in a day without a shot being fired, had larger ramifications. Not only did they feature many of the 'usual suspects' like Honasan and defence minister Juan 'Ponce' Enrille, but the complete failure subsequently to punish any of the plotters established an unfortunate precedent and 'seems to have convinced [Enrile and the RAM colonels] that they could plot against Aquino with impunity' (McCoy 1999: 268). Even though subsequent coup attempts were more serious and involved the proposed assassination of Aquino, Enrile was simply dismissed from his post, while Honasan was made commander of the special forces school – where he was ideally placed to recruit more followers amongst the ranks of the next generation of officers. Perhaps the most consequential outcome of this period was a significant reorientation of the Aquino government's priorities. Most immediately, military spending was increased, especially for middle level officers who had the potential to decide the outcome of future coups. The military's ranks actually expanded as a consequence, and the policy of negotiation with secessionists in the south and with the NPA – policies the military had never liked – were abandoned.

It is indicative of the military's continuing institutionalised power and the inherent threat they pose to civilian authorities that the only period of substantial economic and political stability came under the administration of Fidel Ramos, Aquino's former defence secretary and head of the constabulary under Marcos. Significantly, the Ramos administration was distinguished by the number of former military men who took up key civilian positions in defence and security, as well as in less obvious fields like transport and local government (Hedman 2001: 183). It is also significant that the Ramos administration oversaw a period of sustained economic development and reform (Hutchcroft 1999). The other particularly significant initiative of the Ramos government from a narrower military perspective, was the proposal to undertake a major modernisation programme – something that had been a simmering cause of discontent within the services. The fact that the modernisation programme took so long to even formulate, let alone implement, highlights two crucial issues that continue to shape the trajectory of Philippine development in general and civil–military relations in particular: the state of the economy and ties with the United States.

We have already suggested that the Philippines compares unfavourably as far as economic outcomes and state capacities are concerned to the other countries considered in this book, but also to much of the rest of East Asia for that matter. However, given that the failure of economic development has such direct implications for both the stability and security of the nation, and the capacity to modernise and equip the military, it is worth spelling out briefly just how parlous the situation is. Not only has the Philippines been burdened with a massive foreign debt as a consequence of the corrupt practices of the Marcos regime and the willingness of foreign lenders to underwrite his regime, to a point where debt repayments account for nearly 30 per cent of government expenditures, but tax revenues have also contracted, compounding the government's dire fiscal position (Hutchison 2006). Despite the praise heaped upon the Ramos administration for instituting a range of market-oriented reforms, the reality is that poverty, inequality and development failures remained endemic (Bello 2000).

The comparative developmental failure and chronic indebtedness of the Philippines would have been a major problem for the military and its prospects for modernisation under any circumstances, but it was made especially acute by a broader reconfiguration of the Philippines' geopolitical position. In 1991 the Philippine senate rejected the Philippine–American Cooperation Treaty and thus effectively terminated the Americans' long-standing basing rights. Previously considered unthinkable, the end of the cold war made an American withdrawal possible, but placed an added responsibility on the AFP, which suddenly found itself responsible for the external defence of the Philippines in addition to maintaining internal order. The significance of this transformation cannot be underestimated, as American military assistance in the form of loans or grants was thought to account for 90 per cent of spending on operations and maintenance prior to 1992. Equally significantly, the Ramos government was not prepared to finance an expensive modernisation programme of the AFP's conventional warfare capability, but 'required any modernisation programme to be subordinated to its domestic economic agenda' (Cruz de Castro 1999: 127). Indeed, it took another shock in the Philippines' strategic environment – China's occupation of mischief reef in 1995 – to overcome political opposition to significantly increased spending on the AFP.

Even though China's actions triggered an initial rethink of government priorities and an apparent willingness to fund a more conventional defensive role for the military, the state of the economy meant that this was effectively impossible. Economic constraints have recently combined with an upsurge of more immediate, domestically generated security threats and culminated in a new National Military Strategy, which proposes that the AFP should concentrate its limited resources in addressing internal threats, and that 'external threats will have to be overlooked until the AFP can redirect its resources toward them' (Cruz de Castro 2005a: 11). At one level, then, this is a reflection of the state of the Philippine economy and the inability of government to fund the military's conventional external defence capacity. At another level, however, it is indicative of just how pressing domestic security issues have become.

Insurrection, instability and the US

There is, of course, nothing new about this: economically , ideologically or religiously inspired insurrection movements have presented major challenges to the achievement of national stability and coherence since independence. In the aftermath of the Marcos era, violence and insurrection remained major problems. The Aquino government had to cope with the continuing actions of the NPA, as well as a widespread outbreak of vigilantism across the archipelago – something the new government was complicit in encouraging. Ostensibly such groups were allowed to mobilise in response to the activities of the NPA, but they appeared to be an extension of earlier forms of private armies and paramilitary bands. Although the vigilante groups eventually disbanded, they were entirely in keeping with the pervasive 'violent practices of Philippine political life' (van der Kroef 1988: 649). What is of particular significance for our purposes is the military's failure to make much headway in dealing with various sources of domestic instability, despite the massive increase in manpower, if not hardware, noted above. In reality the military's heavy-handed, brutal and repressive tactics actually inflamed insurrectionary pressures. Given that the Aquino government's attempts to achieve a negotiated settlement with rebel factions were not supported by either the AFP or – equally importantly, perhaps – the US (Bello 1987), it is not surprising that such attempts were abandoned.

While the threat posed by the NPA may have become negligible as a consequence of the ending of the cold war and the sheer length of the struggle (SarDesai 1997), the challenge posed by radical Islam has grown and proliferated. It is important to remember that no country in Southeast Asia has suffered more from the inherent artificiality of colonially inspired national borders than the Philippines. Indeed, there has been a secessionist movement of some sort in the southern islands for hundreds of years. Consequently, Philippine unity as an independent nation has from the outset been overlaid on, and compromised by, separatist struggles in the predominantly Muslim island of Mindanao. Although renewed attention has been given to this conflict as a consequence of the war on terror and the area's apparent role in the training of Islamic militants from around the Southeast Asian region, it is important to recognise that Mindanao has long constituted one of the main heartlands of Islam in Southeast Asia (Chalk 2001: 247). Resentment among Mindanao's Muslims has been inflamed by a Catholic transmigration programme, by efforts at assimilation, as well as a more general lack of economic development; factors that have fuelled a long-standing effort to secure greater autonomy if not independence. What is noteworthy about the current situation is the sheer number of different groups that have emerged, the radical nature of some of their agendas, and the capacity some of them have to destabilise the Philippine state. It is also important to note that the failure of the Philippine economy has exacerbated the problem and swelled the ranks of potential terrorists: not only does poverty fuel discontent, but some of the 8 million Filipinos who have to work overseas and make a living in places like Saudi Arabia become converts to Islam, potential recruits for radical groups, and sources of instability in the north of the country as well (ICG 2005b: 3).[9]

The strength of these insurrectionary groups has posed a direct challenge to the AFP. The Moro National Liberation Front (MNLF), which was founded in 1968 was within ten years able to field an estimated 30,000 soldiers, tying down some 70 to 80 per cent of the Philippine armed forces in the process. Equally significantly, high casualty rates and low morale amongst AFP forces led to mass desertions (Abuza 2003: 38). There were, however, tensions within the MNLF itself, which culminated in the formation of the Moro Islamic Liberation Front (MILF). The MILF adopted a more overt and radical doctrinal position, and rapidly became the most important vehicle pushing for greater autonomy. Two points are worth making briefly about these secessionist groups in the south. First, they represent a continuing challenge to the authority of the central government and the competence of the AFP. This challenge has provoked a variety of responses as a consequence, from attempts at negotiation by Aquino and Ramos, to outright confrontation under the troubled Estrada administration. The second point to make is that the MILF, which marked the further Islamisation of the conflict in the Philippines, is now thought to be cooperating with even more radical, transnational terrorist networks that have security implications that extend beyond the Philippines itself. It is claimed that the MILF has provided training facilities for Jemaah Isamiyah (JI), and organisational links to the Abu Sayyaf Group (ASG), all of which is further radicalising the domestic insurrectionary movement (ICG 2005a). In short, religion has come to be a more prominent, if not more primordial part of conflict in the Philippines.[10]

As a consequence, military ties with the US have been reinvigorated as America attempts to contain radical Islam across Southeast Asia. Despite the fact that some observers consider the threat posed by the region to be somewhat overstated (Gersham 2002; Hamilton-Hart 2005), the reinvigoration of US–Philippine military ties marks a major change of direction in the overall relationship, and one that has direct implications for the AFP. Even before the attacks on the US in 2001, the Philippines and the US had been moving toward concluding a Visiting Forces Agreement (VFA) in 1999, which not only allowed joint exercises with, and visits by, American forces, but saw the development of new programmes to re-equip the AFP, which was unable to maintain even basic equipment.[11] Despite this, there is continuing scepticism about the government's ability to deliver on its promises of renewal – partly because of the perennial budgetary constraints, but partly because of the rapid turnover of senior personnel in AFP ranks under Arroyo.[12]

In Cruz de Castro's (2005b) view, renewed strategic cooperation with the US came about because of a recognition on the Philippine government's part that they were incapable of maintaining the spending required for domestic security, let alone responding to the potential threat posed by the rise of China. While the US' own possible desire to contain the development of China and remain strategically engaged in the Asia-Pacific clearly meshes with the Philippine government's own agenda, it is the Philippines place as a 'front line state' in the war on terror that has seen funding rapidly increase, and overtake more general development assistance. Of the US$131.2 million assistance package for 2006, US$58 million was to go into defence programmes and equipment upgrades, with a further US$25 million set aside to support the Mindanao peace process (Contreras 2006).

And yet despite this partial rejuvenation of the AFP's finances, its future status, legitimacy and relationship with the civil authorities remains as problematic and uncertain as ever. Revelations about massive corruption amongst some of the AFP's senior financial controllers further undermined the credibility of the overall organisation (Rivera 2004: 130). While there had been a long-standing cynicism on the part of many Filipino politicians about corruption in the military and a concomitant reluctance to fund them (Cruz de Castro 2005b: 420), what is more surprising is the impact such revelations had within the military itself – or upon some of its more youthful and idealistic members, at least. The great paradox of the contemporary AFP is that, despite its own inglorious history, some of its members see themselves as bulwarks against the spread of corruption and the undermining of democracy. While such rhetoric is not necessarily to be taken at face value (Reid 2006), the contemporary debate about the role of the AFP and the continuing threat of direct intervention in the political process reveals much about both the current state of the military and the future prospects for reform.

The ever mutinous military?

In July 2003, the Philippines experienced its first coup attempt since 1989. The interim period had been one of relative stability under Ramos, followed by a gradual return to instability under the corrupt and incompetent Estrada administration. Current president Arroyo was formerly Estrada's vice president, and came to power following the latter's impeachment over corruption charges (Magno 2001). Significantly, she had the backing of the army during this process and fairly widespread popular support, although Estrada remains popular amongst the poor, despite the fact that he still languishes in custody. From the outset, therefore, the Arroyo presidency has been mired in controversy and lacking legitimacy – especially as Arroyo had initially indicated she would not run for the top job. The circumstances of her ascension – which some observers have also described as a coup in that it replaced an elected leader with an un-elected one (Neumann 2003a) – arguably helped re-establish a pattern of non-democratic regime transition in which the military has played an important part. Even if we accept that the military were broadly supportive of democratic impulses and reflected broadly based sentiment, its actions have tended to undermine the authority of the civilian administration and may help to explain the military's renewed enthusiasm for subverting the political process.

The first signs of this renewed proclivity for intervention in the political process were more a consequence of the military's failings, rather than the government's, however. The so-called Oakwood mutiny[13] was emblematic both of the tensions within the military and a more generalised sense of disillusion and frustration about the nature of the Philippine political-economy. Led by apparently idealistic young officers with connections to perennial coup instigator Gregorio Honasan, the main objective of the mutineers was to draw attention to pervasive corruption within the Philippines' security sector. The leader of the mutiny, navy lieutenant Antonio Trillanes, was both a persuasive spokesman for the disillusioned officers and a perceptive analyst of many of the military's problems. Trillanes had written a Masters dissertation on corruption in the navy, which detailed the extensive, pervasive nature of a culture of dishonesty, incompetence and kick-backs in the purchase of military equipment.[14] Even more seriously, Trillanes claimed that naval forces were in the pay of smugglers and pirates, and may have even been involved in directly assisting MILF and Abu Sayyaf operations (Neumann 2003b).

Although this episode ended non-violently, it was a huge embarrassment for the Arroyo government as it tried to convince prospective international investors that the country was stable. It also revealed both the continuing extent of military ill-discipline, as well as the lack of respect, if not contempt, many in the military have for the conventional political system. As Neumann (2003a) perceptively points out, 'That raising grievances through force of arms is considered a viable option by elite young officers is itself a dramatic example of how far the rule of law has been eroded in the Philippines and how deeply corruption undermines confidence in the country's many failed institutions.' There was an equally predictable failure of the country's political and security institutions to respond decisively to this challenge: not only has little been done to implement reforms and address the officers grievances (Kaufman 2004), but the officers themselves have received little if any punishment (Laude 2005). The failure to act decisively against the mutineers is especially significant and troubling given that the government-commissioned Feliciano Commission (2003: 33) concluded that the rebellion was not simply a spontaneous act but part of a long-standing attempt to 'achieve political change by military force'. More significantly in the long run, perhaps, the Commission (2003: 35 & 39) concluded that the renewed coup activity was a consequence of 'a general decline of professionalism in the AFP officer corps', on one hand, and a 'failure on the part of the government to enforce the law', on the other.

This indulgent or timid approach to the military on the part of successive administrations has been highlighted by successive post-coup investigative Commissions. While this attitude to the military may be understandable given its history, the Arroyo government is especially vulnerable and lacking in independence and legitimacy in this context. Not only did Arroyo's own accession to the presidency occur in controversial circumstances and necessitate military acquiescence in its realisation,[15] but her subsequent behaviour has further undermined her standing and authority. In what became known as the 'Hello Garci' scandal, the president was accused of electoral fraud after tapes emerged of her apparently attempting to rig the vote during a conversation with electoral commissioner Virgillo 'Garci' Garcillano. This scandal came on top of earlier accusations against Arroyo's son, brother-in-law, and husband, who were believed to be receiving money from illegal gambling activities (Son 2005). Despite a plunge in her popularity and a failed impeachment attempt, Arroyo refused to quit.

It was against this backdrop of a highly unpopular, polarising presidential figure, faced with the prospect of yet another display of 'people power', that the latest 'coup attempts' emerged. Although some of the details remain confused and uncertain, what is clear is that a number of prominent figures, including five members of the House of Representatives, 'communist rebel leaders', members of the military and – almost inevitably – coup veteran Honasan, were arrested and charged with plotting to overthrow the government (International Herald Tribune 2006; Ubac and del Puerto 2006). The divisions within, and lack of discipline of, the military had been evident when Trillanes, the leader of the failed Oakwood mutiny, was able to conduct press interviews on the shortcomings of the Arroyo administration from the Villamor Air Base, where he was in detention. Even more bizarrely, opportunistically and alarmingly, four of his fellow plotters were able to escape from custody and seek sanctuary with what appeared to be a resurgent NPA.

The most significant short-term consequence of what seems to have been yet another poorly organised coup attempt with only limited popular or – more importantly – military support, was the declaration of state of national emergency. Given the history of martial law under Marcos this was a highly unpopular step and appeared to many observers in the Philippines to presage a significant diminution of its democratic traditions. High profile Philippine columnist Amando Doronila (2006: 1) argued that martial law

> [G]ave the military a franchise to implement repressive security measures and to reassert messianic interventionism that had been lurking just underneath the surface since 1986. The state of emergency allowed the soldiers, on whom the civilian government is more dependent than ever, to enforce repressive measures on society and to hold the government hostage.

Such views were far from uncommon. Former president Fidel Ramos, for example, described the declaration of martial law as the 'beginnings of authoritarianism' (Diaz 2006). Although significant parts of the military appeared to remain loyal to Arroyo, she remained a seriously compromised figure whose continuance in office seemed to be entirely dependent on the support of key 'loyal' senior officers. Indeed, AFP spokesperson colonel Tristan Kison claimed, in a widely noted and resented announcement, that 'we [the military] are one of the strong pillars holding the nation. If we break, the nation will collapse' (Pazzibugan and Tubeza 2006). However, it was not simply the ubiquity and prominence of military and police figures in the aftermath of the coup that irritated many Filipinos, but the military's self-serving hypocrisy. The remarks of current AFP chief of staff Generoso S Senga, who was largely responsible for defusing the coup attempt, were important and representative. On the one hand Senga (2006: B 11) rather sanctimoniously claimed that 'the political culture based on patronage that persists in our society clashes with the military system based on merit and competence', whilst simultaneously conceding that 'we may not have seen that last of the attempts at power grab' [sic].

Given that this could be read as a none too subtle threat to the civilian authorities, there is no small irony in the fact that the alleged coup plotters led by brigadier Danilo Lim – like so many of his colleagues, a veteran of several earlier coup efforts – claimed to be acting in defence of democracy and against rampant fraud and corruption. Despite that fact that Lim and the other alleged plotters have been arrested, and despite the declared intention of not offering the ringleaders amnesties as has invariably happened in the past (Bergonia 2006), there is little reason to be confident that the offenders will be punished, or that this episode will mark the end of such challenges to civilian authority. The culture of insubordination and ill-discipline is deeply entrenched and likely to remain so. As an editorial writer in the *Philippine Star* (2006) wearily observed, continued mutinies are 'what happens when you punish coup plotters with 20 push-ups, reinstate them and even promote them'.[16]

When even seasoned and sober observers like former President and military leader Fidel Ramos observe that 'there would be no end to mutinies because the AFP was "dangerously politicised" ' (Balana 2006), then it is safe to assume that a renewed enthusiasm for political interventionism on the part of the military is unlikely to disappear. When seen in the context of a factionalised, ill-disciplined military then the reform efforts that have been undertaken thus far look hopelessly inadequate and almost certain to fail. Although the AFP has developed a comprehensive reform plan which it assiduously promotes,[17] it does not specifically address the problem of corruption in the military (Pamintuan 2005). There are consequently no independent mechanisms with which to ensure that such practices are controlled. Given that this is plainly one of the most serious obstacles to making the AFP a more professional and accountable body then it is difficult to see how meaningful reform is to be achieved under the current regime.

There are, however, even more formidable, systemic obstacles to reforming the military. Not only is the Philippine economy still incapable of supporting the mass of the people, let alone the cost of re-equipping and adequately training the military, but the country itself remains mired in political crisis. In addition to the problems that flow from having a president who is widely seen as illegitimate and corrupt, the Philippines appears to be moving toward major constitutional change and embracing a parliamentary system of government. While such initiatives may be understandable given the political paralysis that often characterises the current American-based system, some observers consider that such a change – if it can be realised – will simply concentrate power, entrench corruption and do nothing to address the underlying economic and social problems that plague the Philippines and profoundly compromise its overall security (de Leon 2006).

Reform initiatives that have been made have been driven largely by US influence and originated in the 1999 Joint Defence Assessment conducted by the AFP and American defence officials. The assessment identified deficiencies within the Philippines' security sector and identified potential long-term institutional reforms.[18] This initiative has delivered some progress in terms of fine-tuning reforms to the internal budgetary process. For example, in collaboration with the US, the AFP has reformed its internal budgetary process, separating the budgets for internal security operations and 'national development' (building roads, bridges, schools and so on), decentralising the budgets of each element of the armed forces, and introducing internal and external auditing.[19] However, even though the government formally committed itself to security sector reform in the wake of the 2003 coup attempt, trumpeting its appointment of a civilian as Defence Minister as an indication of its commitment to reform,[20] it remains to be seen whether this will have much of an impact in practice and there remain few details about substantive reforms in the pipeline.

Conclusion

Despite Thailand's recent problems, the Philippines arguably confronts the most intractable challenges in the area of security sector reform of any Southeast Asian nation. No other country in the region faces the prospect of continuing military intervention in the political process in quite the way the Philippines does. Indeed, at the time of writing there is still the very real prospect of a complete military take-over – something that has been publicly called for by one prominent former defence secretary (Antiporda 2005).[21] Perhaps it is fortunate for the civilian authorities in the Philippines that the military itself is so politicised, divided and lacking in the coherence and competence needed to mount an effective coup, let alone actually run a country as complex as the Philippines. In this context it was highly revealing that AFP chief of staff Senga, who effectively ended the most recent coup attempt, declared that 'I'm not capable of running the government, even if it's for a day' (Pazzibugan 2006a).

At one level this admission may help to explain a more generalised aspect of contemporary civil–military relations: running a modern political and economic system, especially one with complex international linkages and a reliance on external assistance and investment, is simply beyond the capacity of military officers. Unfortunately for the Philippines, it seems to be beyond the capacity of most of its civilian administrations, as well. Undoubtedly there are some competent and skilled public officials in the Philippines, but the state itself is weak and ineffective by comparison with its neighbours and often simply a vehicle for self-enrichment. True, this has been the case in our other case studies, too, to some degree, but they have managed to achieve a level of development that has generally eluded the Philippines, something that has compounded all its other problems and profoundly undermined the authority of its national government.

The outbreaks of 'people power' that have attracted such attention, and which are such a dramatic expression of popular sovereignty, are also emblematic of the incompetence and failure of the Philippines' political class. Corruption and maladministration have opened the door for a military that was politicised by the Marcos period and incapable of adjusting to its new status as a servant of civilian power. We need to remember that before the Marcos period, however, the military was a far more disciplined institution and not a threat to the civil authorities. We also need to remember that this was a consequence – in part, at least – of the benign influence of the American exemplar on the strategic culture and self-identity of the Philippine military. It is not entirely fanciful to suggest that the influence of a more professional, disciplined military like America's might once again instil values that might discourage the sort of political intervention and adventurism for which the AFP has become infamous. There are, in fact, some encouraging signs: at the time of writing, new chief of staff General Hermogenes Esperon Jr. has overruled the recommendation of a military panel to dismiss mutiny charges against 38 officers implicated in the February 24 coup attempt and ordered Major General Renato Miranda, Brigadier General Danilo Lim and 28 others to face a court-martial. Esperon stated that ' "adventurism" would no longer be tolerated within the military' (Pazzibugan 2006b). Unfortunately, such hopeful signs have been overshadowed by the abrupt, unexpected resignation of the Philippine defence secretary, Avelino Cruz, fuelling further speculation about rifts in the government about the direction of military reform (Landingin 2006).

Even more troublingly in the longer-term, and despite the fact that the American model of professionalism has once again been taken up as part of the mooted reform programm in the AFP (Pamintuan 2005), the possible benefits of such initiatives may be diluted by historically contingent geopolitical circumstances. Because of the Philippines' prominence in the 'war on terror', it is all too likely that concerns about reform and the cultivation of more professional attitudes will be subordinated to the perceived need to clamp down on supposed threats to national security – despite the fact that sources of insecurity long pre-date the war on terror and revolve around the feeble nature of key domestic institutions (Kraft 2003). The leverage that the Americans might have used to encourage greater professionalism within the Philippine security sector may be obviated by the need of AFP assistance in counter terrorism operations. Consequently, the marked shift toward a more authoritarian form of government (Ubac and de Puerto 2006) – in which the military appears to be an essential and increasingly influential partner – may be consolidated and actually facilitated by the contemporary geopolitical situation. In short, the Philippines may face the unappetising prospect of an increasingly illegitimate, incompetent government presiding over an under-performing economy, while remaining wholly dependent for its survival on a military that is increasingly politicised and beyond civilian control. In such circumstances the prospects for meaningful security sector reform look remarkably bleak.

Conclusion

In this brief conclusion, we will limit ourselves to offering some tentative answers to the questions we posed at the outset, namely to what extent has security sector reform taken hold in Southeast Asia and what are the main drivers and inhibitors of reform? The overall conclusions are fairly gloomy. Although the region's governments and security forces have, to a greater or lesser extent, adopted the language of professionalism and reform there have been few, if any, fundamental changes. To return to the schema that we introduced, it is fair to say that has plenty of 'fine-tuning' but this has not resulted in profound changes in the way that security sectors do their business or relate to other institutions. There are two sets of reasons for this. The first are domestic and relate back to the theme of path dependency raised at the beginning of the book and elaborated in Chapter 3. In short, the region's particular history and its place within the global economy and international society have helped create identities, institutions and relations that are both quite different to those that underpin civil–military relations in other parts of the world and which are deeply entrenched. Because, as currently conceived, the reform agenda implies a significant reworking of those identities, institutions and processes, it has inevitably struggled to find broad acceptance.

Nowhere was this contradiction between declaratory policy and underlying strategic cultures made more clear than in the 2006 Thai coup which installed the country's most prominent advocate of security sector reform, General Surayud, as unelected prime minister. As we pointed out in Chapter 5, the coup demonstrated that whilst security sectors might adopt the language of reform, it will only be embedded if it is internalised and becomes constitutive of the collective identities and interests of relevant groups and institutions. But surely, one might ask, didn't regions such as West Africa and South America confronted similar structural obstacles? Why have they had such a profound effect in Southeast Asia?

This brings us to our second set of reasons which relate to the international environment. On the one hand, for much of the post-independence era, the region's states have avoided outside pressure for reform. During the cold war, American military assistance was primarily geared towards defeating communism by whatever means possible. Arms and funds were transferred without much concern about the governance structures set up to control them. Similar trends have become apparent in the post-9/11 world. Not only has American attention shifted from reform to winning the 'war on terror', so too has that of other key states in the region such as Australia. The recent 'Treaty of Lombok' between Australia and Indonesia provides testimony to the changed priorities of the world's liberal democracies. Without external pressure, there has been little domestic impetus to do much beyond rhetorical fine-tuning. On the other hand, even in the brief periods where outside states have been actively engaged in promoting reform, we failed to find a case wherein progress on reform was linked to *serious* conditionality relating, for instance, to funding from the IMF or World Bank. Instead, outside actors have tended to pay lip service to security sector reform, which has tended to produce similarly, half-hearted, tokenistic responses.

The extent of SSR in Southeast Asia

Of our four case studies, Indonesia has – somewhat surprisingly – gone furthest in adopting the rhetoric, if not the reality, of security sector reform. In the course of our research we continually met academics and activists who were familiar with the SSR literature, keen to apply its potential insights, and doing their utmost to ensure that Indonesia's civil–military relations were reformed in line with international best practice. Such efforts are plainly encouraging and to be applauded. And yet the Indonesian exemplar highlights all of the problems that confront those who wish to make the transition from theory to practice. As we saw in Chapter 6, there are powerful, institutionalised impediments to SSR in Indonesia, which mean that little of substance has actually changed as far as the implementation of real reform is concerned. To move beyond the merely cosmetic to the substantive would require a transformation of Indonesia's larger, embedded and institutionalised structures of governance. Even more fundamentally, perhaps, meaningful change of Indonesia's security sector is unlikely to occur while the economy languishes and is unable to provide jobs and economic security for Indonesia's rapidly expanding population.

The inescapable reality in Indonesia is that the military performs a function and is organised in a manner that is inescapably antipathetic to serious reform. At one level, this is simply a consequence of the military's pivotal role as an instrument of governance with an unparalleled reach into every part of the Indonesian archipelago and society. It is also, of course, a not inconsiderable source of employment in a country that is struggling to provide jobs for its rapidly expanding, increasingly youthful population. At another level, however, the distinctive structural logic of territorial system and the associated patterns of patronage this has encouraged, means that there are powerful vested interests who at best are unenthusiastic, or at worst, actively hostile to reform. Crucially, the central government has little leverage with which to change the extant incentive structures or patterns of resource distribution. As a consequence, the sobering reality is that the Indonesian government is simply incapable of providing the economic resources that would allow a substantive transformation of the current system.

Many of the same problems confront the Philippines. Like Indonesia, the Philippine military is also currently involved in processes of internal review that are superficially in accord with the broad principles of SSR, and yet, as in Indonesia, the reality is frequently at odds with the rhetoric. Not only is the military seemingly just as great a potential threat to civilian authorities as it has ever been, but its capacity for meaningful internal reform and even discipline has yet to be demonstrated and sustained. There are, it should be acknowledged, a few encouraging signs and, as in Indonesia, there are some well-intentioned individuals who are attempting to bring about reform. Yet the underlying reality is that the obstacles to serious and sustainable reforms remain formidable. In the Philippines, we suggest, this is not simply a consequence of the military defending its entrenched interests – although there is, of course, plenty of that, too. In the Philippines' case, much of the blame for the repeated failures to reform the military must be attributed to the government. Despite the robust democratic traditions that exist in the Philippines, effective governance and leadership has invariably not been provided by the central government itself. At one level, this is an unfortunate consequence of the weak Philippine state that emerged after independence. At another level, however, it has been a direct consequence of a series of governments that have often been either corrupt, incompetent, or simply lacking in the authority and capacity to implement meaningful reform.

One potential bright spot as far as SSR is concerned was found in Malaysia, although even here, the picture was more complex and less rosy than we might have hoped. While Malaysia's military compares favourably in organisational and historical terms with its counterparts in most parts of the world, and is a beacon of professionalism by comparison with our other case studies, even here there is cause for concern. If the purpose of effective SSR is to ensure that the security services and apparatus do not constrain the development of civil society and undermine a more broadly conceived notion of human security, then even in Malaysia SSR clearly has some way to go – and not just as far as the formal process of reform is concerned. Malaysia serves as a salient reminder of the possibility that it is not simply the military that needs to be considered when thinking about the problem of SSR. On the contrary, unless we recognise that the security sector may be configured differently as a consequence of distinctively realised, contingent historical forces, and that it may serve particular, non-traditional functions as a consequence, then SSR initiatives are likely to miss their mark.

As we saw in Chapter 4, the most active and important element of Malaysia's security sector has been the police rather than the army. In some ways this is, perhaps, unsurprising: if there is one common denominator in the way Southeast Asia's security sectors have developed and operated, it is that throughout the region, the security services have been pre-occupied with *internal* threats to security, not with external challenges. That such perceived threats might have been met by the police rather than the army is consequently not as aberrant as it might seem at first blush, especially when we remember the circumstances in which Malaysia achieved independence: the negotiated, non-violent nature of Malaysia's independence process meant that a putative national army did not play a key role in its achievement as it did in Indonesia, and to a lesser extent the Philippines. Not only has the military in Malaysia not played the same historical role in independence struggles as its counterparts elsewhere, but neither has it played much part in maintaining domestic security in its aftermath. The particular structures of Malaysian society, and the political and economic practices and relations that have crystallised there, have meant that it has been the police and a compliant judiciary, rather than the military, that have assumed a conspicuous role in the maintenance of internal stability in particular, and the ruling regime more generally. This does not mean that the SSR agenda is irrelevant in Malaysia, but it does mean that it needs to be appropriately targeted.

If there was any doubt about the continuing importance of, and need for, SSR in Southeast Asia, the recent, entirely unexpected coup in Thailand dispelled it.

Drivers and inhibitors of reform

Our analysis of SSR in some of Southeast Asia's most important countries may make for somewhat dispiriting reading, but we want to conclude by suggesting – more in hope than expectation, perhaps – that there are at least some grounds for cautious optimism; a claim that may seem less outlandish if we briefly rehearse some of the key drivers and inhibitors of reform we have identified in the preceding pages. The obstacles are, alas, all too numerous, easy to identify and seemingly implacable. We suggest that, contrary to much of the prevailing wisdom in the literature on civil–military relations, however, the origins of many of the apparently most intractable problems in Southeast Asia's security sectors can be found, not within the ranks of the militaries themselves and their particular strategic cultures, but within the wider social and institutional milieu of which they are a part.

Some of the most distinctive features of the structures of security in Southeast Asia are a consequence, we have suggested, of the unique historical circumstances from which they emerged. The multiple, inter-connected challenges of nation-building, economic development and political consolidation encouraged an all-too-predictable preoccupation with security – especially internal security – across the region. In such circumstances, the military in particular or the security services more generally, were able to position themselves as bulwarks of stability. Even where this legitimacy was spurious and their ascendancy was contested, the lack of alternative institutions or actors with sufficient capacity often had the effect of consolidating military power. Even more disappointingly, perhaps, a willingness on the part of civilians or ex-army personnel to opportunistically align themselves with what was often the most powerful and capable organisation in the country, ensured that the military remained a dominant force, even where it was not actually running the government.

While the passing of Marcos, Suharto, and Mahathir may have marked the end of Southeast Asia's authoritarian 'strong men', as recent events in Thailand remind us, democracy remains fragile. Governments across the region may still be susceptible to capture by particularistic interests or lacking in the capacity to govern effectively and legitimately. In such circumstances, the threat of military intervention in the 'national interest' cannot be ruled out; consequently, the prospects for meaningful SSR appear rather dim.

At the heart of the region's difficulties in definitively overthrowing the old order in which the military and authoritarian rule have played such prominent parts, is a continuing dialectic between structure and agency. On the one hand, structural changes in the international and domestic systems have completely transformed the circumstances in which Southeast Asian politics, economics and security takes place. While there has been remarkable economic development in much of the region, formidable challenges remain and the development process in general – arguably more so than any other issue – remains the most formidable obstacle and inhibitor of effective SSR. Until and unless underlying structural constraints are overcome, which allow the region's militaries to be funded by central governments, and which provide alternative employment and economic opportunities, there is little likelihood of serious change.

And yet the very forces that have presented such a challenge to the region's post-independence political elites – international economic and political restructuring – may have also presented opportunities for those within and outside the region to promote reform and change. On the one hand, the integration of Southeast Asia into an increasingly global economy has presented opportunities for development. We need to remember that pre-crisis Southeast Asia was associated with remarkable and largely unexpected economic expansion, and although the quality and sustainability of that development may look to have been oversold in hindsight, nevertheless, real development did occur. It is possible – all other things being equal – that similar patterns of economic expansion could occur in the future. If so, there is compelling evidence to suggest that this will do more than anything else to consolidate democratic rule and thus civilian oversight of the military. It is a process that might also mean that external actors and agencies, as well as externally oriented domestic forces, could have an opportunity to encourage reform, although there is clearly a debate to be had about the nature and goals of the reform process itself.

Unfortunately, the relatively benign conditions that underpinned the earlier growth spurt look unlikely to be repeated. Although a consideration of the intimidating environmental problems that confront the region is beyond the scope of this book, we need to recognise that the pressures on Southeast Asia's fragile environment are mounting, unlikely to lessen because of population pressures, and have the potential to become a source of major insecurity and thus possible military intervention. Southeast Asia's modest record in managing intra-regional environmental challenges, and the frequently negative impact of external economic forces in exacerbating such problems, suggest that they will not be easily remedied.

The one potentially optimism-inducing conclusion we can draw from our case studies and the challenges that currently confront Southeast Asian governments is that the very process of governing effectively – even moderately effectively – may be beyond the capabilities of the region's militaries. The sheer complexity of running a modern economy seems well beyond the capabilities of many military personnel, as the disarmingly frank admission of the Philippines' chief of staff we quoted in Chapter 7 reminds us. Even 'national' economic management and development may prove too difficult given the nature of the challenge confronting

Indonesia and the Philippines in particular, and the necessity of placating powerful vested interests in the process. But when this process is made even more complex by the nature of manifold international linkages and relationships, then the problems are compounded. This is not to suggest that the governments of the region will, of necessity, assume a similar, functionally determined form, but it is to suggest that there are potentially powerful constraints operating on regional elites, whoever they may be. There are consequently potential points of entry for external actors who wish to encourage reform.

While this is potentially important from the perspective of encouraging SSR, at least, the historical record suggests that this may not be an unambiguous boon. On the one hand, external actors have often acted opportunistically, promoting reforms that suited their interests, but which were not necessarily beneficial for the region. The East Asian financial crisis remains the prime example of this possibility. On the other hand, crises in the broadly conceived security sector may trigger very different responses from those in the economic sphere, and actually *reduce* the reformist pressure on local governments and the militaries they ostensibly command. The increased prominence of the 'war on terror' in the policy agenda of the United States in particular has meant that earlier attempts at encouraging reform on the part of regional militaries have been largely displaced by more immediate security concerns. Whether this short-term calculus will deliver long-term security is a moot point; what is important for our purposes is that one potentially promising avenue of reform – well-intentioned external pressure – appears to have been curtailed for the foreseeable future.

The complexity of the multiple political, economic and security challenges facing Southeast Asia means that the 'foreseeable future' tends to be very short indeed, and always likely to throw up surprises like the Thai coup. Nevertheless, it is safe to predict that the militaries of Southeast Asia will continue to play pivotal roles in the development of the countries and region of which they are a part. The big question is whether this role will be in 'the national interest', or in the interests of the military elites that run them. Thus far, the record has generally not been good. But we need to remember that the militaries remain potentially one of the most effective institutions in countries with limited state capacities and infrastructure. They could still be a powerful force for modernisation and development, in precisely the way that some of their own doctrines and an earlier generation of civil–military scholars would have us believe. Security sector reform could offer one way forward. Given the stakes and the alternatives, there is little to be lost in trying.

Notes

Introduction

1 ABRI (Angkatan Bersenjata Republik Indoensia) was re-badged in1999 as the TNI (Tentara Nasional Indonesia).
2 One of the authors conducted extensive confidential interviews with a number of public officials and think-tank members in Indonesia who have been instrumental in shaping the course of military reform in Indonesia. They are generally familiar with, and have drawn inspiration from, the security sector reform literature.
3 This may reflect the fact that, according to one observer, the Reform Bill was mainly drafted by the TNI itself. See Lane (2004).

2 Civil–military relations and institutional change

1 Where 'external' refers to external to the bureaucracy – such shocks may be either national or international.
2 Though it may be sustained over a number years or even decades depending on the state's capacity to coerce and/or bribe.
3 Similar studies have been conducted on Southeast Asia. Crouch and Morley (1999) for instance argue that the propensity for future military intervention is dependent on the levels of factionalism and unity among military and civilian elites, a theme raised in some detail by Desch.
4 Thanks to Nicholas J. Wheeler for this point.

3 The historical origins of Southeast Asian security

1 For very different views on the significance of 'the West' see Huntington (1996) and Hall (1992).
2 For overviews of what is now a substantial literature, see Hall and Taylor (1996); Beeson (2002).
3 Costa Rica, for example, disbanded its army in 1949, suggesting that there is nothing inevitable about the form or even the existence of broadly similar institutions, and that they reflect specific patterns of social understanding and accommodation.
4 About 60 per cent of Malaysia's population are indigenous Malays or *Bumiputeras*, with the rest being made up of Chinese (27 per cent), Indians (7 per cent) and other indigenes.
5 Patron–client ties or patrimonialism refers to the personal ties and loyalties that exist between superiors and subordinates, and which may be the basis of power and patronage when part of a wider social and political system. See Brown (1994: 114–117).

6 Gaddis (1997: 35) argues that the distinction between 'benign' and 'malignant' forms of authoritarianism that US policymakers made in the context of the cold war allowed them to overcome their own isolationism and actively support non-democratic regimes.

7 Some of the most important and influential champions of Asian values were Malaysia's Mahathir and Singapore's Lee Kuan Yew – both noted authoritarians and strident critics of the West and its values. For a useful discussion of the issues and the significance of Asian values see Rodan (1996).

8 There is now a vast literature on the crisis and its aftermath. See Noble and Ravenhill (2000) and Robison *et al.* (2000) for useful samples.

9 'Globalisation' is, of course, a highly contested and rather imprecise concept. However, for our purposes it is a useful shorthand for what Held *et al.* (1999: 16) describe as 'A process (or set of processes) which embodies a transformation in the spatial organisation of social relations and transactions – assessed in terms of their extensity, intensity, velocity and impact – generating transcontinental or interregional flows and networks of activity, interaction, and the exercise of power'.

10 There is a substantial literature on new modes of governance and the growth of transnational, non-state policy networks. For important examples see Rosenau (1997).

11 There is a striking tension between America's unilateral and multilateral impulses, but two general points are worth making. First, the US is possibly the only country with the freedom to choose between them and utilise them in different circumstances. Second, the limits of unilateralism, and the possible long-term damage to America's authority and legitimacy are becoming more apparent to even the most hawkish and independently-minded of neoconservatives. See Kagan (2004).

4 Malaysia: constitutionalism corrupted?

1 Confidential interview Australian defence force official, Kuala Lumpur, 29 March 2005.

2 Interview with Zakaria Ahmad, 26 March 2005.

3 Significantly, the civil service, like the military, is dominated by Malays and there are frequently close personal and family ties between members of both institutions.

4 Interview with Zakaria Ahmad, 26 March 2005.

5 It is also worth noting that, unlike in Indonesia, the Malaysian military was seriously affected by the Japanese occupation in World War II. Whereas the indigenous military the Japanese controlled in Indonesia went on to form the backbone of the post-independence army, in Malaysia they were disbanded.

6 Interview with Mohammed JB Hassan, Institute of Strategic and International Studies, Kuala Lumpur, 25 March 2005.

7 Interview with Zakaria Ahmad, 26 March 2005.

8 Interview with Chris Forbes, Assistant Military Attaché, Australian High Commission, Kuala Lumpur, 23 March 2005.

9 Our understanding of the early development of the Malaysian military was influenced by discussions with Zakaria Ahmad in particular.

10 On the international background and the attitude of the British in this period, see Hack (2001).

11 Interview with Mohammed JB Hassan, Institute of Strategic and International Studies, Kuala Lumpur, 25 March 2005.

12 We are indebted to Chandran Jeshrun for highlighting the importance of Mahathir's personal 'anti-militarism' when accounting for the relatively subordinate position of the armed forces.

13 One of the most widely noted and distinctive features of security practices in East Asia generally has been their 'comprehensive' nature. Following the Japanese exemplar in particular, security issues are routinely considered to have economic and even political

components, as well as the more familiar military and strategic aspects that are central to 'Western' conceptions. See Alagappa (1998); Beeson (2007).

14 Interview with Zakaria Ahmad, 26 March 2005.

15 Confidential interview, Australian Embassy, Kuala Lumpur, 29 March 2005.

16 Indeed, Slater (2003: 93) argues that the Malaysian press is little more than a 'semi-privatized appendage of the information ministry'.

17 Interview with Mohammed JB Hassan, Institute of Strategic and International Studies, Kuala Lumpur, 25 March 2005.

18 Interview with foreign officials connected to the police, Kuala Lumpur, 29 March 2005

19 It is noteworthy that the most useful sources of information about the police and to a lesser extent the military are to be found in various online journals and internet outlets which operate fairly effectively outside of the control of the mainstream media. The major media outlets remain dominated and frequently owned by the government and consequently provide little useful information about, or scrutiny of, the role of the security sector generally.

20 Interview with foreign officials connected to the police, Kuala Lumpur, 29 March 2005.

21 Interview with Mohammed JB Hassan, Institute of Strategic and International Studies, Kuala Lumpur, 25 March 2005.

22 Confidential interview, Australian Embassy, Kuala Lumpur, 29 March 2005.

23 Confidential interview, Australian Embassy, Kuala Lumpur, 29 March 2005.

24 UMNO is a crucial source of funding for BN candidates and corrupt payments are a central component of the intense, factionalised power struggles within UMNO itself.

25 See 'The blurring of corruption and money politics', at the website of veteran journalist MGG Pillai (*MGGPillai.com*), a very useful – if generally un-testable – source of information on corruption in the police and government more generally that is not found in the government controlled mass media.

26 Malaysia has purchased arms from Britain, the US, Poland, Pakistan, Russia and is currently evaluating weapons systems from a number of other countries. There have already been a number of high profile scandals involving defence purchases, but Tan (2002: 34) believes that 'rampant corruption has been somewhat curtailed'.

27 Interview with Mohammed JB Hassan, Institute of Strategic and International Studies, Kuala Lumpur, 25 March 2005.

5 Thailand: military rule, there and back again?

1 We are grateful to Kevin Smith for this insight.

2 Interview with Suchit Bunbongkarn, Institute of Security and International Studies, Bangkok, 7 April 2005.

3 One of the best analyses of the rise and operation of Thaksin's government is provided by Pasuk and Baker (2004).

4 According to General Niyom, for example, the army is 'really thinking about the country. And in fact the army personnel brought democracy into Thailand'. Interview with General Niyom, Bangkok, 4 April 2005.

5 Changes in Thai politics has always involved a relationship between internal and external factors and this is also one of the core themes of this chapter. See Pitsuwan (2003).

6 The phrase 'extra-bureaucratic' belongs to Girling (1981: 120–121). As Ockey (2004: 144) argues, it is important to acknowledge the role of non-state state political actors in Thailand's political development. In relation to our argument, it is important to note that external and internal shocks could not have been translated into crises of legitimacy in the absence of non-state actors interpreting events and mobilising political support.

7 Interview with Arsa Sarasin, former Thai Foreign Minister, Bangkok, 5 April 2005.

8 Although there is no space here to go into detail about the early development of the Thai military, the definitive work on the matter is Battye (1974).
9 Fred Riggs (1966) famously argued that Thailand was governed exclusively by civilian and military bureaucrats for the furtherance of their own interests and he coined the phrase 'bureaucratic polity'. This has been rightly criticised by Kevin Hewison (1996: 75) for overlooking persistent civil society based resistance and for offering a static conception of government that failed to account for deep divisions and factionalism within the governing elite.
10 A position endorsed by Riggs (1966: 113).
11 The contrast between Thailand and Burma was emphasised by Sunait Chutintaranod, Chulalongkorn University, interviewed in Bangkok, 8 April 2005.
12 Interview with P. Sukhumbhand, Bangkok, 14 April 2005.
13 Thanks to Kevin Smith for this insight.
14 Interview with Suchit Bunbongkarn, Institute of Security and International Studies, Bangkok, 7 April 2005.
15 Confidential interview with Australian consular official, Bangkok, 7 April 2005 and Sunait Chutintaranod, Chulalongkorn University, interviewed in Bangkok, 8 April 2005.
16 Interview with General Niyom, Bangkok, 4 April 2005.
17 Interview with Sunait Chutintaranod, Chulalongkorn University, Bangkok, 8 April 2005.
18 Interview with General Niyom, Bangkok, 4 April 2005.
19 Interview with Dr. Panitan.
20 According to McCargo (2006), around 2002, 'the Thai government began to believe that violent incidents in the South were no longer fundamentally political, but reflected a complex pattern of criminal activity'.
21 Interview with Suchit Bunbongkarn, Institute of Security and International Studies, Bangkok, 7 April 2005. In this regard, evidence of rivalry in 2004–06 between the army and police in relation to jurisdiction in the south is important. Echoing informal opinions in the army, one leading commentator described the police as being 'like Mafia in uniform'.
22 Interview with Dr. Panitan.
23 Interview with Richard Ellis, RPA Services, Bangkok, 5 April 2005.
24 Interview with Dr. Panitan.
25 Though, by contrast, Bunbongkarn argued that public and parliamentary scrutiny of military procurement is 'quite strong'. Interview with Suchit Bunbongkarn, Institute of Security and International Studies, Bangkok, 7 April 2005.
26 Interview with Dr. Panitan.

6 Indonesia: from concordance to constitutionalism?

1 Since 1999 ABRI (Angkatan Bersenjata Republik Indoensia) has been known as the TNI (Tentara Nasional Indonesia). This latter term is generally used in what follows.
2 Early military leaders in Indonesia had quite different views about what the army's role should be, with some like Sudirman seeing it as a revolutionary force, while others like Nastution were more 'technically inclined' and in keeping with the orthodox military thinking. We are indebted to Bob Elson for highlighting this point.
3 Corporatism is characterised by state bureaucratic domination, monopolistic political representation, ideologically exclusive executive authorities, and anti-liberal, authoritarian or mercantilist states. See, Schmitter (1979: 22).
4 The 5 principles were: 'Belief in the One and Only God'; 'Just and Civilised Humanity'; 'the Unity of Indonesia'; 'Democracy Guided by the Inner Wisdom in the Unanimity

Arising out of Deliberation amongst Representatives'; and 'Social Justice for the Whole People of Indonesia'.

5 There is now persuasive evidence to suggest that the CIA played a prominent role in identifying 'communists' who were slaughtered in the aftermath of the coup.
6 For a detailed analysis of military management practices and the non-transparent nature of their business relations, see Widoyoko *et al.* (2003).
7 There is some debate about the extent of Chinese business interests in Southeast Asia generally, or in Indonesia in particular. Linda Lim (1996) estimates that ethnic Chinese business interests amount for only 4 per cent of Indonesia's population and yet control 75 per cent of private sector economic activity, with similar ratios in the Philippines (2 to 40 per cent), Thailand (10 to 85 per cent) and Malaysia (30 to 65 per cent).
8 Interview with K. S. Nathan, Institute of Southeast Asian Studies, Singapore, 14 April 2005.
9 Personal communication.
10 Suharto established his own *yayasan* while in Central Java, and was instrumental in establishing Kostrad's too.
11 Given the inter-connected nature of political, economic and even security issues in Indonesia, any reform initiatives were inevitably going to have a multidimensional impact, however they may have been couched – a reality that was insufficiently appreciated by agencies like the IMF which took a remarkably narrow, abstract and ahistorical view of the reform process.
12 Murdani brought about his own downfall after making the fatal mistake of drawing Suharto's attention to the excesses of his children's business interests. See Schwartz (1994: 285).
13 It is widely believed that military personnel linked to Probowo were behind a series of bombings and assignations that added to the overall instability around the time of Suharto's fall – lacing increased pressure on Wiranto who was responsible for overall security. See Honna (2003, ch. 7).
14 Probowo was demoted to head Sesko TNI, the army's Joint Staff and Command College.
15 For an overview of this complex period, see Case (2002).
16 This outline draws on Honna (2003: 166) and Rinakit (2005: 105–106).
17 There have been numerous examples of the military violently intervening in the political process, one of the most notorious of which was its invasion of Megawati Sukarnoputri's PDI headquarters in 1996. See Randall (1998).
18 Interview with Andi Mallarangeng, Presidential Spokesman, Jakarta, 18 March 2005.
19 Interview with Andi Mallarangeng, Presidential Spokesman, Jakarta, 18 March 2005.
20 It is not clear at this stage how the increased preoccupation with security will affect US–Indonesian relations, with some observers believing that the Bush administration's 'clumsy' conduct of the war on terror in Southeast Asia is alienating a rising generation and sowing the seeds of future tensions. See Bourchier (2006).
21 Interview with K. S. Nathan, Institute of Southeast Asian Studies, Singapore, 14 April 2005.
22 Interview with Marcus Meitzner, USAID, Jakarta, 17 March 2005. Also interviews with senior foreign defence officials in Jakarta.
23 According to one analyst, for instance, NGOs played a crucial role in lobbying for the TNI Reform Bill. Interview with J. Kristiadi, Centre for Strategic and International Studies, Jakarta, 16 March 2005.
24 At the time of writing there is a continuing struggle between the DPR, TNI and the government which wants to stop members of the military from being tried in civil courts for crimes committed 'outside the line of duty'. See *Tempo Magazine*, No 30/VI 28 March–03 April 2006.
25 Interview with Marcus Meitzner, USAID, Jakarta, 17 March 2005.

26 Group interview with Edy Prasetyono, Philips J. Vermonte, Andi Widjajanto and Makmier Kelial, Centre for Strategic and International Studies, Jakarta, 21 March 2005.
27 Interview with Andi Mallarangeng, Presidential Spokesman, Jakarta, 18 March 2005.
28 Group interview with Edy Prasetyono, Philips J. Vermonte, Andi Widjajanto and Makmier Kelial, Centre for Strategic and International Studies, Jakarta, 21 March 2005.
29 Yudhoyono's Democratic Party controls only 56 seats out of 500 and must rely on other parties for support to pass legislation. See *The Economist* (2004b).

7 The Philippines: the politics of polyarchy

1 On the difference between developmental and predatory states, see Evans (1995).
2 Interview with Ana Marie Permantual, *Philippine Star*, Manila, 13 May 2005.
3 It is called the EDSA revolution because many of the main events – especially the defence of some of the key conspirators in a military base – took place in or around the Epifanio de los Santos Avenue, popularly known as EDSA.
4 We are indebted to Jane Hutchison for highlighting the importance of the military's support of democratic processes during this period.
5 Estrada was elected mayor of Metro Manila in the late 1960s and became a senator in 1987.
6 At the time of writing, Honasan had recently been arrested for his part in the Oakwood Mutiny.
7 The Philippines is the most dangerous country in the world for journalists to work outside a war zone (*Manila Bulletin* 2006).
8 Honasan, for example, became a senator upon retiring from the army, despite his well documented involvement in numerous coup plots.
9 Ten per cent of Manila's growing Muslim population are estimated to be converts.
10 Thanks to Jane Hutchison for highlighting this point.
11 Indicative of the parlous state of the AFP's finances was the fact that equipment failures and shortages meant that the AFP was considered to be only capable of operating at 50 per cent of its potential capacity (Spaeth 2005).
12 Between 2001, when the Arroyo administration came to power, and 2006, when the latest coup attempts were instigated, there were no fewer than eight AFP chiefs of staff and four police chiefs (Cabacungan 2006).
13 Oakwood is the name of the apartment building in the heart of Manila's business district that was taken over by the mutineers.
14 Trillanes' MA thesis has been published by the Philippine centre for Investigative Journalism. See Trillanes (2001).
15 A combination of politicians, church leaders and the military decided to move against Estrada. Crucially it was the 'withdrawal of support' on the military's part that sealed his fate and led to what many commentators saw as the illegal installation of Arroyo in his place. See Neumann (2006).
16 Significantly, this is also the view of vice chief of staff Ariston Decos Reyes, chairman of the AFP Reform Implementation Group, who stressed that if the reform process was to prove effective and a new culture was to be instilled within the military, then mutineers would have to be punished effectively. Interview, Manila, 13 May 2005.
17 See, for example, *Philippine Defence Reform*, Department of Defence, Quezon City. This short document is necessarily short on detail, but the principal focus is on 'operational capabilities', rather than rooting out the long-standing sources of corruption and indiscipline.
18 Interview with Ernesto Carlino, AFP officer and UN peacekeepers, Manila, 13 May 2005.

19 Interview with Ariston Decos Reyes, AFP vice chief of staff, Manila, 13 May 2005.
20 Interview with Ana Marie Permantual, *Philippine Star*, Manila, 13 May 2005.
21 Despite calling for the violent overthrow of a democratically elected government, the police decided only to 'evaluate' the remarks of former Ramos government member, Fortunato Abat.

References

Abernathy, David B. (2000), *Global Dominance: European Overseas Empires, 1415*–1980 (Yale: Yale University Press).

Abrahamsen, Rita (2000), *Disciplining Democracy: Development Discourse and Good Governance in Africa* (London: Zed Books).

Abrahamsen, Rita (2001), 'Development Policy and Democratic Peace in Sub-Saharan Africa', *Conflict, Security and Development*, 1(3): 79–103.

Abuza, Zachary (2003), *Militant Islam in Southeast Asia: Crucible of Terror* (Boulder, CO: Lynne Rienner).

Acharya, Amitav (2001), *Constructing a Security Community in Southeast Asia: ASEAN and the Problems of Regional Order* (London: Routledge).

Acharya, Amitav and Richard Stubbs (1999), 'The Asia-Pacific Region in the Post-Cold War Era: Economic Growth, Political Change and Regional Order', in Louise Fawcett and Yezid Sayigh (eds), *The Third World beyond the Cold War: Continuity and Change*, pp. 118–133 (Oxford: Oxford University Press).

Adler, Emanuel and Michael Barnett (eds) (1998), *Security Communities* (Cambridge: Cambridge University Press).

Agence-France Presse (2004a), 'Philippines says Thai Muslim Deaths "Unfortunate," No Comment on Unrest', 28 October.

Agence-France Presse (2004b), 'US Concerned over New Violence in Southern Thailand', 29 October.

Agence-France Presse (2005), 'ASEAN Troops in Indonesia's Tsunami-hit Aceh to Remain', 17 January.

Alagappa, Muthiah (1988), 'Military Professionalism and the Developmental Role of the Military in Southeast Asia', in J. Soedjati Djiwandono and Yong Mun Cheong (eds), *Soldiers and Stability in Southeast Asia*, pp. 15–48 (Pasir Panjang, Singapore: Institute of Southeast Asian Studies).

Alagappa, Muthiah (1998), 'Asian Practice of Security: Key Features and Explanations', in Muthiah Alagappa (ed.), *Asian Security Practice: Material and Ideational Influences*, pp. 611–676 (Stanford, CA: Stanford University Press).

Alagappa, Muthiah (2001), 'Asian Civil-Military Relations: Key Developments, Explanations and Trajectories', in Muthiah Alagappa (ed.), *Coercion and Governance: The Declining Political Role of the Military in Asia*, pp. 433–497 (Stanford, CA: Stanford University Press).

Anatara News (2004), 'U.S. Demands Settlement of Timika Case to Recover Mily Ties', 22 November.

Anderson, Benedict R. (1978), 'Studies of the Thai State: The state of Thai Studies', in Eliezer B. Ayal (ed.), *The Study of Thailand* (Athens, OH: Ohio Center for International Studies, Southeast Asia Program), pp. 193–247.

Anderson, Benedict R. O'G. (1990), 'Old Society, New Society', in Benedict R. O'G. Anderson (ed.), *Language and Power: Exploring Political Cultures in Indonesia*, pp. 94–122 (Ithaca, NY: Cornell University Press).

Anderson, Mary (1999), *Do no Harm: How Aid can Support Peace – or War* (London: Lynne Rienner).

Antiporda, Jefferson (2005), 'Abat: We need a Junta', *Sunday Times*, 1 May.

Anwar, Dewi Fortuna (1998), 'Indonesia: Domestic Priorities define National Security', in Muthiah Alagappa (ed.), *Asian Security Practice: Material and Ideational Influences*, pp. 477–512 (Stanford, CA: Stanford University Press).

Anwar, Dewi Fortuna (2001), 'Negotiation and Consolidating Civilian Control of the Indonesian Military', *East-West Center Occasional Papers*, No. 4, February (Honolulu: East-West Center).

Aphornsuvan, Thanet (2005), *The Search for Order: Constitutions and Human Rights in Thai Political History* (Canberra, ACT: Asia-Pacific Cross-Border Online Rights Network, Australian National University).

Asmarani, Devi (2004), 'Jakarta Military bows out', *Straits Times*, 27 September.

Asmus, Ronald D. (2002), *Opening NATO's Door: How the Alliance Remade Itself for a New Era* (London: Columbia University Press).

Azar, Edward (1991), 'The Analysis and Management of Protracted Social Conflict', in Vamik D. Volkan, Joseph V. Montville and Demetrios A. Julius (eds), *The Psychodynamics of International Relationships: Unofficial Diplomacy at Work,* Vol. II (Lexington, MA: DC Heath), pp. 91–94.

Baker, Chris (2004), 'Civil-Military Relations in Thailand', interview with Kevin Smith, Bangkok.

Baker, Chris and Pasuk Phongpaichit (2005), *A History of Thailand* (New York: Cambridge University Press).

Balana, Cynthia D. (2006), 'AFP Dangerously Politicized – FVR', *Philippine Daily Inquirer*, 18 March.

Ball, D. (1993), 'Strategic Culture in the Asia-Pacific Region', *Security Studies*, 3(1): 44–74.

Ball, Nicole (1998), *Spreading Good Practices in Security Sector Reform: Policy Options for the British Government* (London: Saferworld).

Ball, Nicole (2000), 'Good Practices in Security Sector Reform', in *Security Sector Reform*, Bonn International Center for Conversion Brief, No. 15, June.

Ball, Nicole (2002), 'Democratic Governance in the Security Sector', paper presented at a UNDP workshop, 5 February.

Bangkok Post (2004), 'Gunmen Kill Three, Petrol Station Bombs Expected to Increase', 30 August.

Barkawi, Tarak and Mark Laffey (1999), 'The Imperial Peace: Democracy, Force and Globalization', *European Journal of International Relations*, 5(4): 403–434.

Barnett, Michael (1995), 'The United Nations and Global Security: The Norm is Mightier than the Sword', *Ethics and International Affairs*, 9(2): 37–54.

Barnett, Michael (2002), 'Historical Sociology and Constructivism: An Estranged Past, a Federated Future?' in S. Hobden and J. M. Hobson (eds), *Historical Sociology of International Relations* (Cambridge: Cambridge University Press).

Barnett, Michael N. and Martha Finnemore (1999), 'The Politics, Power, and Pathologies of International Organizations', *International Organization*, 53(4): 699–732.

Barnett, Michael and Martha Finnemore (2004), *Rules for the World: International Organizations in Global Politics* (Ithaca, NY: Cornell University Press).

Beeson, Mark (1998), 'Indonesia, the East Asian Crisis and the Commodification of the Nation-State', *New Political Economy*, 3(3): 357–374.

Beeson, Mark (2000), 'Mahathir and the Markets: Globalisation and the Pursuit of Economic Autonomy in Malaysia', *Pacific Affairs*, 73(3): 335–351.

Beeson, Mark (2002), 'Theorising Institutional Change in East Asia', in Mark Beeson (ed.), *Reconfiguring East Asia: Regional Institutions and Organisations after the Crisis*, pp. 7–27 (London: RoutledgeCurzon Press).

Beeson, Mark (2003), 'Sovereignty under Siege: Globalisation and the State in Southeast Asia', *Third World Quarterly*, 24(2): 357–374.

Beeson, Mark (2004), 'US Hegemony and Southeast Asia: The Impact of, and Limits to, American Power and Influence', *Critical Asian Studies*, 36(3): 323–354.

Beeson, Mark (2006a), 'American Ascendancy: Conceptualising Contemporary Hegemony', in Mark Beeson (ed.), *Bush and Asia: America's Evolving Relations with East Asia*, pp. 3–23 (London: Routledge).

Beeson, Mark (2006b), 'Does Hegemony still Matter? Revisiting Regime Formation in the Asia-Pacific', in Helen E.S. Nesadurai (ed.), *Globalisation and Economic Security in East Asia: Governance and Institutions*, pp. 183–199 (London: RoutledgeCurzon).

Beeson, Mark (2006c), 'Southeast Asia and the International Financial Institutions', in Garry Rodan, Kevin Hewison and Richard Robison (eds), *The Political Economy of South-East Asia: An Introduction*, 3rd edn., pp. 238–255 (Melbourne: Oxford University Press).

Beeson, Mark (2007), *Regionalism and Globalisation in East Asia: Politics, Security and Economic Development* (Basingstoke: Palgrave).

Beeson, Mark and Iyanatul Islam (2005) 'Neoliberalism and East Asia: Resisting the Washington Consensus', *Journal of Development Studies*, 41(2): 197–219.

Beeson, Mark and Kanishka Jayasuriya (1998), 'The Political Rationalities of Regionalism: APEC and the EU in Comparative Perspective', *Pacific Review*, 11(3): 311–336.

Beetham, D. (1996), *Bureaucracy*, 2nd edition (Minneapolis, MN: University of Minnesota Press).

Bellamy, Alex J. (2003), 'Security Sector Reform: Prospects and Problems', *Global Change, Peace & Security*, 15(2): 101–119.

Bellamy, Alex J. (2004), *Security Communities and their Neighbours: Regional Fortresses or Global Integrators?* (Basingstoke: Palgrave).

Bellamy, Alex J. (2006), *Just Wars: From Cicero to Iraq* (Cambridge: Polity).

Bellamy, Alex J. and Matt McDonald (2004), 'Securing International Society: Towards an English School Discourse of Security', *Australian Journal of Political Science*, 39(2): 307–330.

Bello, Walden (1987), *Creating the Third Force: US Sponsored Low Intensity Conflict* (San Francisco, CA: Food First Development Report).

Bello, Walden (2000), 'The Philippines: The Making of a Neo-Classical Tragedy', in Richard Robison, Mark Beeson, Kanishka Jayasuriya and Hyuk-Rae Kim (eds), *Politics and Markets in the Wake of the Asian Crisis*, pp. 238–257 (London: Routledge).

Berger, Mark T. (2003), 'Decolonisation, Modernisation and Nation-Building: Political Development Theory and the Appeal of Communism in Southeast Asia, 1945–1975', *Journal of Southeast Asian Studies*, 34(3): 421–448.

Berger, Mark T. (2006), 'From Nation-Building to State-Building: The Geopolitics of Development, the Nation-State System and the Changing Global Order', *Third World Quarterly*, 27(1): 5–25.

Bergonia, Tony S. (2006), 'Now it can be told: Why 'Withdrawal' Plot failed', *Philippine Daily Inquirer*, 11 March, A1.

Berry, William E. (1986), 'The Changing Role of the Philippine Military during Martial Law and the Implications for the Future', in Edward A. Olsen and Stephen Jurika, Jr (eds), *The Armed Forces in Contemporary Asian Societies*, pp. 215–240 (Boulder, CO: Westview Press).

Bonn International Center for Conversion (2004), *Inventory of Security Sector Reform (SSR) Efforts in Developing and Transition Governments* (Bonn: BICC).

Booth, Ken (1979), *Strategy and Ethnocentrism* (London: Croom Helm).

Booth, Ken (1991), 'Security in Anarchy: Utopian Realism in Theory and Practice', *International Affairs*, 67(3): 527–545.

Booth, Ken (1995), 'Human Wrongs and International Relations', *International Affairs*, 71(1): 103–126.

Booth, Ken and Nicholas Wheeler (2007), *The Security Dilemma: Fear, Cooperation and Trust in World Politics* (Basingstoke: Palgrave).

Booth, Ken and Russel Trood (eds) (1999), *Strategic Cultures in the Asia-Pacific Region* (London: Macmillan).

Bourchier, David (1999), 'Skeletons, Vigilantes and the Armed Forces' Fall from Grace', in Arief Budiman, Barbara Hatley and Damien Kingsbury (eds), *Reformasi: Crisis and Change in Indonesia,* pp. 149–171 (Clayton, Australia: Monash Asia Institute, Monash University).

Bourchier, David (2006), 'The United States, Bush and Indonesia: Bitter Memories, New Eggshells', in Mark Beeson (ed.), *Bush and Asia: America's Evolving Relations with East Asia*, pp. 162–178 (London: RoutledgeCurzon).

Brooks, Stephen G. and William C. Wohlforth (2002), 'American Primacy in Perspective', *Foreign Affairs*, 81(4): 20–33.

Brown, Chris (2002), *Sovereignty, Rights and Justice: International Political Theory Today* (Oxford: Polity).

Bruderlein, Claude (2001), 'The End of Innocence: Humanitarian Protection in the Twenty-First Century', in Simon Chesterman (ed.), *Civilians in War*, pp. 221–235 (Boulder, CO: Lynne Rienner).

Bunbongkarn, Suchit (1987), *The Military in Thai Politics 1981–86* (Pasir Panjang, Singapore: Institute of Southeast Asian Studies).

Bunbongkarn, Suchit (1988), 'The Military and Development for National Security in Thailand', in J. Soedjati Djiwandono and Yong Mun Cheong (eds), *Soldiers and Stability in Southeast Asia*, pp. 133–162 (Pasir Panjang, Singapore: Institute of Southeast Asian Studies).

Bunbongkarn, Suchit (1993), 'Thailand in 1992: in Search of a Democratic Order', *Asian Survey*, 33(2): 218–223.

Bunbongkarn, Suchit (1999), 'Thailand's Successful Reforms', *Journal of Democracy*, 10(4): 54–68.

Bunbongkarn, Suchit (2000), 'Of Crown and Swords: The Military and the Monarch in Thai Politics', unpublished paper.

Bunbongkarn, Suchit (2004), 'The Military and Democracy in Thailand', in R.J. May and Viberto Selochan (eds), *The Military and Democracy in Asia and the Pacific* (Canberra: ANU E Press, available at epress.anu.edu.au/mdap/mobile_devices/ch03.html).

Bunbongkarn, Suchit (2005), 'The Military and the Monarch in Thai Politics', interview with Kevin Smith.

Bunbongkarn, Suchit and K. Sukapanich-Kantaprab (1987), 'Civil Service Works of the Thai Army', in Surachat Bamrungsuk (ed.), *The Thai Military System: A Study of the Army in the Context of Society and Politics*, pp. 27–59 (Bangkok: Institute of Security and International Studies).

Burke, Anthony and Matt McDonald (eds) (2007), *Critical Security in the Asia Pacific* (Manchester University Press).

Buzan, Barry (1991), *People, States and Fear: An Agenda for International Security Studies in the Post-Cold War Order* (2nd edn, London: Harvester Wheatsheaf).

Buzan, Barry and Eric Herring (1998), *The Arms Dynamic in World Politics* (London: Lynne Rienner).

Cabacungan, Gil (2006), 'Arroyo backs Fixed Terms for AFP, PNP Chiefs', *Philippine Daily Inquirer*, 4 April.

Callahan, Mary P. (1999), 'Civil-Military Relations in Indonesia: *Reformasi* and Beyond', *Center for Civil-Military Relations Occasional Papers*, No. 4 (Naval Postgraduate School, Monterey).

Campbell, David (1992), *Writing Security: United States Foreign Policy and the Politics of Identity* (Manchester, NH: Manchester University Press).

Capie, David (1998), 'Once were Warriors? Military Entrepreneurship in East Asia', *New Zealand International Review*, 23(2): 21–26.

Caplan, Richard (2005), *International Governance of War-Torn Territories: Rule and Reconstruction* (Oxford: Oxford University Press).

Case, William (1995), 'Malaysia: Aspects and Audiences of Legitimacy', in Muthiah Alagappa (ed.), *Political Legitimacy in Southeast Asia: The Quest for Moral Authority*, pp. 69–107 (Stanford, CA: Stanford University Press).

Case, William (2002), *Politics in Southeast Asia: Democracy or Less* (London: Routledge-Curzon).

Cerny, Philip G. (1995), 'Globalization and the Changing Logic of Collective Action', *International Organization*, 49(4): 595–625.

Chalk, Peter (2001), 'Separatism and Southeast Asia: The Islamic Factor in Southern Thailand, Mindanao and Aceh', *Studies in Conflict and Terrorism*, 24(4): 241–269.

Challis, Roland (2001), *Shadow of a Revolution: Indonesia and the Generals* (Stroud: Sutton).

Chalmers, Malcolm (2000), *Security Sector Reform in Developing Countries: An EU Perspective* (London: Saferworld).

Chalmers, Malcolm (2001), 'Structural Impediments to Security Sector Reform', paper presented at Conference on Security Sector Reform, International Institute of Strategic Studies/DCAF, April.

Chandra, Siddharth and Douglas Kammen (2002), 'Generating Reforms and Reforming Generators: Military Politics in Indonesia's Democratic Transition and Consolidation', *World Politics*, 55(1): 96–136.

Channa, Jane (2002), 'Security Sector Reform: Issues, Challenges and Prospects', *Adelphi Papers*, No. 344.

Chase-Dunn, Christopher (1998), *Global Formation: Structures of the World Economy* (Lanham, MD: Rowan and Littlefield).

Christie, Clive J. (1996), *A Modern History of Southeast Asia: Decolonization, Nationalism and Separatism* (London: I. B. Tauris).

Christie, Clive (2001), *Ideology and Revolution in Southeast Asia 1900–1980: Political Ideas in the Anti-Colonial Era* (London: RoutledgeCurzon).

Clark, Ian (1999), *Globalization and International Relations Theory* (Oxford: Oxford University Press).

Clausewitz C.V. (1993), *On War* (ed. and trans.) M. Howard and P. Paret (London: Everyman's Library).

Cochrane, Joe (2002), 'A Military Mafia', *Newsweek*, 26 August, 30–32.

Cohen, Eliot A. (2002), *Supreme Command: Soldiers, Statesmen and Leadership in Wartime* (New York: The Free Press).

Cohen, Raymond (1994), 'Pacific Unions: A Reappraisal of the Theory that "Democracies Do Not Go to War with Each Other" ', *Review of International Studies*, 20(3): 207–233.

Cohen, Raymond (1995), 'Needed: A Disaggregate Approach to the Democratic-Peace Theory', *Review of International Studies*, 21(3): 323–325.

Colletta, Nat J., Markus Kostner and Ingo Widerhofer (1996), *The Transition from War to Peace in Sub-Saharan Africa* (Washington, DC: World Bank).

Connors, Michael Kelly (1999), 'Political Reform and the State in Thailand', *Journal of Contemporary Asia*, 29(2): 202–226.

Connors, Michael K. (2006), 'Thailand and the United States: Beyond Hegemony?', in Mark Beeson (ed.), *Bush and Asia: America's Evolving Relations with East Asia*, pp. 128–144 (London: Routledge).

Contreras, Volt (2006), 'US giving Manila P6.7B in Aid this year', *Philippine Daily Inquirer*, 4 April, A2.

Cooper, Neil and Michael Pugh (2002), 'Security Sector Transformation in Post-Conflict Societies', *CDS Working Papers*, No. 5 (London).

Cortell A.P. and Davis J.W. (1996), 'How do International Institutions Matter? The Domestic Impact of International Rules and Norms', *International Studies Quarterly*, 40: 451–478.

Cottey, Andrew, Timothy Edmunds and Anthony Forster (eds) (2002), *Democratic Control of the Military in Postcommunist Europe: Guarding the Guards* (Basingstoke: Palgrave).

Crispin, Shawn W. (2006a), 'Military Coup Tumbles Thailand's Thakisn', *Asia Times Online*, 21 September 2006.

Crispin, Shawn W. (2006b), 'All the King's Men', *Asia Times Online*, 21 September 2006.

Crouch, Harold (1978), *The Army and Politics in Indonesia* (Ithaca, NY: Cornell University Press).

Crouch, Harold (1985), 'Indonesia', in Haji Ahmad Zakaria and Harold Crouch (eds), *Military-Civilian Relations in Southeast Asia*, pp. 50–77 (Singapore: Oxford University Press).

Crouch, Harold (1991), 'The Military in Malaysia', in Viberto Selochan (ed.), *The Military, the State and Development in Asia and the Pacific*, pp. 83–120 (Boulder: Westview Press).

Crouch, Harold (1996), *Government and Society in Malaysia* (Cornell: Cornell University Press).

Crouch, Harold (1999), 'Wiranto and Habibie: Military-Civilian Relations since May 1998', in Arief Budiman, Barbara Hatley and Damien Kingsbury (eds), *Reformasi: Crisis and Change in Indonesia*, pp. 127–148 (Clayton, Australia: Monash Asia Institute, Monash University).

Cruz de Castro, Renato (1999), 'Adjusting to the Post-US Bases Era: The Ordeal of the Philippines Modernization Program', *Armed Forces and Society*, 26(1): 119–138.

Cruz de Castro, Renato (2005a), 'The Dilemma between Democratic Control versus Military Reforms: The Case of the AFP Modernization Program, 1991–2004', *Journal of Security Sector Management*, March, 1–24.

Cruz de Castro, Renato (2005b), 'Philippine Defense Policy in the 21st Century: Autonomous Defense or Back to the Alliance?', *Pacific Affairs*, 78(3): 403–422.

Cumming-Bruce, Nick (2005), 'Report finds Malaysia's Police Corrupt and Abusive', *International Herald Tribune*, 17 May.

Cumming-Bruce, Nick (2006), 'Thailand: A Coup for Democracy?', *Open Democracy*, 20 September.

Dandeker, Chris (1990), *Surveillance, Power and Modernity* (New York: St. Martin's Press).

The Davide Fact-Finding Commission (1990), The Final Report (Makati: Bookmark Inc.).

Davies, Sara Ellen (2005), *Legitimising Rejection? Southeast Asia and International Refugee Law* (PhD thesis, University of Queensland, St Lucia).

Deen, Thalif (2006), 'US Faces Dilemma Over Coup', *Inter Press Service*, 6 October.

de Leon, Augusto (2006), 'Cha-cha: Do we really Need It?', *Philippine Daily Inquirer*, 3 April, B2.

Department for International Development (1999), 'Policy Statement on Security Sector Reform', available from www.dfid.gov.uk.

Department of Defense (2006), *Quadrennial Defense Review Report* (Washington, DC: Department of Defense).

de Quiros, Conrado (1997), *Dead Aim: How Marcos Ambushed Philippine Democracy* (Pasig City: Foundation for Worldwide People's Power).

Desch, Michael (1999), *Civilian Control of the Military: The Changing Security Environment* (Baltimore: Johns Hopkins University Press).

Diaz, Jess (2006), 'FVR: GMA Proclamation "Overkill" ', *Philippine Star*, 26 February.

Dillon, Michael (1996), *Politics of Security: Towards a Political Philosophy of Continental Thought* (London: Routledge).

DiMaggio, Paul J. and Walter W. Powell (1991), 'Introduction', in Walter W. Powell and Paul J. DiMaggio (eds), *The New Institutionalism in Organizational Analysis*, pp. 1–38 (Chicago, IL: University of Chicago Press).

Djiwandono, J.S. and Y.M. Cheong (eds) (1988), 'Soldiers and Stability in Southeast Asia', *The Military and Development in Southeast Asia* (Singapore: Institute of Southeast Asian Studies), pp. 49–72.

Doronila, Amando (2006), 'RP Most Endangered Democracy in Asia', *Philippine Daily Inquirer*, 20 March, 1.

Doyle, Michael W. (2001), 'Peacebuilding in Cambodia: Legitimacy and Power' in Elizabeth Cousens and Chetan Kumar (eds), *Peacebuilding as Politics: Cultivating Peace in Fragile Societies* (London: Lynne Rienner), pp. 89–112.

Duffield, Mark (1997), 'NGO Relief in War Zones: Towards an Analysis of the New Aid Paradigm', *Third World Quarterly*, 18(3): 527–542.

Duffield, Mark (2001), *Global Governance and the New Wars: The Merging of Development and Security* (London: Zed Books).

The Economist (2004a), 'Enter a New Star', 25 September, 27–29.

The Economist (2004b), 'Forging a Nation', 23 October, 66.

The Editors (2000), 'Changes in Civil-Military Relations since the Fall of Suharto', *Indonesia*, 80, 123–159.

The Editors (2005), 'Current Data on the Indonesian Military Elite', *Indonesia*, 80: 123–159.

Edmonds, Martin (1988), *Armed Forces and Society* (Leicester: Leicester University Press).

Edmunds, Timothy (2001), 'Defining Security Sector Reform', *TCMR*, 1.11.

Edmunds, Timothy (2007), *Security Sector Reform in Transforming Societies: Croatia and Serbia-Montenegro* (Manchester University Press).

Eklöf, Stefan (1999), *Indonesian Politics in Crisis: The Long Fall of Suharto, 1996–98* (Copenhagen: NIAS).

Eldridge, Philip J. (2002), *The Politics of Human Rights in Southeast Asia* (London: Routledge).

Elliott, David (1987), *Thailand: Origins of Military Rule* (London: Zed Press).

Elman, Miriam Fendius (ed.) (1999), *Paths to Peace: Is Democracy the Answer?* (Cambridge, MA: MIT Press).

Elson, Robert E. (1999), 'International Commerce, the State and Society: Economic and Social Change', in Nicholas Tarling (ed.), *The Cambridge History of Southeast Asia: From c. 1800 to the 1930s*, Vol 3, pp. 127–192 (Cambridge: Cambridge University Press).

Elson, Robert E. (2001), *Suharto: A Political Biography* (Cambridge: Cambridge University Press).

Emmerson, Donald K. (1984), 'Southeast Asia: What's in a Name?', *Journal of Southeast Asian Studies*, 15(1): 1–21.

Evans, Peter (1995), *Embedded Autonomy: States and Industrial Transformation* (Princeton, NJ: Princeton University Press).

Fawthrop, Tom (2002), 'Indonesian Links to Terror', *AsiaTimes*, 7 November, available at: www.atimes.com/atimes/Southeast_Asia/DK07Ae02.html.

Feaver, Peter (2003), *Armed Servants: Agency, Oversight and Civil-Military Relations* (Cambridge, Mass: Harvard University Press).

Feith, Herbert (1962), *The Decline of Constitutional Democracy in Indonesia* (Ithaca, NY: Cornell University Press).

Feld, Maury D. (1968), 'Professionalism, Nationalism and the Alienation of the Military', in J. van Doorn (ed.), *Armed Forces and Society* (The Hague: Mouton), pp. 55–70.

Feliciano Commission (2003), *The Report of the Fact Finding Commission (pursuant to AO No. 78)* (Manila: Republic of the Philippines).

Ferguson, Niall (2003), *Empire: The Rise and Demise of the British World Order and the Lessons for Global Power* (New York: Basic Books).

Finer, Samuel (1962), *The Man on Horseback: The Role of the Military in Politics* (London: Routledge).

Finnemore, Martha and Kathryn Sikkink (1998), 'International Norms and Political Change', *International Organization*, 52(4): 887–917.

Fischel, John and Edmund Cowan (1988), 'Civil-Military Operations and the War for Moral Legitimacy in Latin America', *Military Review*, January: 36–49.

Foot, Rosemary (2004), 'Southeast Asia: The Second Front: Human Rights and Counter-terrorism in America's Asia Policy', *Adelphi Papers*, No. 363.

Forster, Anthony, Timothy Edmunds and Andrew Cottey (2001), 'Professionalisation of Armed Forces in Central and Eastern Europe: A Background Paper', unpublished paper in the possession of the authors.

Forster, Anthony, Timothy Edmunds and Andrew Cottey (eds) (2002), *The Challenge of Military Reform in Postcommunist Europe: Building Professional Armed Forces* (Basingstoke: Palgrave).

Foucault M. (1970), *The Order of Things* (New York: Random House).

Foucault M. (1980), 'Truth and Power' in M. Foucault, *Power/Knowledge: Selected Interviews and Other Writings 1972–1977* (edited by Colin Gordon) (New York: Pantheon).

Freedman, Lawrence (1998), 'Revolution in Military Affairs', *Adelphi Papers*, No. 318.

French, Shannon (2005), *The Code of the Warrior: Exploring Warrior Values Past and Present* (Lanham, MA: Rowman and Littlefield).

Fukuyama, Francis (1992), *The End of History and the Last Man* (New York: Free Press).

Funston, John (2002), 'Thaksin Woos the Military', ASEAN Focus Group, *Asian Analysis*, October, available at www.aseanfocus.com/asiananalysis/article.cfm?articleID=553.

Gaddis, John Lewis (1982), *Strategies of Containment: A Critical Appraisal of Postwar American Security Policy* (Oxford: Oxford University Press).

Ganesan, Nicholas (2000), 'ASEAN's Relations with Major External Powers', *Contemporary Southeast Asia*, 22(2): 258–278.

Ganesan, Nicholas (2001), 'Appraising Democratic Developments in Postauthoritarian States: Thailand and Indonesia', *Asian Affairs: An American Review*, 28(1): 3–17.

Germann, Wilhelm N. (2002), 'Evaluation of Security Sector Reform and Criteria of Success: Practical Needs and Methodological Problems', paper presented at Geneva Centre for Democratic Control of Armed Forces (DCAF) Conference, August.

Gersham, John (2002), 'Is Southeast Asia the Second Front?', *Foreign Affairs*, 81(4): 60–74.

Giddens, Anthony (1985), *The Nation-State and Violence* (Cambridge: Polity).

Gill, Stephen (1998), 'New Constitutionalism, Democratisation and Global Political Economy', *Pacifica Review*, 10(1): 23–38.

Girling, John L.S. (1981), *Thailand: Society and Politics* (Ithaca, NY: Cornell University Press).

Glassman, Jim (2006), 'US Foreign Policy and the War on Terror in Southeast Asia', in Garry Rodan, Kevin Hewison and Richard Robison (eds), *The Political Economy of South-East Asia: An Introduction*, 3rd edn, pp. 219–237 (Melbourne: Oxford University Press).

Goldstein, Judith and Robert O. Keohane (1993), 'Ideas and Foreign Policy: An Analytical Framework', in Judith Goldstein and Robert O. Keohane (eds), *Ideas and Foreign Policy: Beliefs, Institutions and Political Change*, pp. 3–30 (Ithaca, NY: Cornell University Press).

Gomez, Edmund Terence (2002), 'Introduction: Political Business in East Asia', in Edmund Terence Gomez (ed.), *Political Business in East Asia*, pp. 1–33 (London: Routledge).

Gomez, Edmund Terence and Jomo K.S. (1997), *Malaysia's Political Economy: Politics, Patronage and Profits* (Cambridge: Cambridge University Press).

Goodno, James B. (1991), *The Philippines: Land of Broken Promises* (London: Zed Books).

Gray, Colin S. (1986), *Nuclear Strategy and National Style* (Lanham, MD: Hamilton Press).

Guerin, Bill (2005), 'Indonesia Armed for a Fight', *AsiaTimes*, 24 November, available at: www.atimes.com/atimes/Southeast_Asia/GK24Ae01.html.

Haacke, Jurgen (2003), *ASEAN's Diplomatic and Security Culture* (London: Routledge-Curzon).

Haacke J. and P.D. Williams (2006), 'Thinking about Regional Security Culture', unpublished paper.

Haas, Peter M. (1992), 'Introduction: Epistemic Communities and International Policy Coordination', *International Organization*, 46(1): 1–35.

Hadiz, Vedi R. (2004), 'Decentralization and Democracy in Indonesia: A Critique of Neo-Institutionalist Perspectives', *Development and Change*, 35(4): 697–718.

Hall, Peter A. (1986), *Governing the Economy: The Politics of State Intervention in Britain and France* (Oxford: Oxford University Press).

Hall, Peter A. (1993), 'Policy Paradigms, Social Learning and the State: The Case of Economic Policymaking in Britain', *Comparative Politics*, 25(3): 275–296.

Hall, Peter A. and Rosemary C.R. Taylor (1996), 'Political Science and the Three New Institutionalisms', *Political Studies*, 44(5): 936–957.

Hall, Rodney Bruce (2003), 'The Discursive Demolition of the Asian Development Model', *International Studies Quarterly*, 47(1): 71–99.

Hallinan, Conn (2004), 'Terrorism key in US Support for Indonesian Army', *AsiaTimes*, 23 September, available at: www.atimes.com/atimes/Southeast_Asia/FI23Ae01.html.

Hamilton-Hart, Natasha (2005), 'Terrorism and Southeast Asia: Expert Analysis, Myopia and Fantasy', *Pacific Review*, 18(3): 303–325.

Hawes, Gary (1987), *The Philippine State and the Marcos Regime: The Politics of Export* (Ithaca, NY: Cornell University Press).

Hector, Charles (2003), 'Mahathir and the Judges: The Judiciary during the Mahathir Era', *Aliran Monthly*, 23(8).

Hedman, Eva-Lotta E. (2001), 'The Philippines: Not so Military, Not so Civil', in Muthiah Alagappa (ed.), *Coercion and Governance: The Declining Political Role of the Military in Asia*, pp. 165–186 (Stanford, CA: Stanford University Press).

Hedman, Eva-Lotta E. and John T. Sidel (2000), *Philippine Politics and Society in the Twentieth Century: Colonial Legacies, Post-Colonial Trajectories* (London: Routledge).

Hegre, Håvard (2000), 'Development and the Liberal Peace: What Does it Take to be a Trading State?', *Journal of Peace Research*, 37(1): 5–30.

Held, David, Anthony G. McGrew, David Goldblatt and Jonathan Perraton (1999), *Global Transformations: Politics, Economics and Culture* (Stanford, CA: Stanford University Press).

Hendrickson, Dylan (1999), 'A Review of Security Sector Reform', *CDS Working Papers*, No. 1 (London).

Hendrickson, Dylan and Nicole Ball (2002), 'Off-Budget Military Expenditure and Revenue: Issues and Policy Perspectives for Donors', *Centre for the Study of Democratic Government Occasional Papers*, No. 1 (Department of Politics and International Relations, Oxford University).

Henning, C. Randall (2002), *East Asian Financial Cooperation* (Washington, DC: Institute for International Economics).

Hernandez, Carolina G. (1986), 'Political Institution Building in the Philippines', in Robert A. Scalapino, Seizaburo Sato and Jusuf Wanandi (eds), *Asian Political Institutionalization*, pp. 261–287 (Berkeley, CA: Institute of East Asian Studies, University of California).

Hess, Gary R. (1987), *The United States' Emergence as a Southeast Asian Power, 1940–1950* (New York: Columbia University Press).

Hewison, Kevin (1993), 'Of Regimes, State and Pluralities: Thai Politics enters the 1990s', in Kevin Hewison, Richard Robison and Garry Rodan (eds), *Southeast Asia in the 1990s: Authoritarianism, Democracy and Capitalism*, pp. 159–189 (St. Leonards, NSW: Allen & Unwin).

Hewison, Kevin (1996), 'Political Oppositions and Regime Change in Thailand', in Garry Rodan (ed.), *Political Oppositions in Industrialising Asia*, pp. 72–94 (London: Routledge).

Hewison, Kevin (ed.) (1997), *Political Change in Thailand: Democracy and Participation* (London: Routledge).

Hewison, Kevin, Richard Robison and Garry Rodan (eds) (1993), *Southeast Asia in the 1990s: Authoritarianism, Democracy and Capitalism* (St. Leonards, NSW: Allen & Unwin).

Heymann, Phillip B. (2003), *Terrorism, Freedom and Security: Winning Without War* (Cambridge, Mass: MIT Press).

Higgott, Richard (1996), 'Beyond Embedded Liberalism: Governing the International Trade Regime in an Era of Economic Nationalism' in P. Gummett (ed.), *Globalization and Public Policy* (Cheltenham: Edward Elgar), pp. 83–104.

Hilley, John (2001), *Malaysia: Mahathirism, Hegemony and the New Opposition* (London: Zed Books).

Hollingsworth, J. Rogers and Robert Boyer (1997), 'Coordination of Economic Actors and Social Systems of Production', in J. Rogers Hollingsworth and Robert Boyer (eds), *Contemporary Capitalism: The Embeddedness of Institutions*, pp. 1–47 (Cambridge: Cambridge University Press).

Honna, Jun (1999), 'Military Ideology in Response to Democratic Pressure during the late Suharto Era: Political and Institutional Contexts', *Indonesia*, 67: 77–126.

Honna, Jun (2000), *The Military and Democratisation in Indonesia: The Developing Civil-Military Discourse during the late Soeharto Era* (PhD thesis, Australian National University, Canberra).

Honna, Jun (2003), *Military Politics and Democratization in Indonesia* (London: RoutledgeCurzon).

Hood, Ludovic (2006), 'Security Sector Reform in East Timor, 1999–2004', *International Peacekeeping*, 13(1): 60–77.

Horn, Robert (2001), 'Bullets & Ballots', *Time*, 8 January.

Horn, Robert (2003), 'Asian Heroes: Surayud Chulanont', *Time,* 28 April.

Hughes, Christopher (2005), 'Japan's Re-Emergence as a "Normal" Military Power', *Adelphi Papers*, No. 368.

Human Rights Watch (2000), *World Report 2000,* available at: www.hrw.org/wr2k1/asia/indonesia.html.

Human Rights Watch (2003), *World Report 2003,* available at: www.hrw.org/wr2k3/asia7.html.

Human Rights Watch (2006), *Too High a Price: The Human Rights Cost of the Indonesian Military's Economic Activities* (New York: Author).

Huntington, S. (1993), *The Third Wave: Democratization in the late Twentieth Century* (Norman, OK: University of Oklahoma Press).

Huntington, Samuel P. (1957), *The Soldier and the State: The Theory and Politics of Civil-Military Relations* (Cambridge, MA: Belknap Press).

Huntington, Samuel P. (1991), *The Third Wave: Democratisation in the Late Twentieth Century* (Norman: University of Oklahoma Press).

Huntington, Samuel P. (1995), 'Reforming Civil-Military Relations', *Journal of Democracy*, 6(4): 9–17.

Huntington, Samuel P. (1996), 'The West: Unique, not Universal', *Foreign Affairs*, 75(6): 28–46.

Hutchcroft, Paul D. (1998), *Booty Capitalism: The Politics of Banking in the Philippines* (Ithaca, NY: Cornell University Press).

Hutchcroft, Paul D. (1999), 'Neither Dynamo nor Domino: Reforms and Crises in the Philippine Political Economy', in T.J. Pempel (ed.), *The Politics of the Asian Economic Crisis*, pp. 163–183 (Ithaca, NY: Cornell University Press).

Hutchison, Jane (2006), 'Poverty of Politics in the Philippines', in Garry Rodan, Kevin Hewison and Richard Robison (eds), *The Political Economy of South-East Asia: Markets, Power and Contestation*, 3rd edn, pp. 39–71 (South Melbourne, Victoria: Oxford University Press).

Huxley, Tim (2001), 'Reforming Southeast Asia's Security Sectors', *Centre for the Study of Democratic Government Working Papers*, No. 4 (Department of Politics and International Relations, Oxford University).

Ikenberry, G. John (2004), 'Liberalism and Empire: Logics of Order in the American Unipolar Age', *Review of International Studies*, 30(4): 609–630.

International Crisis Group (2001), 'Indonesia: Next Steps in Military Reform', *Asia Report*, No. 24 (11 October).

International Crisis Group (2005a), 'Philippines Terrorism: The Role of Militant Islamic Converts', *Asia Report*, No. 110 (19 December).

International Crisis Group (2005b), 'Thailand's Emergency Decree: No Solution', *Asia Report*, No. 105 (18 November).

International Herald Tribune (2006), '16 Charged in Plot against Arroyo', 27 February.

International Institute of Strategic Studies (2004), *The Military Balance 2003–2004* (London: IISS).

Jakarta Post (2004), 'Carnage in Jakarta', 10 September.

Janowitz, Morris (1960), *The Professional Soldier: A Social and Political Portrait* (London: The Free Press-Macmillan).

Jeshrun, Chandran (1988), 'Development and Civil-Military Relations in Malaysia: The Evolution of the Officer Corps', in J. Soedjati Djiwandono and Yong Mun Cheong (eds), *Soldiers and Stability in Southeast Asia*, pp. 255–278 (Pasir Panjang, Singapore: Institute of Southeast Asian Studies).

Jeshrun, Chandran (1999), 'Malaysia: The Delayed Birth of a Strategic Culture', in Ken Booth and Russell Trood (eds), *Strategic Cultures in the Asia-Pacific Region*, pp. 225–246 (Basingstoke: Macmillan).

Jeshrun, Chandran (2004), 'Malaysian Defense Policy under Mahathir: What has Changed?', in Bridget Welsh (ed.), *Reflections: The Mahathir Years*, pp. 333–342 (Washington, DC: John Hopkins University).

Johnston, Alistair I. (1995), 'Thinking About Strategic Culture', *International Security*, 19(4): 32–64.

Johnson, Chalmers (2001), *Blowback: The Costs and Consequences of American Empire* (New York: Owl Books).

Jomo, K.S. (1997), *Southeast Asia's Misunderstood Miracle: Industrial Policy and Economic Development in Thailand, Malaysia and Indonesia* (Boulder, CO: Westview Press).

Jones, David Martin (1998), 'Democratizatrion, Civil Society and Illiberal Middle Class Culture in Pacific Asia', *Comparative Politics*, 30(2): 147–169.

Jones, David Martin (ed.) (2004), *Globalisation and the New Terror: The Asia Pacific Dimension* (Cheltenham, UK: Edward Elgar Publishers).

Kagan, Robert (2004), 'America's Legitimacy Crisis', *Foreign Affairs*, 83(2): 65–87.

Kaldor, Mary (1999), *New and Old Wars: Organized Violence in a Global Era* (London: Stanford University Press).

Kammen, Douglas and Siddharth Chandra (1999), *A Tour of Duty: Changing Patterns of Military Politics in Indonesia in the 1990s* (Ithaca, NY: Cornell Southeast Asia Program Publications).

Kang, David C. (2002), *Crony Capitalism: Corruption and Development in South Korea and the Philippines* (Cambridge: Cambridge University Press).

Kang, David C. (2003), 'Transaction Costs and Crony Capitalism in East Asia', *Comparative Politics*, 35(4): 439–458.

Katzenstein, Peter J. (ed.) (1996), *The Culture of National Security: Norms and Ideology in World Politics* (New York: Columbia University Press).

Katzenstein, Peter J. (2005), *A World of Regions: Asia and Europe in the American Imperium* (Ithaca, NY: Cornell University Press).

Kaufman, Karl B. (2004), 'Reforms Still a Dream a Year after Oakwood', *Manila Times*, 27 July.

Kebschull, Harvey (1994), 'Operation 'Just Missed': Lessons from Failed Coup Attempts', *Armed Forces and Society*, 20(4): 565–579.

Kennedy, Charles H. and David J. Louscher (1991), 'Civil-Military Interaction: Data in Search of a Theory', in Charles H. Kennedy and David J. Louscher (eds), *Civil-Military Interaction in Asia and Africa* (Leiden: E.J. Brill), pp. 123–147.

Keohane, Robert O. and Joseph Nye (1977), *Power and Interdependence* (Boston: Little Brown).

Kerkvliet, Benedict J. (1977), *The Huk Rebellion: A Study of Peasant Revolt in the Philippines* (Berkeley, CA: University of California Press).

Kerr, Pauline (1998), *Researching Security in East Asia: From 'Strategic Culture' to 'Security Culture'* (Canberra: Centre for Defence and Security Studies, working paper no. 326).

Kessler, Richard J. (1988), 'Development and the Military: Role of the Philippine Military in Development', in J. Soedjati Djiwandono and Yong Mun Cheong (eds), *Soldiers and Stability in Southeast Asia*, pp. 213–227 (Pasir Panjang, Singapore: Institute of Southeast Asian Studies).

Kessler, Richard J. (1989), *Rebellion and Repression in the Philippines* (New Haven, CT: Yale University Press).

Khoo, Boo Teik (1995), *Paradoxes of Mahthirism: An Intellectual Biography of Mahathir Mohamad* (Kuala Lumpur: Oxford University Press).

Khoo, Boo Teik (2003), *Beyond Mahathir: Malaysian Politics and its Discontents* (London: Zed Books).

Kinzer, Stephen (2006), *Overthrow: America's Century of Regime Change from Hawaii to Iraq* (New York: Times Books/Henry Holt).

Klein, James R. (1998), 'The Constitution of the Kingdom of Thailand, 1997: A Blueprint for Participatory Democracy', *Asia Foundation Working Papers*, No. 8 (March).

Knoke, David (1990), *Political Networks: The Structural Perspective* (Cambridge: Cambridge University Press).

Kolko, Gabriel (1985), *Anatomy of a War: Vietnam, the United States and the Modern Historical Experience* (New York: Pantheon).

Kraft, Herman Joseph (2003), 'The Philippines: The Weak State and the Global War on Terror', *Kasarinlan: Philippine Journal of Third World Studies*, 18(1–2): 133–152.

Krasner, Stephen D. (ed.) (1983), *International Regimes* (Ithaca, NY: Cornell University Press).

Krasner, S.D. (1999), *Sovereignty: Organized Hypocrisy* (Princeton, NJ: Princeton University Press).

Krause, Keith and Michael C. Williams (eds) (1997), *Critical Security Studies: Concepts and Cases* (London: UCL Press).

Kristiadi, J. (1999), 'The Armed Forces', in Richard W. Baker, Hadi Soesastro, J. Kristiadi and Douglas E. Ramage (eds), *Indonesia: The Challenge of Change*, pp. 99–114 (Singapore: Institute of Southeast Asian Studies).

Kuhn, Thomas (1996), *The Structure of Scientific Revolutions*, 3rd edition (Chicago: University of Chicago Press).

Kuhonta, Erik Martinez (2006), 'Thaksin Triumphant: The Implications of One-Party Dominance in Thailand', *Asian Affairs*, 33(1), pp. 39–54.

Kuppusamy, Baradan (2005), 'Malaysia: Electoral Honeymoon is Over for Prime Minister', *Inter Press Service*, 1 November.

LaMoshi, Gary (2004a), 'A Win for Indonesia's Military', *AsiaTimes*, 5 November, available at: www.atimes.com/atimes/Southeast_Asia/FK05Ae01.html.

LaMoshi, Gary (2004b), 'Terrorism Links in Indonesia point to Military', *AsiaTimes*, 8 October, available at: www.atimes.com/atimes/Southeast_Asia/FJ08Ae01.html.

Landingin, Roel (2006), 'Philippine Defence Chief unexpectedly Quits', *Financial Times*, 5 November, available at: www.ft.com/cms/s/02957af6-6cd0-11db-9a4d-0000779e2340.html.

Langit, Richel (2004), 'Indonesian Military – The Powers that Be', 1 October, available at: www.atimes.com/atimes/Southeast_Asia/FJ01Ae03.html.

Latham, Michael E. (2000), *Modernization as Ideology: American Social Science and 'Nation Building' in the Kennedy Era* (Chapel Hill, NC: University of North Carolina Press).

Laude, Jamie (2005), '184 Mutineers Ordered Freed', *Philippine Star*, 12 May, 1–8.

Layne, Christopher (1994), 'Kant or Cant: The Myth of the Democratic Peace', *International Security*, 19(2): 5–49.

Legro, Jeffrey (1997), 'Which Norms Matter? Revisiting the "Failure" of Internationalism', *International Organization*, 51(1), pp. 31–63.

Leifer, Michael (1986), 'The Role and Paradox of ASEAN', in Michael Leifer (ed.), *The Balance of Power in East Asia*, pp. 119–131 (New York: St. Martin's Press).

Leifer, Michael (1989), *ASEAN and the Security of Southeast Asia* (London: Routledge).

Levy, Jack S. (1988), 'Domestic Politics and War', *Journal of Interdisciplinary History*, 18(4): 653–673.

Levy, Michael J. (1963), *Modernization and the Structure of Societies* (Princeton, NJ: Princeton University Press).

Lewis, Glen (1998), 'The Television Business, Democracy and the Army', ASEAN Focus Group, *Asian Analysis*, December, available at www.aseanfocus.com/asiananalysis/article.cfm?articleID=99.

Liddle, R. William (1999), 'Regime: The New Order', in Donald K. Emmerson (ed.), *Indonesia Beyond Suharto: Polity, Economy, Society, Transition*, pp. 39–70 (New York: M.E. Sharpe).

Lim, Linda C. (1996), 'The Evolution of Southeast Asian Business Systems', *Journal of Asian Business*, 12(1): 51–74.

Lissak, Moshe (1976), *Military Roles in Modernization: Civil-Military Relations in Thailand and Burma* (Beverley Hills, CA: Sage).

Loh, Francis K.W. (2005), 'National Security, the Police and the Rule by Law: Militarisation by Other Means in Malaysia', in Jayadeva Uyangoda (ed.), *TBA* (London: Zed Books).

Longhurst, Kerry (2004), *Germany and the Use of Force: The Evolution of German Security Policy, 1990–2003* (Manchester: Manchester University Press).

Lowry, Robert (1996), *The Armed Forces of Indonesia* (St. Leonards, NSW: Allen & Unwin).

Luttwak, Edward N. (1990), 'From Geopolitics to Geo-economics: Logic of Conflict, Grammar of Commerce', *The National Interest*, Summer: 17–23.

McBeth, John (2003), 'Elite Force', *Far Eastern Economic Review*, 13 November, 18.

McCargo, Duncan (2005), 'Network Monarchy and Legitimacy Crises in Thailand', *Pacific Review*, 18(4): 499–519.

McCargo, Duncan (2006), 'Thaksin and the Resurgence of Violence in the Thai South: Network Monarchy Strikes Back?', *Critical Asian Studies*, 38(1): 39–71.

McCoy, Alfred W. (1995), ' "Same Banana": Hazing and Honour at the Philippine Military Academy', *Journal of Asian Studies*, 54(3): 689–726.

McCoy, Alfred W. (1999), *Closer than Brothers: Manhood at the Philippine Military Academy* (New Haven, CT: Yale University Press).

MacDonald, Brian (1996), *Military Spending in Developing Countries: How Much is Too Much?* (Carleton: Carleton University Press).

McDougall, Walter A. (1997), *Promised Land, Crusader State: The American Encounter with the World since 1776* (Boston: Mariner Books).

MacFarling, Ian (1996), *The Dual Function of the Indonesian Armed Forces: Military Politics in Indonesia* (Canberra: Australian Defense Studies Center).

Machmud, Benjamin (1993), 'The Malaysian Army in Transition', *Asian Defence Journal*, March, 6–10.

McMahon, Robert J. (1999), *The Limits of Empire: The United States and Southeast Asia since World War II* (New York: Columbia University Press).

Magno, Alexander R. (2001), 'Philippines: Trauma of a Failed Presidency', in Daljit Singh and Anthony L. Smith (eds), *Southeast Asian Affairs 2001*, pp. 251–262 (Singapore: Institute of Southeast Asian Studies).

Mahoney, James (2000), 'Path Dependence and Historical Sociology', *Theory and Society*, 29(4): 507–548.

Manilla Bulletin (2004), 'Solon – Balikatan, US Aid Proves Government Moving to Maintain Peace', 17 February.

Manila Bulletin (2006), 'Philippines Most Dangerous Country for Journalists – IPI', 31 March, 15.

Manila Standard (2005), 'Terror Suspects Free on Bail', 17 August.

Mann, Michael (1988), *States, War and Capitalism* (Oxford: Blackwell).

March, James G. and Johan P. Olsen (1989), *Rediscovering Institutions: The Organizational Basis of Politics* (New York: Free Press).

Marshall, Andrew (2001), 'An Army Man turns to Education', Norwegian Centre for International Cooperation in Higher Education, available at siu.no/vev.nsf/O/SIU= publications+Global+Knowledge-Schools+in+the +line.

Mektrairat, Nakharin (1992), *The 1932 Revolution in Siam* (Bangkok: Project on Social Sciences and Humanities Textbook Foundation).

Mietzner, Marcus (2002a), 'Politics of Engagement: The Indonesian Armed Forces, Islamic Extremism and the "War on Terror" ', *Brown Journal of World Affairs*, 9(1): 71–84.

Mietzner, Marcus (2002b), 'Military Reform and Civilian Conflict in Indonesia', *Developing Alternatives*, 8(1): 23–26.

Mietzner, Marcus (2004), *Indonesian Civil-Military Relations: The Armed Forces and Political Islam in Transition, 1997–2004* (PhD thesis, Australian National University, Canberra).

Mill, John Stuart (1874), *Dissertations and Discussions: Political, Philosophical and Historical* (New York: Henry Holt).

Milne, R.S. and Diane K. Mauzy (1999), *Malaysian Politics under Mahathir* (London: Routledge).

Moravcsik, Andrew (1999), 'A New Statecraft? Supranational Entrepreneurs and International Cooperation', *International Organization*, 53(2): 267–306.

Morell, David (1986), 'Political Dynamics of Military Power in Thailand', in Edward A. Olsen and Stephen Jurika, Jr. (eds), *The Armed Forces in Contemporary Asian Societies*, pp. 138–152 (Boulder, CO: Westview Press).

Morell, David and Chai-anan Samudavanija (1981), *Political Conflict in Thailand: Reform, Reaction, Revolution* (Cambridge, MA: Oelgeschlager, Gunn & Hain).

Moskos, Charles, John Allen Williams and David Segal (eds.) (2000), *The Postmodern Military: Armed Forces after the Cold War* (Oxford: Oxford University Press).

Nathan, K.S. (1998), 'Malaysia: Reinventing the Nation', in Muthiah Alagappa (ed.), *Asian Security Practice: Material and Ideational Influences*, pp. 513–548 (Stanford, CA: Stanford University Press).

Nathan, K.S. and Geetha Govindasamy (2001), 'Malaysia: A Congruence of Interests', in Muthiah Alagappa (ed.), *Coercion and Governance: The Declining Political Role of the Military in Asia*, pp. 259–275 (Stanford, CA: Stanford University Press).

Nesadurai, Helen (2006), 'Malaysia and the United States: Rejecting Dominance, Embracing Engagement', in Mark Beeson (ed.), *Bush and Asia: America's Evolving Relations with East Asia*, pp. 179–195 (London: RoutledgeCurzon).

Neumann, A. Lin (2003a), 'Absurd Coup has Sting in the Tail', *AsiaTimes*, 29 July, available at: www.atimes.com/atimes/Southeast_Asia/EG29Ae08.html.

Neumann, A. Lin (2003b), 'Philippines: Academic Roots of Rebellion', *AsiaTimes*, 2 August, available at: www.atimes.com/atimes/Southeast_Asia/EH02Ae05.html.

Neumann, A. Lin (2006), 'Philippines: Military on the Move', *AsiaTimes*, 28 February, available at: www.atimes.com/atimes/Southeast_Asia/HB28Ae05.html.

Noble, Gregory W. and John Ravenhill (eds) (2000), *The Asian Financial Crisis and the Architecture of Global Finance* (Cambridge: Cambridge University Press).

Nordholt, Henk Schulte (2002), 'A Genealogy of Violence', in Freek Colombijn and J. Thomas Lindblad (eds), *Roots of Violence in Indonesia: Contemporary Violence in Historical Perspective*, pp. 33–62 (Lieden: KITLV Press).

Ockey, James (1998), 'Crime, Society, and Politics in Thailand,' in Carl A. Trocki (ed.), *Gangsters, Democracy, and the State in Southeast Asia* (Ithaca, NY: Cornell University Press), pp. 39–53.

Ockey, James (2001), 'Thailand: The Struggle to redefine Civil-Military Relations', in Muthiah Alagappa (ed.), *Coercion and Governance: The Declining Political Role of the Military in Asia*, pp. 187–208 (Stanford, CA: Stanford University Press).

Ockey, James (2004), 'State, Bureaucracy and Polity in Modern Thai Politics', *Journal of Contemporary Asia*, 34(2): 143–162.

Ohmae, Kenichi (1990), *The Borderless World: Power and Strategy in the Interlinked Economy* (New York: Harper Business).

Olsen, Edward A. and Stephen Jurika, Jr. (eds) (1986), *The Armed Forces in Contemporary Asian Societies* (Boulder, Co: Westview Press).

Osborne, Milton (2000), *Southeast Asia: An Introductory History*, 8th edn. (Crows Nest, NSW: Allen & Unwin).

Owen, John M. (1994), 'How Liberalism produces Democratic Peace', *International Security*, 19(2): 87–125.

Painter, Martin (2006), 'Thaksinisation or Managerialism? Reforming the Thai Bureaucracy', *Journal of Contemporary Asia*, 36(1): 26–47.

Pamintuan, Ana Marie (2005), 'The Road to Reforms', *Philippine Star*, 11 May, 14.

Panaspornprasit, Chookiat (2003), 'Democratization in Thailand: Bust or Boon?', Institute for Security and International Studies, Chulalongkorn University, Thailand.

Panaspornprasit, Chookiat (2004), 'Thailand: Politicized Thaksinization', *Southeast Asian Affairs*, 257–266.

Parry, Richard Lloyd (2002), 'The Shark Cage', *Dissent*, 49(2): 73–84.

Pasuk, Phongpaichit and Chris Baker (1995), *Thailand: Economy and Politics* (Kuala Lumpur: Oxford University Press).

Pasuk, Phongpaichit and Chris Baker (2004), *Thaksin: The Business of Politics in Thailand* (Chiang Mai: Silkworm Books).

Pathmanand, Ukrist (2001), 'Globalization and Democratic Development in Thailand: The New Path of the Military, Private Sector and Civil Society', *Contemporary Southeast Asia*, 23(1): 24–42.

Pauker, Guy J. (1962), 'The Role of the Military in Indonesia', in John J. Johnson (ed.), *The Role of the Military in Underdeveloped Countries*, pp. 185–230 (Princeton, NJ: Princeton University Press).

Pazzibugan, Dona Z. (2006a), 'Senga: Military Council will Never Happen', *Philippine Daily Inquirer*, 12 March.

Pazzibugan, Dona Z. (2006b), 'Military Court to try 30 Officers for Mutiny', *Philippine Daily Inquirer*, 2 November.

Pazzibugan, Dona Z. and Philip C. Tubeza (2006), 'We hold Nation Together', *Philippine Daily Inquirer*, 15 March, A1.

Pearson, Donald (2002), 'Radical Islam in Indonesia: Its Potential Impact on International Islamic Terrorism', *Journal of Counterterrorism and Homeland Security International*, 8(2): 40–42.

Perlmutter, Amos (1977), *The Military and Politics in Modern Times: On Professionals, Praetorians and Revolutionary Soldiers* (New Haven, CT: Yale University Press).

Philippine Star (2006), 'Endless Cycle', 28 February.

Pillai, M.G.G. (2004), 'Is UMNO Serious about the Corruption in Its Ranks?', 25 August, available at: www.mggpillai.com/article.php3?sid=1993.

Pobre, Ceasar P. (2000), *History of the Armed Forces of the Filipino People* (Quezon City: New Day Publishers).

Polidano, Charles (2000), 'Measuring Public Sector Capacity', *World Development*, 28(5): 805–822.

Pongsudhirak, Thitinan (2003), 'Thailand: Democratic Authoritarianism', *Southeast Asian Affairs*, 277–290.

Przeworski, Adam, Michael E. Alvarez, Jose Antonio Cheibub and Fernando Limongi (2000), *Democracy and Development: Political Institutions and Well-Being in the World, 1950–1990* (Cambridge: Cambridge University Press).

Pye, Lucian W. (1962), 'Armies in the Process of Political Modernization', in John J. Johnson (ed.), *The Role of the Military in Underdeveloped Countries*, pp. 69–90 (Princeton, NJ: Princeton University Press).

Pye, Lucian W. and Mary W. Pye (1985), *Asian Power and Politics: The Cultural Dimensions of Authority* (Cambridge, MA: Harvard University Press).

Quinlivan, James (1999), 'Coup-Proofing: Its Practices and Consequences in the Middle East', *International Security*, 24(2): 131–165.

Rabasa, Angel M. (2003), 'Political Islam in Southeast Asia: Moderates, Radicals and Terrorists', *Adelphi Papers*, No. 358.

Rabasa A. and Haseman, J. (2002) *The Military and Democracy in Indonesia: Challenges, Politics and Power* (Rand Corporation).

Randall, Jesse (1998), 'Political Gangsters', *Inside Indonesia*, January–March.

Reid, Ben (2006), 'Bush and the Philippines after September 11: Hegemony, Mutual Opportunism and Democratic Retreat', in Mark Beeson (ed.), *Bush and Asia: America's Evolving Relations with East Asia*, pp. 145–161 (London: RoutledgeCurzon).

Report of the Fact Finding Commission (2003), (Manila: Republic of the Philippines).

Reus-Smit C. (2003), 'Constructivism', in S. Burchill, R. Devetak *et al.*, *Theories of International Relations*, 2nd edition (Basingstoke: Palgrave).

Reus-Smit, C. (2007), 'International Crises of Legitimacy', *International Politics*, 44(2–3), pp. 157–174.

Rieffel, Lex (2004), 'Indonesia's Quiet Revolution', *Foreign Affairs*, 83(5): 98–110.

Riggs, Fred Warrem (1966), *Thailand: The Modernization of a Bureaucratic Polity* (Honolulu: East-West Centre Press).

Rinakit, Sukardi (2005), *The Indonesian Military After the New Order* (Singapore: ISEAS Press).

Rivera, Ternario C. (2005), 'The Philippines in 2004: New Mandate, Daunting Problems', *Asian Survey*, 45(1): 127–133.

Robinson, Geoffrey (2001), 'Indonesia: On a New Course?', in Muthiah Alagappa (ed.), *Coercion and Governance: The Declining Political Role of the Military in Asia*, pp. 226–256 (Stanford, CA: Stanford University Press).

Robison, Richard (1986), *Indonesia: The Rise of Capital* (Sydney: Allen & Unwin).

Robison, Richard and Vedi R. Hadiz (2004), *Reorganising Power in Indonesia: The Politics of Oligarchy in an Age of Markets* (London: RoutledgeCurzon).

Robison, Richard, Mark Beeson, Kanishka Jayasuriya and Hyuk-Rae Kim (eds) (2000), *Politics and Markets in the Wake of the Asian Crisis* (London: Routledge).

Rodan, Garry (1996), 'The Internationalisation of Ideological Conflict: Asia's New Significance', *Pacific Review*, 9(3): 328–351.

Rodan, Garry (2004), *Transparency and Authoritarian Rule in Southeast Asia: Singapore and Malaysia* (London: Routledge).

Roosa, John (2003), 'Brawling, Bombing and "Backing" ', *Inside Indonesia*, January–March.

Rosenau, James N. (1997), *Along the Domestic-Foreign Frontier: Exploring Governance in a Turbulent World* (Cambridge: Cambridge University Press).

Ross, Robert S. (2005), 'Assessing the China Threat', *The National Interest*, Fall, 81–87.

Royal Thai Army (1994), 'The Defense of Thailand', paper prepared for the ASEAN Regional Forum summit, Bangkok.

Rueschemeyer, Dietrich, Evelyne Huber Stephens and John D. Stephens (1992), *Capitalist Development and Democracy* (Cambridge: Polity Press).

Ruggie J.G. (1998), *Constructing the World Polity: Essays on International Organization* (London: Routledge).

Rusli, Evelyn (2004), 'Indonesia Court voids 4 Convictions in 1999 East Timor Strife', *New York Times*, 7 August, A2.

Russett, Bruce (1993), *Grasping the Democratic Peace: Principles for a Post-Cold War World* (Princeton, NJ: Princeton University Press).

Samudavanija, Chai-Anan (1985), 'Implications of a Prolonged Conflict on Internal Thai Politics', in William Turley (ed.), *Confrontation or Coexistence: The Future of*

ASEAN – Vietnam Relations (Bangkok: Institute of Security and International Studies, Chulalongkorn University).

Samudavanija, Chai-Anan (1997), 'Old Soldiers Never Die, They are Just Bypassed: The Military, Bureaucracy and Globalisation', in Kevin Hewison (ed.), *Political Change in Thailand: Democracy and Participation*, pp. 42–57 (London: Routledge).

Samudavanija, Chai-Anan and Suchit Bunbongkarn (1985), 'Thailand', in Haji Ahmad Zakaria and Harold Crouch (eds), *Military-Civilian Relations in South-East Asia*, pp. 78–117 (Singapore: Oxford University Press).

Scarpello, Fabio (2004), 'Indonesians fear increased Military Role in Politics', *Indonesia Media Online*, available at: www.indonesiamedia.com/2004/10/English/English-1004-fear.htm.

Scarpello, Fabio (2005), 'Politicizing Indonesia's Military', *AsiaTimes*, 21 October, available at: www.atimes.com/atimes/Southeast_Asia/GJ21Ae01.html.

Schaller, Michael (1982), 'Securing the Great Crescent: Occupied Japan and the Origins of Containment in Southeast Asia', *Journal of American History*, 69(2): 392–414.

Schiff, Rebecca L. (1995), 'Civil-Military Relations Reconsidered: A Theory of Concordance', *Armed Forces and Society*, 22(1): 7–25.

Schmitter, Philippe C. (1979), 'Still the Century of Corporatism?', in Philippe C. Schmitter and Gerhard Lehmbruch (eds), *Trends toward Corporatist Intermediation*, pp. 7–48 (Beverly Hills: Sage).

Schwarz, Adam (1994), *A Nation in Waiting: Indonesia in the 1990s* (St. Leonards, NSW: Allen & Unwin).

Scott, W. Richard (1995), *Institutions and Organizations* (London: Sage).

Searle, John R. (2005), 'What is an Institution?', *Journal of Institutional Economics*, 1(1): 1–22.

Searle, Peter (1999), *The Riddle of Malaysian Capitalism: Rent Seekers or Real Capitalists?* (St. Leonards, NSW: Allen & Unwin).

Sedra, Mark (2006), 'Security Sector Reform in Afghanistan: The Slide towards Expediency', *International Peacekeeping*, 13(1): 94–110.

Selochan, Viberto (1989), 'The Armed Forces of the Philippines: Its Perceptions of Governing and the Prospects for the Future', *Centre for Southeast Asian Studies Working Papers*, No. 53 (Clayton, Victoria: Monash University, Centre of Southeast Asian Studies).

Senga, Generoso S. (2006), 'Never Again', *Manila Bulletin*, 24 March, 10–11.

Shalom, Stephen Rosskamm (1981), *The United States and the Philippines: A Study of Neocolonialism* (Philadelphia, PA: Institute for the Study of Human Issues).

Shambaugh D. (1996), 'Containment or Engagement of China? Calculating Beijing's Response', *International Security*, 21 (2).

Shearer, David (2000), 'Aiding or Abetting? Humanitarian Aid and Its Economic Role in Civil War', in Mats Berdal and David M. Malone (eds), *Greed and Grievance: Economic Agendas in Civil Wars*, pp. 189–203 (London: Lynne Rienner).

Shore S.M. (1998), 'No Fences Make Good Neighbours: The Development of the US–Canadian Security Community' in E. Adler and M. Barnett (eds), *Security Communities* (Cambridge: Cambridge University Press).

Sidel, John T. (1999), *Capital, Coercion and Crime: Bossism in the Philippines* (Stanford, CA: Stanford University Press).

Sikkink, Kathryn (1991), *Ideas and Institutions: Developmentalism in Brazil and Argentina* (Ithaca, NY: Cornell University Press).

Singh, Bilveer (2000), 'Civil-Military Relations in Democratizing Indonesia: Change amidst Continuity', *Armed Forces and Society*, 26(4): 607–633.

Singh, Bilveer (2001), 'The Indonesian Military Business Complex: Origins, Course and Future', *Strategic and Defence Studies Centre Working Papers*, No. 354 (Canberra: Australian National University).

Sipress, Alan (2006), 'Thailand Protests Mounting: Embattled Premier Refuses to Budge in Face of Uproar', *Washington Post*, 21 March, A09.

Slater, Dan (2003), 'Iron Cage in an Iron Fist: Authoritarian Institutions and the Personalization of Power in Malaysia', *Comparative Politics*, 36(1): 81–101.

Slim, Hugo (2001), 'Violence and Humanitarianism: Moral Paradox and the Protection of Civilians', *Security Dialogue*, 32(3): 325–339.

Smith, Steve (2000), 'The Increasing Insecurity of Security Studies: Conceptualizing Security in the Last Twenty Years', in Stuart Croft and Terry Terriff (eds), *Critical Reflections on Security and Change* (London: Frank Cass).

Snyder, Jack L. (1977), *The Soviet Strategic Culture: Implications for Limited Nuclear Options* (Santa Monica, CA: RAND Corporation).

Son, Johanna (2005), ' "Cheater" Arroyo faces people's wrath', *Asia Times* on-line, 29 June.

Soontornpipet, Pichet (2004), 'Is a Culture of Accountability Developing in Thailand?', available at: www.cdi.anu.edu.au/CDIwebsite_1998-2004/thailand/thailand_downloads/Culture%20of%20Accoutability.pdf.

Spaeth, Anthony (2005), 'Under the Gun', *Time International*, May, 16.

Spear, Joanna (1996), 'Arms Limitation, Confidence Building Measures and Internal Conflict', in Michael E. Brown (ed.), *The International Dimensions of Internal Conflict* (London: MIT Press), pp. 377–410.

Spiro, David (1994), 'The Insignificance of the Liberal Peace', *International Security*, 19(2): 50–86.

Spruyt, Hendrik (1994), *The Sovereign State and Its Competitors: An Analysis of Systems Change* (Princeton, NJ: Princeton University Press).

Sreshthaputra, Laurence W. (2000), 'A Thai Crusade for Clean Politics', *UNESCO Courier*, December.

Stockwell, A.J. (1999), 'Southeast Asia in War and Peace: The End of European Colonial Empires', in Nicholas Tarling (ed.), *The Cambridge History of Southeast Asia: From World War II to the Present*, Vol 4, pp. 1–58 (Cambridge: Cambridge University Press).

Straits Times (2002), 'Militants will be Hunted Down, says Mahathir', 7 January.

Stubbs, Richard (2005), *Rethinking Asia's Economic Miracle: The Political Economy of War, Prosperity and Crisis* (Basingstoke: Palgrave).

Sucharat, B. (1996), *Submarine: Naval Expansion in the Asia-Pacific* (Bangkok: Kebfire).

Sucharat, B. (2002), 'From Domination to Transformation: Civil-Military Relations in Thailand Toward 2020', paper presented at the Bilateral Conference on United States-Thailand Relations in the 21st Century, Washington, DC, 11–13 March.

Suriya, S. (1998), 'Soldiers Banned from Canvassing', *The Post*, 2 November.

Suwannathat-Pian, Kobkua (2003), *Kings, Country and Constitution: Thailand's Political Development, 1932–2000* (London: RoutledgeCurzon).

Tan, Andrew (2002), 'Malaysia's Security Perspectives', *Strategic and Defence Studies Centre Working Papers*, No. 367 (Canberra: Australian National University).

Tan, Andrew (2004), 'Force Modernisation Trends in Southeast Asia', Institute of Defence and Strategic Studies, Singapore, *Working Papers*, No. 59, January.

Tarling, N. (1998), *Nations and States in Southeast Asia* (Cambridge: Cambridge University Press).

Tarling, Nicholas (2001), *Imperialism in Southeast Asia: 'A Fleeting, Passing Phase'* (London: RoutledgeCurzon).

Tasker, Rodney (2006), 'Thailand's Man Behind the Throne', *Asia Times Online*, 2 November.

Thakur, Ramesh and Albrecht Schnabel (eds) (2001), *United Nations Peacekeeping Operations: Ad Hoc Missions, Permanent Engagement* (Tokyo: UNU Press).

Thomas, Caroline (1987), *In Search of Security: The Third World in International Relations* (London: Lynne Rienner).

Thomas, Caroline (2000), *Global Governance, Development and Human Security: The Challenge of Poverty and Inequality* (London: Pluto).

Thomas, Ward (2001), *The Ethics of Destruction: Norms and Force in International Relations* (Ithaca, NY: Cornell University Press).

Thomson, James C., Peter W. Stanley and John Curtis Perry (1981), *Sentimental Imperialists: The American Experience in East Asia* (New York: Harper and Row).

Tilly, Charles (1990), *Coercion, Capital and European States, AD 990*–1992 (Oxford: Blackwell).

Trillanes, Antonio (2001) 'A Study on Corruption in the Philippine Navy', available at: http://www.pcij.org/HotSeat/trillanes.html.

Trocki, Carl A. (1999), 'Political Structures in the Nineteenth and early Twentieth Centuries', in Nicholas Tarling (ed.), *The Cambridge History of Southeast Asia: From c. 1800 to the 1930s*, Vol 3, pp. 75–126 (Cambridge: Cambridge University Press).

Ubec, Michael and Luige del Puerto (2006), 'Arroyo cracks down on Foes', *Philippine Daily Inquirer*, 28 February.

Ukrist, Pathmanand (2001), 'Globalization and Democratic Development in Thailand', *Contemporary Southeast Asia*, 23(1), pp. 24–42.

United Nations Development Programme (1994), *Human Development Report 1994* (New York: Oxford University Press).

United States Senate and the Committee on Appropriations of the US House of Representatives (1999), 'Annual Report on Military Expenditures, 1998 by the Department of State', 19 February.

van der Kroef, Julius M. (1988), 'The Philippines: Day of the Vigilantes', *Asian Survey*, 28(6): 630–649.

van Doorn, Jacques (1975), *The Soldier and Social Change: Comparative Studies in the History and Sociology of the Military* (London: Sage).

Vatikiotis, Michael R.J. (1998), 'The Military and Democracy in Indonesia', in R.J. May and Viberto Selochan (eds), *The Military and Democracy in Asia and the Pacific*, pp. 29–46 (Bathurst, NSW: Crawford House Publishing).

Voice of America Press (2004), 'Thai Government Cracks Down on Southern Violence as Monday's Death Toll Shoots Upward', 25 October.

Wade, Robert (2001), 'The US Role in the long Asian Crisis of 1990–2000', in Arvid J. Lukauskas and Francisco L. Rivera-Batiz (eds), *The Political Economy of the East Asian Crisis and Its Aftermath: Tigers in Distress*, pp. 195–226 (Cheltenham: Edward Elgar).

Walker, R.B.J. (1993), *Inside/Outside: International Relations as Political Theory* (Cambridge: Cambridge University Press).

Wattanayagorn, Panitan (1998), 'Thailand', in Muthiah Alagappa (ed.), *Asian Security Practice: Material and Ideational Influences* (Stanford, CA: Stanford University Press), pp. 417–444.

Weber, Max (1978), 'Bureaucracy' in H.H. Gerth and C. Wright-Mills (eds), *From Max Weber: Essays in Sociology* (Oxford: Oxford University Press).

Welch, C. (ed.) (1976), Civilian Control of the Military: Theory and Cases from Developing Countries (Albany, NY: State University of New York Press).

Wendt, A. (1999), *Social Theory of International Politics* (Cambridge University Press).

Widoyoko, Danang, Irfan Muktiono, Adnan Topan Husodo, Barly Haliem N. and Agung Wijay (2003), *Military Businesses in Search of Legitimacy* (Jakarta: Indonesian Corruption Watch and National Democratic Institute).

Williamson, Oliver E. (1993), 'Transaction Cost Economics and Organization Theory', *Industrial and Corporate Change*, 2(1): 107–156.

Winter, Jeffrey A. (1996), *Power in Motion: Capital Mobility and the Indonesian State* (Ithaca, NY: Cornell University Press).

World Bank (1994), *Governance: The World Bank's Experience: Development in Practice* (Washington, DC: World Bank).

World Bank (1997a), *The State in a Changing World: The World Development Report 1997* (Washington, DC: World Bank).

World Bank (1997b), *A Framework for World Bank Involvement in Post-Conflict Reconstruction* (Washington, DC: World Bank).

World Bank (2003), *Thailand Country Development Partnership: Governance and Public Sector Reform (Phase I)* (Bangkok and Washington, DC: World Bank).

Yahuda, M. (2003), *The International Politics of the Asia-Pacific* (London: Routledge-Curzon).

Yee, Chen May (1998), 'US Support makes Anti-Mahathir Movement Uneasy', *Asian Wall Street Journal*, 18 November, 8.

Young, Oran R. (1994), *International Governance: Protecting the Environment in a Stateless Society* (Ithaca, NY: Cornell University Press).

Yuen, Foong Khong (1997), 'ASEAN and the Southeast Asian Security Complex', in David A. Lake and Patrick M. Morgan (eds), *Regional Orders: Building Security in a New World*, pp. 318–339 (Philadelphia, PA: Pennsylvania State University Press).

Zakaria, F. (1994), 'Culture is Destiny: A Conversation with Lee Kuan Yew', *Foreign Affairs*, 73(2): 109–126.

Zakaria, Haji Ahmad (1985), 'Malaysia', in Haji Ahmad Zakaria and Harold Crouch (eds), *Military-Civilian Relations in South-East Asia*, pp. 118–135 (Singapore: Oxford University Press).

Zysman, John (1994), 'How Institutions create Historically Rooted Trajectories of Growth', *Industrial and Corporate Change*, 3(1): 243–283.

Index

References such as '178–179' indicate (not necessarily continuous) discussion across a range of pages, whilst '183c6n5' indicates a reference to note 5 to Chapter 6 on page 183 and '183c6nn' refers to multiple notes to Chapter 6 on page 183. Wherever possible in the case of topics with many references, these have either been divided into sub-topics (indented below the main heading) or the most significant discussion of the topic is indicated by page numbers in bold.

For Product Safety Concerns and Information please contact our EU
representative GPSR@taylorandfrancis.com
Taylor & Francis Verlag GmbH, Kaufingerstraße 24, 80331 München, Germany

www.ingramcontent.com/pod-product-compliance
Lightning Source LLC
Chambersburg PA
CBHW050432280326
41932CB00013BA/2088